THE WATERLOO ARCHIVE

Dutch, Brunswick and Scottish troops fighting to defend Bossu Woods

THE
WATERLOO
ARCHIVE

Previously unpublished or rare journals and letters
regarding the Waterloo campaign and
the subsequent occupation of France

Volume II
German Sources

Edited by Gareth Glover

Translated by Martin Mittelacher

Introductory Letter from
Nikolaus Fürst Blücher von Wahlstatt

FRONTLINE
BOOKS

The Waterloo Archive: Volume II

This edition published in 2010 by Frontline Books,
an imprint of
Pen & Sword Books Limited, 47 Church Street,
Barnsley, S. Yorkshire, S70 2AS
www.frontline-books.com
email info@frontline-books.com

ISBN: 978-1-84832-541-8

For more information on our books, please visit
www.frontline-books.com, email info@frontline-books.com
or write to us at the above address.

Typeset by Palindrome

Printed in the UK by MPG Books Limited

CONTENTS

Contents

ILLUSTRATIONS

Plates may be found between pages 112 and 113

Colour Plates

Plates 1 and 2 are from the Editor's collection. Plates 3–8 are paintings by Charles Turner Warren and were originally published in 1818. They are reproduced here with the kind permission of the Anne S. K. Brown Military Collection, Brown University Library.

Black and White Illustrations

INTRODUCTORY LETTER

From Nikolaus Fürst Blücher von Wahlstatt

Dear Mr Glover,

I have been learning from your book how many Germans fought under other flags than just the Prussian and it is making me think how this is relevant for our own times.

In fact the Napoleonic wars were the cause that saw the awakening of a German nationality, which is the reason for so many of these German principalities fighting in the alliance against Napoleon, even before something like 'Germany' actually existed.

What was it, against which the allies had risen in such a joint effort? It was against some element in Napoleon – the will to subjugate vastly different tribes and traditions under one French rationality. It was not some superior government which aroused resistance, it was the violation of local traditions.

The Prussian king hesitated to oppose Napoleon: he weighed the sufferings of war against a loss of sovereignty. General York submitted his decision to ignore the king's command together with Blücher at Tauroggen to the judgement of the king who initially saw a traitor in York. So the whole start of the Napoleonic wars in East Prussia was a delicate balance of rightful defence and high treason.

Hence the victory at Waterloo (or La Belle Alliance) has two elements: the redressing of local European independence and also presaging a European unity, of which Napoleon was the first to dream.

Nikolaus Fürst Blücher von Wahlstatt

FOREWORD

Readers of Volume I of the *Waterloo Archive*[1] will already be aware of the reasons why I have embarked upon this crusade to bring into the public domain such a mass of new material relating to the Waterloo campaign and the subsequent occupation of France by the allied forces from 1815–18; however a short recap for new readers will not go amiss.

A huge amount of material has been written regarding the Waterloo campaign, perhaps more than any other campaign before or since, so what can possibly be new, and is there anything more to learn? Having spent years surveying the existing material published over the last nearly two hundred years, the answer will perhaps be surprising to many, a resounding yes.

In the first volume, I explored the archives of Britain and those of our ex-colonial[2] brothers where much material including art works that have never previously been published were discovered, along with some astonishing finds of truly historical significance. I shall return to this treasure trove in Volume III in due course.

But what of Volume II? This time it is the turn of the German troops who actually formed the majority of the forces present at the Battle of Waterloo, including the troops of Nassau, a small German state, some of whom actually served in the Dutch army at the battle. Some record of the actions of the troops of the King's German Legion, which was considered as an integral part of the British army and thus partly officered by British citizens, has therefore been published in English, but to a very limited degree. Herbert Siborne[3] published two letters by Lieutenant Graeme; a few KGL officers had their memoirs published in English, such as Ompteda[4] and Wheatley;[5] and, of course, Ludlow Beamish included a small number of letters from officers in his history,[6] including the famous (and often misquoted) account of the defence of La Haye Sainte by Major Baring. However, until very recently this tiny portion of German material was virtually all that was available to students of this campaign who did not possess a high level of German language skill; it is therefore not very surprising that early British histories of the battle have largely sidelined the achievements of the German troops, and this stance has been reiterated by most that have followed. This situation did not change at all until the 1990s when Peter Hofschröer[7] published his two-volume version of the campaign from the German perspective, which included numerous snippets of various German documents published for the first time in English to support his view of the campaign; but even this is not satisfactory, as it left much more still to be translated and published and did not provide whole documents to allow further interpretation. There is thus still a great need to provide an English version of much of the original German source material to aid historians redress this imbalance.

Such a task is truly daunting, not just because of the scale of the task, but also because of the inordinate amount of time needed by a translator with the appropriate level of language skills and grasp of military history and terminology to produce a coherent, meaningful translation. I made a small venture into this area when I published *Letters from the Battle of Waterloo* in 2004,[8] the remaining Siborne letters, when I needed to obtain translations of the numerous German letters in the files. I experimented with various means but all had their problems: professional translators proved extortionately expensive and charitable organisations, which one still felt honour-bound to recompense, or friends and acquaintances who required no fee but forced me to accept interminable delays were all unsatisfactory. I was therefore perhaps understandably not very keen to venture into translation work again.

That is, until I had the luck to begin a correspondence with Martin Mittelacher, who is of German extraction, living in retirement in the United States of America and an expert on the Waterloo campaign. He had previously liaised with Peter Hofschröer on his translation work, which also gave me great confidence in his abilities. Having had the audacity to ask him if he would consider translating the vast amount of German material that I was able to obtain from obscure sources and explaining the project, I was overjoyed to hear of his acceptance. Since then Martin has worked tirelessly and diligently to translate all of this material and our combined expertise has been utilised to edit the material and provide learned footnotes.

Much of the German material is derived from *Belle-Alliance: Reports and Information on the Participation of German Troops of Wellington's Army in the Action at Quatre Bras and in the Battle of Belle-Alliance* by Dr Julius von Pflugk-Harttung, Privy Archive Councillor at the State Archive in Berlin, published in German in 1915. This book is a veritable gold mine of primary source material from German units, particularly as many of these records were then unfortunately destroyed during the Second World War. It is truly amazing and a great loss to many historians that it has never previously been published to any great extent in the English language. However, this volume is not intended merely to form a translation of Pflugk-Harttung's book and although his material will eventually be published in total, it will span both German volumes of the *Waterloo Archive* and will not be published in exactly the same format. Pflugk-Harttung broke up the reports into sections in his work covering Quatre Bras, the Retreat and the Battle of Waterloo [Belle-Alliance]. For ease of use I have joined these various portions back together to form one coherent report, but have clearly annotated each with the numbers of the letters they come from in his work.

The material has been set out in a very similar format to Siborne's *Waterloo Letters* and the editor's *Letters from the Battle of Waterloo* for ease of use and all cross references are annotated in the notes virtually making all of these works one huge reference source on the Waterloo campaign.

These reports and letters do bring some aspects of the accepted history of the Waterloo campaign into question, such as the role of Prince Bernhard of Saxe-Weimar at Quatre Bras; it is clear from these sources that the credit for retaining the crossroads on the 15th may have more to do with the orders of Major Normann than the prince, who, it is clear, was not well-loved: his later statements often drew an acrimonious correspondence from his officers. Further correspondence provides information on the apparent retreat of Kielmannsegge's Brigade that ultimately led to his arrest after the battle, an incident that seems to have been lost for the last two centuries. Primary material from the Nassau contingent reminds us of their valuable but forgotten contribution in the stubborn defence of Hougoumont and confirms that some of their troops were in the front line from the commencement of the battle, but are not so represented on maps of the initial deployment of the troops at Waterloo. British accounts of the defence of Hougoumont rarely mention 1st Battalion 2nd Nassau Regiment (or mention them only cursorily), who initially were the only defenders of the actual buildings and certainly did not retire soon after, as is usually represented, but remained throughout the battle, gallantly repelling all French assaults: this provides clear evidence of the French making a second break-in to the farm complex, which has seemingly been missed by all previous historians.

These German Reports are also noticeably much more frank and open with regard to their failings, honestly describing mistakes or errors of deployment that led to losses and even name and shame both officers and men who failed to perform their duties, something that must have happened in every unit involved in such carnage, but such honesty is virtually unknown in contemporary British accounts.

I am therefore very proud to present this volume of German primary source material of which only small parts have ever to my knowledge been published in the English language before, for both the use of eminent historians and those who are simply interested in gaining a greater understanding of that whirlwind campaign nearly 200 years ago.

Gareth Glover

ACKNOWLEDGEMENTS

A project of this complexity cannot be accomplished without the willing support of many others. Particular thanks must be offered to Mr Gary Cousins who identified and helped to obtain copies of various obscure articles and Mr Michael-Andreas Tänzer who very kindly copied to me a large number of very rare German publications for Martin to translate. My grateful thanks must also extend to the staff of the British Library who have been incessantly bombarded by me for copies of various publications and their granting so freely, permission to publish translations of the same. I must also thank Mr Stefan Felleckner, archivist for the County of Gifhorn, for permission to publish the letters of Private Schacht and Lieutenant Hemmelmann of the Gifhorn battalion, originally published in *Erinnerungen an Waterloo: Weg und Schicksal des Landwehrbataillons Gifhorn*, published by Gunter Weinhold in 1985, and to Mr Volkner Schwichtenberg, managing director of the Mönch Group, for kindly granting permission to publish translations of excerpts from Joachim Kannicht's book *Und alles wegen Napoleon: Aus dem Kriegstagebuch des Georg von Coulon, Major der Königlichen Legion, und die Briefe seiner Frau Henriette 1806–1815*, published by Bernard & Graefe in 1986. Also to Guntram Muller-Schellenberg for his permission to publish the extracts of Private Leonhard of the Nassau contingent, which he originally jointly published with the late Peter Wacker in *Das herzoglich-nassauische Militär 1813–1866* (Schellenberg'sche Verlags-buchhandlung, Taunusstein, 1998), as well as for the use of bio-graphical data on Nassau officers. Thanks are also extended to him for offering for inclusion in the present work the letters of Captain Eberhard of the Orange Nassau Regiment and Lieutenant von Gagern of the 1st Nassau Regiment. Guntram Muller-Schellenberg also kindly allowed the use of the illustration of troops in Bossu woods, which is reproduced as the frontispiece to this volume.

But more than anyone else, I must thank my wife Mary and children Sarah and Michael for their forbearance and encouragement, all my work is dedicated to them.

This work, entailing a mountain of translation and research, is as accurate as I can possibly make it, but errors will occur and I take full responsibility for any that may be discovered.

Gareth Glover
Cardiff

THE STAFF

No. 1 From *Belle-Alliance*

Pflugk-Harttung's letter no. 2. List of the troop bodies of the German Legion and of the Hanoverians. Information on the various detachments of the German Legion and of the Hanoverian troops.

A – King's German Legion

1 Infantry

1st Brigade (Colonel du Plat) consisting of the 1st, 2nd, 3rd, and 4th Line Battalions: part of the 2nd Infantry Division (Clinton).

2nd Brigade (Colonel von Ompteda) consisting of the 1st and the 2nd Light Battalions, 5th and 8th Line Battalions: part of the 3rd Infantry Division (Alten).

2 Cavalry

1st Light Dragoon Regiment, 2nd Light Dragoon Regiment. The two Regiments and the 23rd British Dragoon Regiment formed the 3rd Cavalry Brigade (Major General von Dornberg).

1st Hussar Regiment: part of the 6th Cavalry Brigade (Major General Vivian).

3rd Hussar Regiment: part of the 7th Cavalry Brigade (Colonel von Arentschildt).

Note: The 2nd Hussar Regiment, being part of the 5th Cavalry Brigade, was on detached duty and thus did not directly participate in the battle.

3 Artillery

Major Kuhlmann's Horse Battery; part of the 1st Infantry Division (Cooke).

Major Sympher's Horse Battery; part of the 2nd Infantry Division (Clinton).

Major Cleeves's Foot Battery: part of the 3rd Infantry Division (Alten).

B – Royal Hanoverian Troops

1 Infantry.

1st Infantry Brigade (Major General Count von Kielmansegge) consisting of the Bremen, Verden, Duke of York, Grubenhagen, Luneburg Field Battalions and 2 Companies of Feldjägers: part of the 3rd Infantry Division.

3rd Infantry Brigade (Colonel Halkett) consisting of the Bremervorde, Salzgitter, Osnabrück and Quackenbruck[9] Landwehr Battalions: part of the 2nd Infantry Division.

4th Infantry Brigade (Colonel Best) consisting of the Luneburg, Verden, Osterode and Munden Landwehr Battalions: part of the 6th Infantry Division.

5th Infantry Brigade (Colonel von Vincke) consisting of the Hameln, Hildesheim, Peine and Gifhorn Landwehr Battalions: part of the 5th Infantry Division.

Note: The 6th Infantry Brigade (Major General Lyon) and the Hanoverian Reserve Corps (Lieutenant General von der Decken) did not participate in the battle.

2 Cavalry

Duke of Cumberland's Hussar Regiment: part of the Reserve Corps but on this day assigned to the 3rd Cavalry Brigade.[10]

Note: Colonel von Estorff's Brigade was on detached duty during the battle.

3 Artillery.

1st Foot Battery (Captain Braun): part of the 5th Infantry Division.

2nd Foot Battery (Captain von Rettberg): part of the 4th Infantry Division but on this day assigned to the 5th Division.[11]

No. 2 From *Belle-Alliance*

Pflugk-Harttung's letter no. 4. Report on the participation of the Hanoverian Troops and the German Legion in the action at Quatre Bras.[12]

Letter no. 19. Report on the participation of the Hanoverian Troops and the German Legion in the Battle of La Belle Alliance.

Notes on the participation of the Royal Hanoverian Troops and the King's German Legion in the Campaign in the Netherlands in 1815, and particularly in the Battle of Waterloo.

Introduction

As shown in the attached state of the army under the command of the Duke of Wellington, the Royal Hanoverian troops and the King's German Legion were jointly part of the corps and divisions with the British troops. The Reserve Corps under the command of Lieutenant General von der Decken, consisting only of Hanoverian troops, was not under orders to immediately move into the field with the other troops. It consisted of newly formed battalions and, at first, was intended only to garrison the most important Belgian cities. It did not take part in the events of the war.

The strength of the Hanoverian Troops on the active list of the Army was:

Infantry	12,700 men	
Cavalry	1,000 "	
Artillery	300 "	with 12 guns
Total	14,000 men with 12 guns	

The strength of the King's German Legion was:

Infantry	4,000 men	
Cavalry	2,500 "	
Artillery	500 "	with 18 guns
Total	7,000 men with 18 guns	

The Reserve Corps consisted of:

Infantry	8,500 men
Cavalry	500 "
Total	9,000 men

On receipt of the information of the advance of the French army across the border on 15 June, the Duke of Wellington's Army was cantoned as follows:

1 Corps of the Prince of Orange: Headquarters at Nivelles.
 1st British-Hanoverian Division: Enghien and surroundings.
 3rd British-Hanoverian Division: Soignies and surroundings.
 2nd Netherlands Division: Nivelles, Frasnes and surroundings.
 3rd Netherlands Division: Tay,[13] Haine Saint Paul, etc.

2 Corps of Lieutenant General Hill: Headquarters at Ath.
 2nd British-Hanoverian Division: Ath and surroundings.
 4th British-Hanoverian Division: Hal and surroundings.
 1st Netherlands Division: Hyzenzellen, Vardeghur, Velseke

Ruddershove, Balegem, etc.
Indian Brigade: Erpe, etc.

3 Troops not being part of a Corps:
5th Division: Brussels and surroundings.
6th Division: Brussels and surroundings.
7th Division: Antwerp.

4 Cavalry: Headquarters at Grammont.— All regiments at Grammont
and surroundings. Four of these at the French border between
Tournai and Mons. The Netherlands cavalry at Goegnies-
[Chaussee], Haire,[14] Gottignies, etc.

5. Brunswick Troops: Headquarters at Laeken.
Troop Corps between Mechelen and Brussels.

Events involving the army under the command of the
Duke of Wellington in the period from 15–19 June

15 June
The French troops made their first attack against the brigade of the 2nd
Netherlands Division cantoned at Frasnes, on the highway from
Charleroi to Brussels. On that day, it retired to Quatre Bras where it
maintained its position. Towards evening, all other troops of the army
received orders to quickly move off to Quatre Bras.

16 June: Action at Quatre Bras
Description of the terrain
At the single farmstead of Quatre Bras, the highways from Brussels to
Charleroi and from Nivelles to Namur intersect at a right angle. The area
is almost a plain and covered with cornfields. Next to Quatre Bras and
only 100 paces to the right of the Charleroi highway, there is the wood
of Bossu. It starts at the farm and extends for about a quarter of an hour
in the same direction as the highway. At the left of the same highway and
about 2,000 paces from Quatre Bras towards Charleroi, there is the
Gemioncourt farm, and when walking on the highway for about
2,000 paces from Quatre Bras to Namur, one finds the little village of
Pireaumont about 800 paces to the right of the highway. A wood extends
from near the highway past the left of this village towards the direction
of Charleroi.

The action at Quatre Bras took place on the terrain from the left of
this wood to the right of the wood of Bossu, and was bordered at its rear

by the highway from Nivelles to Namur.

The troops under the command of the Duke of Wellington had the wood of Bossu as a point of support on their right flank, and that near the village of Pireaumont, as well as the village itself, as a point of support on their left flank. The [army's battle] line ran partly on the highway from Nivelles to Namur, partly in parallel to it. Since the two woods extend, as already noted, at right angles from that highway towards the enemy position, they provided the same favourable points of support to the enemy. A sole section of terrain between the two woods, the Gemioncourt farm, was occupied by the French troops.[15]

Summary of the action

The morning of the 16th passed by without any serious fighting. The 2nd Netherlands Division had at this time been deployed near Quatre Bras and was even able to press the enemy back towards Frasnes.

At about two o'clock in the afternoon, Marshal Ney attacked it in earnest with 20,000 to 25,000 men and more than 30 cannon. The Netherlands troops are thrown back to Quatre Bras, with the loss of their battery,[16] and partly retreat into the wood of Bossu. The action is brought to a standstill immediately in front of Quatre Bras at three o'clock by the recently arrived Brunswick infantry, the 5th British Hanoverian Division and a regiment of Belgian hussars.

The Brunswick infantry takes its place at the right flank of the position together with the Netherlands troops, leaning against the wood of Bossu; the 5th Division marches several hundred paces up the highway from Nivelles to Namur from behind the left flank of the Brunswick troops. The Belgian cavalry regiment advances along the left of the Charleroi highway against the enemy cuirassiers, which are about to attack. It becomes completely dispersed; the Brunswick infantry stands its ground by forming square and by moving closer to the wood. The enemy cavalry pushes on against the Namur highway, from where the 1st Battalion of the Scottish 42nd Regiment counter attacks with levelled bayonets. The cavalry falls upon [the battalion] and causes severe losses, and then advances towards the highway, where it is eventually repulsed by the troops on the spot.

Shortly after this attack, two brigades of the 3rd British Hanoverian Division arrive and extend the line on the left flank. They drive back the enemy, who had taken possession of the village of Pireaumont and had advanced up to the highway, and retake the village.

On the right flank, the enemy follows up on the charge of the cavalry with an attack of his infantry between the wood of Bossu and the Charleroi highway. Only with difficulty does our infantry maintain its position at that section, even with the support of a Brunswick battery that had just arrived, and from Brunswick cavalry. But the enemy's superiority ended with this attack. All his attacks made against different points of the line are repulsed.

By seven o'clock in the evening the troops under the Duke of Wellington can go over to the offensive due to the arrival of several corps of infantry, despite the continued lack of artillery and, particularly, of cavalry. The entire line advances and drives the enemy back several thousand paces. The left flank stays in possession of the village of Pireaumont. After the onset of darkness, the enemy is forced to give up the Gemioncourt farm before the position. The enemy retires in disorder as far as Frasnes; the troops under the Duke of Wellington maintain their position on the battlefield during the night.

The Royal Hanoverian troops in the action

4th Hanoverian Brigade

The brigade under the command of Colonel Best arrived towards three o'clock near the battlefield, together with the other troops commanded by Lieutenant General Picton. It had marched off from Brussels at three o'clock in the morning. Upon the enemy's advance on Quatre Bras, the two Luneburg and Osterode Battalions had to be deployed within range of the enemy artillery fire; the sharpshooters formed a chain of skirmishers in front of the line. The remainder of the brigade followed in second line. The line advanced to the highway from Nivelles to Namur where it halted and took position in the ditch alongside the roadway. The Verden Battalion now still had to link up with the British brigade which moved beyond the highway on the left flank of the Hanoverians. One of its companies was detached to the skirmish line.

The enemy's advance was in full swing. His cavalry just now attacked and rode through the 42nd Scottish Regiment which, in rushing against it, had been overly bold. It [the cavalry] then charged into the skirmish line. The dispersed part of the Verden Battalion was unable to retire quickly enough and, for the most part, was struck down or taken prisoner. As the cavalry continued its advance, it was about to ride across the highway when the two battalions in the ditch fired at them at close range and with such effect that they immediately turned around. In this way, a breakthrough in the centre was fortunately prevented and, moreover, at moderate losses, without the brigade's remaining battalions having to do battle. Another enemy cavalry detachment also moved up again at this point, but was likewise repulsed by the battalions from their favourable position.

In the evening, the brigade advanced with the [troops of the] centre, but was not engaged in any further actions.

The losses on this day were as follows: killed, 1 subaltern officer, 43 men; wounded, 2 captains, 2 subaltern officers, 1 NCO, 1 drummer, 77 men; missing, 2 subaltern officers, 6 NCOs, 90 men.

1st Hanoverian Brigade

The 3rd Division under the command of Lieutenant General C[harles, or Karl] von Alten to which the brigade belonged, had been concentrated at Soignies in the evening of the 15th, from where it took off again at two o'clock in the morning and marched to Nivelles by way of Braine le Comte. At Nivelles, the 2nd Brigade of the King's German Legion and the horse battery were detached on observation duty on the road to Charleroi.[17] The other two brigades of the division and the foot battery arrived at the battlefield at about five o'clock in the evening, after a forced march of about 9 *lieues*[18] which they had covered in about fifteen hours, including their halt at Nivelles. They were ordered to reinforce the left flank of our position and there to drive back the enemy. In order to reach their assigned position they had to pass the entire enemy battle line while moving along the Namur highway. On that march, they were fired at by all the enemy guns, but their losses were relatively low, as most balls went too high. A British light battalion and two companies of Brunswick Jäger were the only force that until now had put up resistance against the enemy on the left wing. They just then were forcefully attacked, were driven out of the village of Pireaumont, and had to retire so far back that the enemy tirailleurs were able to fire at the head of the column of the 1st Hanoverian Brigade on the highway. The Luneburg Light [Field] Battalion, being at the head, was immediately ordered to deploy for an attack. It carried out the attack with such forceful dash that, despite the enemy's determined resistance, it drove him not only out of the hedges and fields bordering the highway, but also out of the village of Pireaumont and the tip of the adjoining wood; only in the last minute was he able to salvage a battery he had moved up next to the village. As the resistance stiffened, in the wood in particular, the Grubenhagen Battalion was sent to support the Luneburg Battalion. Towards seven o'clock in the evening, the enemy made another energetic attempt to retake the village he had lost. He did not succeed, and through our holding it, our left wing remained secured. We abandoned the tip of the wood at the onset of darkness.

On the arrival of the 3rd Division at the battlefield, the British brigade had followed the Hanoverian brigade on the highway and moved to its right against the enemy while the Hanoverians attacked the village.

Posted at the centre of the battle line, it repulsed several charges of cavalry and gained terrain. In order to fully restore the liaison with the [British brigade], a company of the Jäger corps of the 1st Brigade was sent off, which then drove the enemy back some 1,000 paces and thus achieved its objective. During the action, the other three battalions of the brigade remained in reserve on the highway. During the night, we held on to the position that we had taken. Between nine and ten o'clock, the Verden Battalion relieved the two battalions that had been engaged in the action. Two companies of the Duke of York Battalion occupied the village of Pireaumont. The Bremen Battalion moved into the position that had been seized by the Jäger, and sent one company ahead on picket duty. The two Jäger companies then moved further to the right.

There was only scattered small arms fire during the night. The losses of the brigade on this day were as follows: killed, 1 captain, 1 NCO, 2 hornists, 33 men; wounded, 1 captain, 8 subaltern officers, 8 NCOs, 121 men.

Artillery

Captain von Rettberg's[19] *9-pounder Foot Battery*
On arrival at three o'clock in the afternoon at Quatre Bras with the 5th Division, the battery had to take position to the left of that farm and close behind the Namur highway. It was the first one, besides a British battery,[20] that it was possible to field against the enemy. It greatly contributed to throwing back the enemy cavalry, which it struck in its right flank. At five o'clock it advanced beyond the highway, together with the infantry, where, now at the centre, it was engaged with three enemy batteries, and successfully took part in the battle until the evening. Its losses were: killed, 1 NCO, 1 man; wounded, 3 men, 3 horses.

Major Kuhlmann's 9-pounder Horse Battery (King's German Legion)
The battery arrived with the British Guards Division at the battlefield at four o'clock, from its quarters between Ath and Enghien. It had to hurry ahead of the infantry and take position directly in front of the Quatre Bras farm. It was just at this time that the enemy made his first forceful cavalry attack, which the battery's fire helped drive back off the highway. After this first crisis had been met, the battery advanced with the infantry along the side of the Charleroi highway and had to keep firing at the enemy artillery until darkness set in.

Captain Cleeves's[21] *9-pounder Foot Battery (King's German Legion)*
Being part of the 3rd Division, it followed, at around half past five

o'clock, the division's British brigade which had advanced at the centre, and unlimbered next to Captain von Rettberg's Battery that had already driven up. Through their joint efforts they succeeded in overpowering the enemy artillery at that spot, which then retired. Several enemy cavalry attacks were thrown back by the infantry with the support of the artillery.

17 June

At the break of dawn, the enemy made an attack against our advance posts, no doubt for reconnoitring purposes, and was repulsed everywhere, and thereafter did not appear again in full force. But he continuously kept the troops in and near Pireaumont on alert with small detachments, so that it was impossible to cease firing at this place.

The greater part of the troops under the command of the Duke of Wellington had arrived at the battlefield during the night and in the morning, except for most of the cavalry.[22] They were ready for another battle, when the news of the advance of the main French force against the left flank required a change in dispositions.

At 12 noon, the troops received the order to retreat. Those troops still on the march towards Quatre Bras, proceeded on the highway from Nivelles to Brussels. The larger column of the troops gathered at Quatre Bras moved on the highway through Genappe, the smaller one, consisting of the Brunswick corps and the 3rd Division, marched on a side road which by passed Genappe to its right. The advance posts remained in place for some time. The march became quite fatiguing from a heavy downpour.

The enemy had not become aware of the retreat and undertook no pursuit during the first few hours. Later on, near Genappe, his cavalry began to drive against the main column, but was repulsed by our cavalry, which had gradually turned up and protected the infantry during its march.

At eight o'clock in the evening (17 June), all retiring troops took up, in the best order, the positions assigned to them in advance on the plateau before the village of Mont St Jean, which is crossed at a right angle by the highway from Brussels to Genappe. The enemy moved up a few batteries near the farm of La Belle Alliance and cannonaded the line. Several [of our] batteries responded from their emplacements on both sides of the highway. The day ended with this insignificant cannonade. The troops bivouacked on the spot. The rain came down in torrents. Only later on were the men allowed to start watch fires.

On this day, of the Hanoverian troops only the 1st Brigade was engaged for some time in the morning against the enemy's reconnoitring towards the village of Pireaumont. The picket of the Bremen Field Battalion in particular suffered from the skirmish fire. The losses of the brigade on this day were: Killed: 10 men. Wounded: 5 subaltern officers, 2 NCOs, 2 hornists, 79 men. Missing: 23 men.

18 June: Battle of Waterloo
Description of the terrain
Before Mont St Jean, a small village where the highways from Nivelles and from Charleroi to Brussels merge, there is a plateau which extends across both highways. The Charleroi highway runs through the exact centre of the plateau. On following the highway for several thousand paces one comes to a ridge which is similar and runs almost parallel to the first one. The army of the Duke Wellington had taken up position on the first of these ridges, and the French army on the second one. The two ridges were separated by low ground, which in some places was deeper than in others. In general, the slope before the enemy position was less steep than that before ours, but was no obstacle anywhere, not even for artillery and cavalry.

The right flank of the Duke of Wellington was to the right of the Nivelles highway, where the plateau ended, but the hamlet of Braine l'Alleud was also occupied, which lies still further to the right and beyond the low ground; the left flank was leaning on the farmsteads of Papelotte and la Haye. The parts of the terrain in front of, and within, the position were formed as follows: At the right flank, the low ground formed a right angle with that before the front, as seen from our side. It was under full control of the troops of the right wing and those at Braine l'Alleud, and was thus secured against a turning movement, but at the same time also caused the right flank to form a hook.

Before the front, where the centre joined the somewhat retired right flank, there was the farmstead of Hougoumont, which was lying slightly below the level at which the troops were posted. Its buildings and a garden attached to their left were surrounded by a wall, in which loopholes were made during the morning, which were also made on the upper floor of the building. There was an orchard and a wood of elm trees, in size about 150 square *ruten*,[23] encompassed for the most part by a wet ditch.

Before the centre and next to the Charleroi highway, in the low ground that separated the two positions, there was the farmstead of La Haye Sainte. It was adjoined by an orchard on the enemy side and by a small kitchen garden on ours, both surrounded by fairly dense hedges. The buildings had not been prepared for defence (an oversight that caused significant losses to the troops posted therein).

There were hedges in a straight direction from the [Charleroi] highway towards Papelotte, along the slope of the plateau on which the left wing was positioned. [Papelotte] formed the end point of this wing. Parts [of the hedges] could be used by the troops posted in the line as parapets, other parts as cover for the skirmishers stationed before the front. Along the best part of the hedge ran a rural road from the highway to Smohain, which was a hollow way for a good a distance. The Charleroi highway had been closed by an abattis near La Haye Sainte, at the beginning of the hedges.

It is thus seen that the retired right wing and the left wing, protected by hedges, represented the better secured parts [of the line], whereas that section between La Haye Sainte and Hougoumont farms was the most suitable part for the [enemy's] attack. It was, however, stiffened somewhat by these strong points. A successful attack could also be conducted against Papelotte, the end point of the left wing, because it was in low ground and not dominating the surrounding terrain, as was the end point of the right wing. The plateau, on which the troops were positioned, was not particularly wide and was sloping to the rear and the front. The second line could thus partly stand in an area where it was protected from artillery fire.

The attached plan [not included] shows in greater detail the deployment of the army under the Duke of Wellington on the terrain described in the foregoing. The end point of the right wing of the enemy line was on the ridge opposite from Papelotte, that of the left wing was the Nivelles highway. The Charleroi highway also crossed the centre of his position. His first line on the left of this highway was formed by the corps of General Reille, that on its right by the corps of General D'Erlon, both in division units. The cavalry divisions were evenly deployed by units in the second line behind both corps, with the exception of a few regiments which had been detached to the far right wing. The cavalry and infantry of the Guard stood in close reserve formation behind the cavalry of the 2nd Corps near the highway. The 6th Corps of Count Lobau stood in massed formation in reserve behind the 1st Corps next to the highway, the artillery reserve still farther to the rear and also close to the highway. The village of Plançenoit behind the right wing was also occupied. The artillery had been evenly distributed and emplaced in front of the entire enemy line.

Summary of the battle
The battle, if viewed from the point of view of the army of the Duke of Wellington (as it is done here), occurred in four phases during its course. Its first, from 11.30 a.m. to 2 p.m., encompasses the prelude and the

initial attacks at the flanks, its second, from 2 to 7 p.m., the enemy's repeated attacks against different sections of the line and the actual set battle, its third, from 7 to 8 p.m., the enemy's attempt to break through the centre, its fourth, from 8 to 9.30 p.m., the offensive movement of the army of the Duke of Wellington.

11.30 a.m.–2.00 p.m.

By 11.30 a.m., the enemy had ended his preparations for the attack, and two infantry columns moved up to the attack, one of these against Papelotte, the other against Hougoumont. As these columns advanced to within firing range, the artillery at the centre opened fire, to which the enemy soon responded. Before long, the cannonading spread along the major part of the line. The attempt to take Papelotte failed and was not vigorously pursued, which was a sign that the enemy's principal attention was not directed at this vulnerable part of the line. The attack against Hougoumont was made with greater determination. At this time, it was defended by a battalion of British Guards, a grenadier company of the Nassau Regiment, a company of the Hanoverian Feldjäger Corps and a detachment of 100 men of the 1st Hanoverian Brigade.[24] The enemy took the small adjoining wood, was expelled again, took it again and advanced to the gate of the farmstead. A forceful sortie with levelled bayonets foiled his prospect of conquering the buildings.

2.00 p.m.–7.00 p.m.

Shortly before two o'clock, the battle expanded into a general affair; the enemy commenced his attacks with large formations against several points of the line. In the right hand area, the Hougoumont farm was still the object of heavy fighting. The buildings go up in flames from the projectiles of an enemy battery, but the farmstead still remains in the hands of our troops; they also regain part of the nearby terrain. A murderous skirmishing fire continues here throughout the day. Meanwhile, infantry columns advance against our troops posted behind the farm, bypassing it to their left. The enemy gradually moves two entire divisions into battle while supported by his cavalry's repeated attacks, which are always repulsed. On our side, the greater part of the troops of the retired right wing move into action, and almost all the Netherlands troops posted at Braine l'Alleud are moved up and positioned behind the centre. Throughout the fighting, the enemy is unable to gain any terrain near the Hougoumont farm. Towards two o'clock, infantry columns, supported by a cavalry division, also move against the La Haye Sainte farm. Attacked several times until after six o'clock in the evening, the 2nd Light Battalion of the King's German

Legion and the Light Company of the 5th Line Battalion of the King's German Legion tenaciously hold on to the farm. It is eventually abandoned because of lack of ammunition. While the fighting at the farmstead continues, the enemy cavalry carries out multiple attacks against the troops standing at the centre on the plateau. But it is thrown back each time by the squares of the infantry or by counter-attacking cavalry. This kind of action continues on the plateau in the same manner, after the La Haye Sainte farm has been taken.

On the highway itself, fighting continues all day for the possession of the abattis. During the first attack on the farm, an infantry column advanced in massed formation along the side of the highway, leaving the farm to their left. After they are repulsed at great loss by the troops at the abattis and at its side, only swarms of enemy tirailleurs move into action [at this point]. The enemy succeeds several times to take possession of the abattis, until it disappears entirely after a few hours. But as soon as he advances beyond it, he is driven back by the troops in the ditches of the highway and in the low spots nearby.

The left wing, extending to the centre at the highway, is attacked by the infantry of the French 1st Corps, concurrently with the first attack on La Haye Sainte. After partly succeeding in its advance up to the position, its front is held up by heavy fire. A British brigade that moves out of the position threatens its right flank with a bayonet attack, and the cavalry brigade of Major General Ponsonby hurries forward from the extreme left flank and throws it completely into a rout. Although [then] retiring in great disorder, it has taken many prisoners and has captured two eagles. One regiment of the cavalry brigade rushes towards the rear of the infantry and disables three batteries by killing the horses, before the enemy cavalry is able to hurry up in support. As the latter moves towards the position to attack our infantry, it is forced back before the parapet like hedges, not having accomplished anything. After the total failure of this assault on the left wing, the enemy does not launch any more serious attacks [against it]. He nevertheless keeps up a heavy cannonade and persistent skirmishing by tirailleurs until the evening, both at this point and at the highway. He only succeeds, at about 6.30 p.m., to expel the weak defending force from Papelotte.[25]

7.00 p.m.–8.00 p.m.

Although the battle began to turn worse for the enemy, due to the arrival and the attack on his right flank by the Royal Prussian troops that had already lasted for several hours, he persisted in his attempts to break through the line of the Duke of Wellington. The most violent attacks, until now, were directed against the centre, in which also the cavalry of the enemy right wing, that was unable to operate on its front participated. At seven o'clock there occurred here one last desperate attack, which involved the entire corps of the Imperial Guard, supported by the simultaneous advance of the troops already engaged in the battle. The major part of the enemy cavalry has rallied in the lower ground, with its right flank next to La Haye Sainte, and now moves up to the plateau. To its left it has infantry and on its flanks and in the intermediate spaces light [horse] artillery. At the same time, the troops in Hougoumont wood are reinforced. Supported by fresh cavalry units, the infantry passes by the farm and moves against the troops in the position. The most violent action of the day now erupts on the plateau, but the enemy's advance is halted for the time being.

8.00 p.m –9.30 p.m.

The Duke of Wellington considers that the proper moment has now come to make a decisive move against the enemy army with the assistance of the Prussian troops, and to end the precarious situation of his troops on the plateau. He orders the left wing to advance in parallel with the Prussian troops that had arrived by way of Ohain and had driven the enemy out of Papelotte. At the same time, he has the troops on the right wing that are not yet engaged in battle to advance towards Hougoumont. He draws two cavalry brigades from the left wing and orders them to attack, together with the troops standing on the ridge near Hougoumont. He indicates the farm of La Belle Alliance at the centre of the enemy position as the point where they have to direct their advance. Renewed courage inspires the troops upon receiving this order; the cavalry commences its attack that achieves the most splendid success; behind it, the infantry presses on. The enemy formations, the Guards among them, do the best they can to conduct their retreat in good order; yet those formed units are soon dispersed.

As the enemy's left wing is driven back, those of his troops in the centre and on the plateau near La Haye Sainte continue the battle, which, so far, has not turned against them yet. Upon becoming aware of the retreat of the flank, they join in, although too late for their escape, because they are also dispersed by the troops moving up from the sides, and only a few fugitives of the large mass can escape. La Haye Sainte is easily retaken by the troops of the left wing near the highway; the other troops of that wing advance without meeting an enemy.

In this way, the army of the Duke of Wellington arrives at the position that the enemy had held in the morning. It stays here during the night while the Royal Prussian troops continue the pursuit.

The Part of the Royal Hanoverian Troops and of the King's German Legion in the Battle[26]

1 Infantry

3rd Hanoverian Brigade

Until three o'clock in the afternoon, the 3rd Brigade under the command of Colonel Hugh Halkett[27] stood in closed columns in the retired right wing, where it suffered somewhat from the cannonade. It then advanced several hundred paces up to the hollow way which in this area joins the Nivelles highway. At five o'clock the two Osnabrück and Salzgitter Battalions were drawn up, past the hollow way, towards the Hougoumont farm and formed squares on a ridge, while under heavy fire. There they remained, without having faced an attack at close quarters, until the time that the line received orders to advance.

The Salzgitter Battalion had to force the wood of Hougoumont, in which Brunswick infantry and other troops battled against the enemy. When he would not yield upon receiving a heavier skirmish fire, the battalion advanced against him with levelled bayonets in closed company front and took possession of the entire wood. Once past the wood, the battalion formed up again and, driving the enemy back [all the time], moved at dusk into the enemy position, where there were already troops from the left wing.

The Osnabrück Battalion, commanded by the brigadier in person, advanced against the enemy, leaving Hougoumont to its right. It ran into a square of the enemy Guard in the lower ground and dispersed it in a bayonet attack. On this occasion, Colonel Halkett in person took General Cambronne prisoner. The battalion moved into the enemy position, also always driving the enemy ahead, who was in the greatest disorder.

The two Bremervorde and Quackenbruck Battalions remained in the position taken up at three o'clock until evening, then followed the advancing line to the edge of the Hougoumont wood, without having done battle. They there spent the night.

The losses of the brigade in the battle were: killed, 1 captain, 3 subaltern officers, 2 NCOs, 53 men; wounded, 2 staff officers, 2 captains, 9 subaltern officers, 6 NCOs, 3 drummers, 157 men.

1st Brigade of the King's German Legion

The brigade under the command of Colonel du Plat stood at the retired right wing. It remained there after three o'clock, having wheeled into open column to be protected as much as possible against the artillery fire.

The enemy cavalry repeated its attacks on the plateau, forced the artillery to go back, and moved on between the squares of infantry almost to the left flank of the brigade, which had to change front, together with the British brigade that was part of the [2nd] Division. The column then changed direction towards Hougoumont. But since the enemy cavalry remained on the plateau on this side of Hougoumont, the battalions immediately formed squares. The rearmost ones moved to the left from the column, while steadily advancing towards the plateau. The brigade commander was shot dead as this happened.

The square of the 2nd Battalion, being in front and just moving towards Hougoumont, was about to open fire against the line of enemy cavalry, when [that cavalry] already leaving the field, they were induced to do so by the advance of the squares and the fire of the batteries that had moved up at the same time. The square now moved close to Hougoumont, where it became exposed to the vigorous fire of the enemy tirailleurs in the orchard. There was little choice but to quickly assault the enemy in the ditches and to seize the orchard. This was then done, and after the battalion had gained a part of the broken terrain in this way, it gradually seized more of it from the enemy. However, his resistance stiffened to a point that some Brunswick battalions were sent in support. The battalion now fought on the broken terrain for the rest of the day with varying success, until in the evening the enemy was completely driven out with the help of the Salzgitter Battalion that had been drawn up. As soon as that had happened, the battalion formed up on the other side of the wood and then advanced as far as La Belle Alliance.

The squares of the 3rd and 4th Battalions remained at first on the plateau from which the enemy cavalry had departed. The 1st Battalion was now moving onto the terrain where several of our batteries had been standing before the charges of the enemy cavalry, and where a number of unmanned artillery pieces had been left. An enemy infantry column, supported by cavalry, attempted to regain this position, but was driven back by the battalion, and then moved sideways into the wood at Hougoumont. The cavalry, however, had charged twice but was beaten back. As the square had suffered heavily, it was combined into a single square with the 3rd Battalion that was standing next to it. A short time later, the squares were forcefully charged by the cavalry of the enemy Guard. The men, having loaded with two balls, fired calmly and at point blank range so that this cavalry had to fall back with great loss, which was still increased by the two divisional batteries. Towards seven o'clock the two squares moved back a short distance on the plateau to reform their ranks. This had hardly been completed, when the Duke of Wellington gave the order in person to move in line against, and seize, the batteries on the opposite side. This was done immediately. The battalions still received a few canister rounds before the artillery crews left their pieces. The enemy was fleeing everywhere in great disorder and the battalions moved into the enemy position.

The losses of the brigade were: killed, 1 colonel, 5 captains, 2 subaltern officers, 7 NCOs, 2 drummers, 93 men; wounded, 3 staff officers, 3 captains, 14 subaltern officers, 24 NCOs, 327 men.

1st Hanoverian Brigade
The brigade under the command of Major General Count von Kielmansegge stayed at the position in the first line of the centre, about 200 paces to the right of the Genappe highway, which it had taken on the previous evening. The area of the plateau, on which it was standing, was level and without any obstructions on the terrain. Upon the beginning of the enemy artillery fire, it moved behind a country road which here connects the Genappe and Nivelles highways. It now stood about 300 paces off the crest of the plateau. The brigade had to form closed columns of two battalions standing side by side, one of these in left in front, the other in right in front formation to allow a rapid deployment in line or square. In the latter case, it was decided that two battalions were to form a single square because of their low strengths. The Brigade's 5th Battalion stood by itself to be used according to circumstances. One of the two Jäger companies formed a line of advance posts before the brigade on the slope of the plateau; the other, together with a detachment of 100 riflemen, half of them each, from the Luneburg and Grubenhagen Battalions, was sent to the wood of Hougoumont, where there was a lack of light troops.[28] This detachment stayed there throughout the day and contributed to the tenacious defence of this outpost.

12.00 p.m–2 p.m.
From the beginning of the battle, the enemy kept up a heavy cannonade against the part of the line that was held by the brigade. However, the ricocheting fire inflicted greater damage on the Nassau infantry regiment that stood in the 2nd line, than on the brigade. The two batteries attached to the 3rd Division and a third one[29] had been placed at the crest of the elevation in front of the brigade, and suffered heavily. They were relieved several times by other batteries, which either quickly ran out of ammunition or were demolished within a short time and left some pieces standing. Several powder wagons blew up in front of, and close to, the brigade.

2 p.m.–7 p.m.
At two o'clock, the enemy attacked the farm of La Haye Sainte to the left

of the brigade in the lower ground. It was tenaciously defended by its garrison. The Luneburg Battalion was sent there as a reinforcement. On approaching the farm, it found it already surrounded by the enemy. With the help of the defenders of the building, it drove the enemy infantry out of the orchard. But before being able to fully occupy the orchard, a column of enemy cuirassiers suddenly fell upon them and, being in open order, was completely dispersed. Many men were killed or taken prisoner; others saved themselves on the highway. Only a small part of the battalion remained together during the rest of the day. The commander, Lieutenant Colonel von Klencke, was wounded, and the battalion major was taken prisoner.[30]

A short time later, the just mentioned column of enemy cuirassiers, probably a division in General Kellermann's corps, moved up to the plateau at the area where the brigade was standing, but not before the Jäger company, posted in open order in front of the brigade, had retreated. The brigade quickly formed two squares, of which that on the right was made up of the Bremen and Verden Battalions, and that on the left of the Grubenhagen and Duke of York Battalions. Without delay and in massed ranks, the cavalry made a forceful attack, which, however, was easily repulsed by the squares with effectively withheld fire. The enemy cavalry lost many horses, but it reformed while still on the plateau. After halting for a short time, it again moved up to the attack. When it did not receive fire at an early [favourable] moment, it turned towards the flanks and rode round all four sides. But fire was opened only after it had completed the circle, and the horsemen were again forced into a hasty retreat, which was gaining more speed upon being pursued by our cavalry.

From now on, our cavalry which stood in the 2nd or 3rd line took care, as a rule, of the defence of the terrain in front of the brigade against the masses of enemy cavalry, which repeated its attacks several times at the same spot. No more than two of [our] regiments, often only one, moved against the enemy who, however, was then forced to retire for reforming, usually in the low ground before the plateau. Our cavalry did the same behind the squares. The enemy resumed his cannonade, each time with renewed vigour, as soon as the cavalry had moved away. At about six o'clock in the evening our cavalry was called off, either because it had been weakened by the repeated attacks and was engaged in reforming or because it was used elsewhere. The enemy cavalry then moved up onto the plateau and sent single skirmishers against the squares, apparently in order to induce them to fire. They rode up close and killed or wounded a number of men. Several marksmen were ordered to drive them away. Now followed a new attack of the massed cavalry, but the closer it came, the more obvious became the weakened resolve that it had. It turned around even before the squares felt a need to fire, and moved off the plateau.

7 p.m.–8 p.m.

During the enemy's last attempt to break through the centre that he now undertook, the brigade was in a serious situation, and that hour was to be its most disastrous. The greatly reinforced enemy cavalry again moved against the plateau in a massive column; to its left it had columns of infantry, and artillery on its right and left flanks. His infantry kept up a well directed fire, which struck primarily the square on the right of the brigade; the artillery was firing case shot. On the right, the Nassau Regiment advanced against the enemy infantry but stopped short of a bayonet attack; still, the enemy now did not push forward anymore. At the same time, the [brigade's] square on the right made a forward move which kept the enemy cavalry from charging at this critical moment. By now, however, the heavy fire had inflicted such a severe loss on the square that its front face had been swept away, reducing the square to the shape of a triangle. The commander and many officers were wounded just now; the ammunition was about to give out. All of this caused it to go back for some distance, together with the Nassau Regiment. Order was soon restored, however, and the former position was taken up again. But now, the enemy case shot and small arms fire became violent to the point, that after less than half an hour all order within the ranks was lost, and whatever remained of the exhausted little troop retired behind the position.

During this last hour, fate was not kinder, either, to the brigade's left square. Two light cannon had been moved up against it on the plateau at a distance of as little as 150 paces, and eventually at less than 100 paces, which fired case shot without interruption. They were too well covered by the cavalry next to them to permit seizing them in a quick forward rush. Just now, assistance from our cavalry or artillery was not to be expected. The entire cavalry had been moved to the right wing, and all batteries had run out of ammunition and gone back to replenish their stores.[31] The losses had to be suffered; firing was impossible out of concern for the cavalry. Lieutenant General von Alten, the commander of the division, was wounded here, and Lieutenant Colonel von Wurmb,[32] commanding the square, was killed, as were many officers and men. The end result was that this square also yielded in disorder. The brigade was reformed as best as possible behind the battle line, was provided with ammunition, and led back to the position. The enemy was prevented from following up by the success already won on the right wing.

The brigade's losses on this day were: killed, 2 staff officers, 1 captain, 2 subaltern officers, 4 NCOs, 159 men; wounded, 3 staff officers, 4 captains, 12 subaltern officers, 16 NCOs, 5 hornists, 375 men.

The total casualties of the last three days, the 16th, 17th and 18th, were: 40 officers and 900 men.[33]

2nd Brigade of the King's German Legion

The brigade under the command of Colonel von Ompteda stood at the centre in the first line, with its left flank adjoining the Charleroi highway. The 2nd Light Battalion, commanded by Major Baring,[34] was detached to the defence of La Haye Sainte. The battalions numbered not even 350 men [each].[35]

Until about two o'clock the brigade suffered from heavy artillery fire. As the enemy infantry and cavalry moved up, the 2nd Light Battalion was soon surrounded in the farm and had to abandon the orchard that had been occupied by 100 men. But it put up a determined defence of the buildings, as the men fired out of the windows and through loopholes in the walls they had opened up with their rifle butts. Around three o'clock, the garrison was reinforced by two companies of the 1st Light Battalion of about 100 men, each, and then by the light company of the 5th Line Battalion, and still later by 200 riflemen of the Nassau Regiment.[36] The enemy attacked three or four times this day, each time in the same pattern with two battalions or regiments. One went straight for the buildings, whereas the other moved against the left side, sending out swarms of tirailleurs. During the last attack, the enemy also moved up artillery against the buildings, and the barn started to burn but the fire was extinguished. Towards six o'clock in the evening the garrison had used up all of its ammunition. As the enemy noticed that there was little return fire, he scaled the wall and forced his way through the entrances of the farm, of which there were five including one that had remained unobstructed during the whole day. The garrison fell back into the building and withdrew by a back door in constant hand-to-hand fighting with the enemy.

The three battalions of the brigade [remaining] on the plateau, standing about 400 paces behind La Haye Sainte, were also ordered to drive back the infantry columns that were moving up. The 1st Light Battalion had, at this time, taken up position in the hollow way which runs from the Charleroi highway to Hougoumont. Disregarding the enemy on its front, it moved to the left of the highway and attacked with great success the left flank of the enemy attack column that had moved against our left wing. When [that column] was attacked at the same time in front by the infantry in the position to the right [left?] by the Scottish

Brigade, and in particular by the cavalry, it soon fell into disorder, and the battalion pursued it for a considerable distance, together with the cavalry. It then returned to its former position in the hollow way, and, for the rest of the day, fired from here at the enemy whenever he appeared on this side of La Haye Sainte, or advanced against him in the ditches of the highway, as soon as he went past the abattis.

The 8th and 5th Line Battalions had to move against enemy infantry, which had attacked and gone past La Haye Sainte in close formation. [Our battalions] had begun their forward move in line when the enemy cavalry fell upon them after roving on the plateau, following the failed charge against the nearby squares of the 1st Hanoverian Brigade. The 5th Battalion still received timely support from the British cavalry to its rear, and thus had minor losses. The 8th Battalion had moved up closer to the enemy infantry and was about to attack it with the bayonet, already seeing it turn around, when it was completely surprised by the cavalry and, for its major part, cut to pieces and dispersed, before the British cavalry was able to drive off the enemy. The officer who carried the colours received three severe wounds, and the colours were then lost. The small remainder of the battalion was reassembled on the ridge behind the hollow way, where it remained for the rest of the day, being unfit for any further attack.

At about three o'clock, the 5th Battalion had to deploy once more and move towards the farm. This time, it was again charged by enemy cavalry and, at great risk, formed square with the support of British cavalry. It now took up position immediately behind the hollow way, where it was protected against the [enemy] cavalry, and remained there until six o'clock. At about this time, the brigade commander led it in line towards the farm for the third time. But on the way there, it suffered the same fate as the 8th Battalion, and was cut down by the enemy cavalry. [Our] horsemen rushing down from the plateau just saved it from complete destruction. The brigade commander was shot and killed during this action,[37] and both colours were lost.

The brigade's losses on this day were: killed, 1 colonel, 1 staff officer, 8 captains, 4 subaltern officers, 10 NCOs, 1 hornist, 122 men; wounded, 1 staff officer, 3 captains, 24 subaltern officers, 32 NCOs, 4 hornists, 321 men; missing, 1 captain, 2 subaltern officers, 4 NCOs, 4 hornists, 56 men.

4th Hanoverian Brigade

On the 18th, the 4th Brigade was part of the left wing and stood to the left of the British troops of the 5th and 6th Divisions in the first line. Towards two o'clock, as the enemy's attacks began to close against this part of the line, the brigade formed squares. Opposite from the brigade, enemy cavalry deployed to charge but was thrown back by the British cavalry, which stood in the 2nd line. During the rest of the day, the brigade was never involved in battling against large formations. It suffered primarily under the artillery fire. Between four and five o'clock, it drew several hundred paces closer to the Charleroi highway and took up position in closed columns on the slope of the plateau. The riflemen stood in the skirmish line and were in action against the enemy all day. After they ran out of ammunition, they were relieved by single companies from the battalions, which were replaced by others after these were also out of cartridges.

In the [general] attack in the evening, the brigade deployed in line and advanced with the entire line on the same front as the Prussian troops, but no longer met the enemy who had already been thrown back by the Prussian cavalry. It found 32 abandoned artillery pieces in the enemy position.

Its losses were: killed, 2 subaltern officers, 1 NCO, 46 men; wounded, 1 staff officer, 4 captains, 12 subaltern officers, 12 NCOs, 284 men.

5th Hanoverian Brigade

At the beginning of the battle, the brigade under the command of Colonel von Vincke was also part of the left wing and stood to the left of the 4th Brigade. Around two o'clock, it formed squares because of the approach of enemy cavalry. After the British cavalry had beaten back that attack, the brigade was ordered to move to the centre to serve as a reserve at the Charleroi highway. The Peine and Hildesheim Battalions took position in closed columns behind the farm of Mont St Jean, the Hameln and Gifhorn Battalions more forward, in line with the cavalry and the Nassau infantry in the second line. Upon the enemy's last attack, they moved up to the plateau, where they deployed and fired at the advancing enemy. As the Duke of Wellington gave the signal to advance, they moved forward along the highway and arrived in the enemy position. The two battalions that were left standing in the rear followed only later.

The brigade's losses were: killed, 1 NCO, 43 men; wounded, 2 staff officers, 3 captains, 5 subaltern officers, 7 NCOs, 2 drummers, 164 men.

2 Cavalry

1st Light Dragoon Regiment of the King's German Legion

The regiment was part of Major General von Dornberg's Brigade and stood, until two o'clock, in the 2nd line at the centre behind the

3rd Division. At this time, the brigade moved further to the right, up to the Nivelles highway. Shortly after four o'clock, the enemy cuirassiers passed between the squares of the infantry in front, and the 1st Regiment, together with the 23rd British Dragoon Regiment, moved against them in squadron columns. The enemy was completely overthrown and pursued energetically so that also the rearmost squadrons engaged the enemy, but this also forced the regiment to retreat as it ran into the enemy reserves. These did not follow too eagerly, giving the regiment time to reform behind the squares. It again repulsed the enemy when he moved up to the plateau. A short time later, [the enemy] appeared again, and this time, the regiment met him in line. It was a violent encounter and a very bloody battle, but the enemy cavalry eventually moved sideways and retreated in good order. The brigade commander received a severe stab wound in this charge.[38] After this action, the enemy cavalry moved two more times against the brigade during the course of the day. But upon being attacked by us, it retreated both times after a brief action, and the regiment returned to its former position behind the squares.

Its losses were: killed, 1 cavalry captain, 2 subaltern officers, 3 NCOs, 1 bugler, 32 men; wounded, 2 staff officers, 3 cavalry captains, 6 subaltern officers, 7 NCOs, 1 bugler, 76 men, 165 horses.

2nd Light Dragoon Regiment of the King's German Legion

It was part of the same brigade as the 1st Regiment and stood next to it until after four o'clock, when it was detached to Braine l'Alleud to observe the enemy cavalry, which had shown up in this area. Once arrived, it found that the enemy cavalry stood behind ditches in an unassailable position. It was therefore kept under observation, only, until it moved off. When this happened at about half past six o'clock in the evening, the regiment went back to the battle line and to the same place it had held at noon. A short time later, it was ordered to charge the enemy cavalry. It passed through the infantry, which was also beginning its forward move, formed in line, and attacked the enemy.

He had halted and received the regiment with fire from carbines; there was a large ditch before his front that was the cause of his stance. But all this did not deter the regiment; it kept sabring him with good success, until forced to turn around by enemy cavalry advancing on its flank. After only a part of the regiment had rallied at great speed, an officer immediately led that part again towards the enemy. The remaining part of the regiment joined in the advance and, as the enemy cavalry was moving up in disorder, it was completely over thrown. At this moment, the enemy cavalry, that had marched up to the side, was charged by the fresh brigades which had been drawn in from the left flank, and all of the enemy cavalry was now taking to flight, and was followed by the infantry.

The regiment lost: killed, 1 captain, 1 subaltern officer, 18 men; wounded, 2 staff officers, 1 captain, 2 subaltern officers, 6 NCOs, 45 men, 89 horses.

Cumberland Hussar Regiment

The regiment was part of the Reserve corps and, on this day, was attached to Major General Dornberg's Brigade. As this brigade moved farther to the right from the centre, the regiment had to halt at the Charleroi highway where it suffered under artillery fire. It did not attack at all. Its commander led it off the battlefield and he was cashiered for that. (This regiment was standing at a forward spot, on whose orders is unknown and poorly positioned in front of the infantry and directly behind La Haye Sainte, where it was exposed to enemy artillery fire for no known purpose. Its commander led it back and forgot to turn it around in time.)[39]

3rd Hussar Regiment of the King's German Legion

The brigade under Colonel von Arentschildt consisted of this and the 13th British Dragoon Regiment. On the day of battle, the two regiments did not join up, however. Of the 10 companies of the 3rd Hussar Regiment, only seven were present, and it stood all by itself at the centre of the battle line behind the Nassau Regiment drawn up in the 2nd line, and had suffered severely under the artillery fire. It had already lost its commander, Lieutenant Colonel Meyer.[40]

After the attacks of the enemy cavalry had commenced and the enemy had driven back the Netherlands Dragoons behind the infantry line in one of its charges, the regiment formed up in the second line, and one half of it repulsed the pursuing enemy cavalry. At this moment, the commanding general of the cavalry [Earl of Uxbridge] ordered the other two squadrons to charge the enemy's reserve that was following up. It consisted of a regiment, each, of cuirassiers, dragoons, and lancers, deployed in line. The squadrons charged part of the first two and broke through them. But in pursuing these, they suffered severe losses because they were outflanked by the rest of the line and attacked in their rear. On reforming behind the squares, the regiment consisted of only 60 *rott*,[41] who were formed into a single squadron.

The regiment made a second charge when, towards six o'clock in the evening, the 5th Line Battalion of the King's German Legion advanced on La Haye Sainte and, on its way, was fallen upon by enemy cuirassiers. It cut the infantry free, but lost severely. Now it numbered only 40 *rott*. They joined two weak squadrons of the British Horse Guards, and this represented the entire cavalry that still stood behind the left part of the centre during the enemy's last attack in the evening. After the regiment's second charge, it deployed only skirmishers against the enemy cavalry, which harassed the squares with its skirmishers. It did not make any further attacks, and advanced as the enemy drew back.

Its losses were: killed, 1 staff officer, 2 captains, 2 subaltern officers, 2 sergeants, 1 bugler, 24 hussars; wounded, 2 captains, 6 subaltern officers, 9 sergeants, 1 bugler, 103 hussars, horses, 143.

1st Hussar Regiment of the King's German Legion
Until half past six o'clock in the evening the regiment stood behind the left wing of the position, together with the two British regiments of Major General Vivian's Brigade, to which it belonged. In the evening, the brigade was moved to the right wing and had to charge the enemy cavalry as the entire line was about to advance. The brigade advanced against the enemy in squadron columns, came upon the cavalry of the enemy Guard and overthrew it completely, whereupon disorder was spread throughout the enemy's ranks. The 1st Hussar Regiment did not cut into the enemy because it was the hindmost in the brigade column.

Its losses were: killed, 2 men; wounded, 1 subaltern officer, 7 men.

3 Artillery

Major Sympher's Horse Battery of the King's German Legion
During the initial part of the battle, it stood at the retired right flank of the position behind the left wing of the 2nd Division, to which it belonged. As the division moved up to the plateau behind Hougoumont and there formed squares, this battery and the British foot battery of the division[42] followed it, took position behind the infantry and fired spherical case shot[43] at the enemy cavalry. It did not engage the enemy artillery that had moved up against this point, because the artillery had received general instructions before the battle to deal only with the infantry and cavalry. Its fire became particularly effective towards evening by which time the enemy cavalry was already exhausted. During the general offensive of the line, the battery joined its advance, at first in the direction of La Belle Alliance, but then had to turn to the right against an enemy battery emplaced near Mon Plaisir, the last one to keep firing at our troops.

The losses of the battery in killed and wounded were: 1 officer and 32 men and 27 horses.

Major Kuhlmann's Horse Battery of the King's German Legion
At the beginning of the battle, the battery and a British battery[44] of the Guards Division, to which it belonged, had moved up onto the plateau behind Hougoumont, about 400 paces to the left of the farm. Right on half past eleven o'clock, it started firing at the advancing infantry, which was forced to move to the left behind the wood of Hougoumont, where it then began its attack. When, after several hours, the enemy cavalry spread out everywhere on the plateau, the much damaged artillery retreated to a ridge further to the rear and, towards evening, moved back to its former position.[45]

The losses of the battery in killed and wounded were: 12 men and 18 horses.

Battery of Captain Cleeves
At the beginning of the battle, the battery with two other batteries had moved up to the crest of the plateau, to the right rear of La Haye Sainte and in front of the 3rd Division. It opened the battle with its firing at the infantry that advanced against Hougoumont. The enemy [cannon] fire towards this point was very effective. Some adjoining batteries had to leave their demolished cannon standing, so had the battery [Cleeves's] in the case of one of its pieces. As the attacks of the enemy cavalry became more numerous, it drew back to a position between the squares where it remained until it had used up all of its ammunition. It then retired to Mont St Jean to replenish its ammunition, but was only able to advance again in the evening,[46] after the enemy had made his last attack. It remained in the position that it had held in the morning.

Its losses were: killed, 1 officer, 1 NCO, 7 men; wounded, 2 officers, 2 NCOs, 10 men, 10 horses.

Captain Braun's Foot Battery
Until three o'clock in the afternoon, the battery stood with Major General Lambert's British Brigade[47] in reserve near Mont St Jean to the right of the Charleroi highway. At that time, it moved with the infantry into the first line. The infantry was positioned with its right flank on the Charleroi highway, and the battery was emplaced before its centre. Covered against attacks in front by the hollow way, on its flank by the high banks of the highway, it remained here throughout the battle. It alternately directed its fire against the enemy's right flank and the attack columns advancing towards La Haye Sainte, together with the other three batteries that had drawn up before the left wing. The enemy's cannonade against this point was particularly heavy. One by one, the greater part of our cannon were demolished, but the fire was kept up

until the enemy's retreat. The battery also lost severely from the fire of the enemy tirailleurs.

Its losses were: killed, 1 subaltern officer, 2 NCOs, 9 men; wounded, 1 captain, 1 subaltern officer, 6 NCOs, 35 men, 57 horses.

Captain von Rettberg's Foot Battery
From the beginning of the battle until its end, it stood at the extreme left flank in front of the 4th Hanoverian Brigade behind the hollow way. The position was almost as good as a regular entrenchment. It fired as heavily at the enemy troops as it could with the available store of ammunition, of which one half had already been used on the 16th.

Its losses: killed, 1 man; wounded, 1 officer and 10 men and 11 horses.

THE CAVALRY

3rd Brigade of Major General William Dornberg

No. 3 From *Belle-Alliance*

Pflugk-Harttung's letter no. 27. Report of the 3rd Mixed Cavalry Brigade (Dornberg) on its participation in the Battle of La Belle Alliance, reported by Lieutenant General von Dornberg.

Celle, 12 November 1824

To the Royal General Staff [War Department] in Hanover

In compliance with the General Order of 28 October 1824, I have the honour to most obediently report that the brigade under my command on 18 June at Waterloo consisted of the 23rd Regiment of English Light Dragoons and the 1st and 2nd Regiments of Light Dragoons of the King's German Legion, and had the designation 3rd Cavalry Brigade, to which in the evening of the 16th the former Cumberland Hussar Regiment, now the 2nd Uhlan Regiment, was attached. Only late on the 17th did I move with the rearguard, which consisted of the 7th Hussars and the 23rd Light Dragoon Regiment, into the bivouac to the right of the Brussels highway close to Mont St Jean. I then received the order to post pickets before the right flank of the army up to the highway which runs from Brussels to Charleroi. Since the enemy army had followed in our footsteps and now stood quite close to us on the opposite heights, these pickets had to be well manned. I therefore fielded 3 squadrons, one of the 23rd Light Dragoons, one from the 2nd Light Dragoons, and one from the Cumberland Hussar Regiment. The latter I posted in front of a small wood on our right flank, that of the 2nd Light Dragoons in the low area in front of the centre of our right flank, and that of the 23rd Light Dragoon Regiment on the highway in the depression between La Haye Sainte and La Belle Alliance. These squadrons detached small troops for maintaining contact with each other, and others in front, as videttes, below the heights occupied by the enemy.

Early on the 18th, about half an hour after daybreak, these pickets were retired. The brigade was then moved slightly to the right and stood in regimental columns, with squadrons marched right shoulders off, behind the division of General von Alten, between the highways from Charleroi and from Nivelles. The terrain consisted of gently rising elevations, with the infantry posted on the forward slope and the crest, and the cavalry standing behind by brigades and somewhat protected by the rearward slope. However, from the cannonade beginning at eleven o'clock we were hit by many cannon balls, and here it was that Captain von Bothmer[48] already lost a leg. The soil had turned very soft from the rains of the 17th. To our left stood the brigade of Lord Edward Somerset, to our right that of General Grant, formed up in the same manner.

At around eleven o'clock, the enemy started his attack on Hougoumont, which was located in front of our right flank. The first cannon shot was fired by the battery placed before the brigade. Masses of cavalry were forming almost directly opposite us, but at a distance of more than a cannon shot; it was probably the heavy division of General Kellermann. At about two o'clock, Lord Uxbridge himself ordered me to move the brigade more to the right, and to leave only the Cumberland Regiment in its place, for the reason that General Grant's Brigade would also have to march more to the right, as more of the [enemy] cavalry was amassing towards our right flank. The brigade thus stood close to the Nivelles highway, with several Brunswick battalions in squares before its right flank, and Kuhlmann's battery before its front.

As, towards four o'clock, the enemy fielded more cavalry on our right flank, Lord Uxbridge ordered me to detach a regiment against it, and I sent off the most senior officer, Colonel de Jonquières,[49] with the 2nd Light Dragoon Regiment. I am unable to give information on his further services on that day because I was not an eyewitness. Soon thereafter, an enemy cuirassier regiment advanced at the trot. It moved straight up to the plateau, between the squares and the battery. Since both of my regiments were light cavalry, I ordered them to stay in column. As soon as I sounded the signal to attack, the 23rd Regiment was to thrust vigorously into the enemy's left flank, and the 1st to do the same against the enemy's right flank. The three rear squadrons were to halt and deploy as soon as the enemy had been repulsed, while only the No. 1 squadrons were to pursue the enemy. This attack fully succeeded, and the cuirassier regiment was completely overthrown. Unfortunately, our rear squadrons could not be held back and they all rushed after the enemy, only to be stopped by his reserve, which then turned us back again. But because this reserve followed only at the trot, I had time to more or less reform the two regiments and to repulse that reserve, which had come up to the plateau. Order had hardly been restored after this attack, when another cuirassier regiment came trotting up to the plateau. We advanced against it in line and at the gallop, whereupon the enemy regiment halted and pointed its swords at us. Our men beat at them with their curved sabres, but without much success, and I heard them shout: 'If only we had again our former old swords!'[50] With some of our men, I attacked that regiment on its right flank and rear. But even then we were unable to accomplish much against the well armoured cuirassiers. They, however, started to move at first to the left, but then retreated in fairly good order. On this occasion I received a stab in my left chest, which penetrated my lung. As blood was coming out of my mouth and my speaking was much impaired, I had to ride off to the rear. I am thus unable to report anything about the conduct of the troops in the later action in the pursuit of the enemy.

How well our troops have fought on this day, is generally known; but what in my opinion redounds most to the honour of our cavalry was the swiftness with which order was restored after each attack, proving the strong discipline prevailing in this corps. My wound kept me from immediately taking notes, and I later missed out on doing that. I therefore have to beg for consideration if this report is quite incomplete, as I no longer can recall all the details.

Dornberg, Lieutenant General and Adjutant General

1st Light Dragoons, King's German Legion

No. 4 From *Belle-Alliance*

Pflugk-Harttung's letter no. 48. Report of the 1st Light Dragoon Regiment of the King's German Legion on its participation in the events of 16 to 19 June.

16 June
At five o'clock in the morning the regiment received an order to move off at once towards Genappe. The regiment accordingly marched off from Malines at nine o'clock, arrived in the Genappe area in the afternoon, and bivouacked near Quatre Bras, thus did not participate in the action.

17 June
The army retired in the afternoon (as did, of course, the regiment). Towards the evening, the five companies had to skirmish alternately (together with the heavy English cavalry) as part of the rearguard, until darkness set in. During the night, the regiment stayed not far away from Mont St Jean, without taking off the horse furniture; Captain von Sichart[51] and his squadron were detached on picket duty. On the 17th,

the regiment lost one man killed, two men and five horses wounded, and Captain George Hattorf[52] lost his horse.

18 June

In the morning, positions were taken up; our brigade (column) consisted of the 23rd Light Dragoon Regiment, the 1st and 2nd Light Dragoon Regiments, King's German Legion, and the Hanoverian Hussar Regiment of His Royal Highness, the Duke of Cumberland, and was commanded by Major General Sir William Dornberg. The 2nd Regiment was detached on orders from Lord Uxbridge; the 23rd also was given a destination further to the left [right?] of us. At the time of the commencement of charges, the regiment thus remained by itself on the position in the centre (by the highway from Nivelles to Brussels) that had been assigned to the four regiments. The cannonade began at eleven o'clock in the morning, and we were exposed all the time to heavy artillery fire. Shortly after one o'clock, the enemy cavalry (cuirassiers) moved up and was charged by us and thrown back. The regiment had hardly retaken its post behind the artillery and infantry that it had left for the charge when a second column of enemy cuirassiers moved up; the regiment charged and likewise drove them back. A third column came up and had already approached to within a short distance from our artillery; this one was also charged and thrown back. Not much later, a fourth cavalry column arrived, which we forcefully charged like the three earlier ones. These four charges occurred within a time period of one and a half hours. All in all, the regiment made nine charges against enemy cavalry on this afternoon; six of these turned into actual combat, whereas in the three others the enemy turned away from our charges. Whatever else did happen in this memorable battle is too well known to be mentioned in this context. The regiment followed the enemy beyond the battlefield and, after nightfall, bivouacked in the enemy position.

19 June

From three o'clock in the morning, the regiment pursued the enemy (with the army).

No. 5 From *Belle-Alliance*

Pflugk-Harttung's letter no. 49. Report of the 1st Light Dragoon Regiment of the [King's] German Legion on its participation in the Battle of La Belle Alliance.

1st Light Dragoon Regiment, King's German Legion, reported by Captain Lewis von Sichart.[53]

Hanover, 10 July 1836

. . . The 1st Dragoon Regiment at first charged in column, but then in line. During this first attack in line, there appeared suddenly on its left flank a detachment of French cavalry (about a squadron strong) while the regiment was already advancing to the charge. On observing the danger of an attack on that flank, the then Major von Reizenstein[54] broke away with part of the regiment's left flank which he quickly pulled together, charged the enemy detachment and threw it back. The 1st Dragoon Regiment and the enemy cavalry then charged each other with such violence that both detachments broke through their respective ranks (at least partially), which turned into a pell-mell melee. In this action, a number of officers of the 1st Dragoon Regiment were wounded, one among them who, in pursuing the fleeing part of the enemy detachment, was wounded in the back by a stab from an enemy horseman . . .

L. von Sichart, Captain, General Staff

No. 6 From *Belle-Alliance*

Pflugk-Harttung's letter no. 50. List of the losses of the 1st Light Dragoon Regiment of the [King's] German Legion reported by Lieutenant General Dornberg.

Report on officers, men, and horses that were killed or wounded in the Battle of Waterloo.

[The following listing is in table format in the original]

Killed on the battlefield: 1 captain, 2 lieutenants, 3 sergeants, 1 bugler, 3 corporals, 23 privates; 12 officer's horses, 53 troop horses.

Wounded: 1 colonel, 1 lieutenant colonel, 1 major, 1 adjutant, 3 captains, 3 lieutenants, 2 cornets, 7 sergeants, 1 bugler, 15 corporals, 67 privates; 5 officer's horses, 95 troop horses.

Note: Of the wounded, 6 men and 24 horses died shortly after the battle.

Names of killed and wounded officers.

Killed: Captain Peters,[55] Lieutenant von Levetzow,[56] Lieutenant Kuhlmann.[57]

Wounded: Colonel (Major General) von Dornberg, Lieutenant Colonel von Bülow,[58] Major von Reizenstein, Lieutenant and Adjutant Fricke;[59] Captains von Sichart, George von Hattorf, von Bothmer; Lieutenants Mackenzie,[60] Bosse,[61] von Hammerstein; Cornets Nanne[62] and Trittau.[63]

Dornberg, Lieutenant General and General Adjutant (former Brigadier)

2nd Light Dragoons, King's German Legion

No. 7 From *Belle-Alliance*

Pflugk-Harttung's letter no. 51. Report of the 2nd Light Dragoon Regiment of the [King's] German Legion on its participation in the Battle of Belle Alliance.

16 June

In the night from the 15th to the 16th, orders were received for an immediate march, as the enemy had already begun his operations. The regiment was first provided with foodstuffs and forage before its departure. It then marched off, passed Brussels around five o'clock in the afternoon, moved along the road to Genappe and Quatre Bras, and camped at night on an open field near Genappe, after having marched 14 leagues, from setting off.

17 June

Engagement with the enemy at Hougoumont. At daybreak, everybody was at arms, and a heavy skirmish fire was kept up by both sides.

Columns of English infantry began to retire, and the entire cavalry was drawn forward in order to cover the retreat. Our brigade was posted on the right flank of the cavalry. In the afternoon towards three o'clock, as the enemy advanced with his reinforcements, our entire cavalry was ordered to retire. A strong thunderstorm, accompanied by a heavy rainfall, soon silenced the enemy artillery. The brigade was not closely pursued, since the enemy columns moved further to the left on the main highway to Brussels. The brigade arrived in the Mont St Jean area around five o'clock in the afternoon. The right flank division of the regiment charged from here with success against part of the French cavalry near Hougoumont and Mon Plaisir, which had already seized the wagons transporting the English General Hospital from Charleroi.[64]

18 June

Battle of Waterloo near Brussels. On this day, the regiment was posted at the centre of the army and was exposed to a continuous heavy cannonade. In the afternoon, the regiment was ordered to cover the town of Braine l'Alleud and the right flank. Later in the afternoon, an order was issued to move [back] to the position held earlier. From here, the regiment soon charged the French cuirassiers, notwithstanding extremely heavy canister fire, and continued its attacks until late in the evening. The regiment had considerable losses.

19 June
The regiment set up camp at Thines near Nivelles.[65]

No. 8 From *Belle-Alliance*

Pflugk-Harttung's letter no. 52. Report of the 2nd Light Dragoon Regiment of the [King's] German Legion on its participation in the Battle of La Belle Alliance, reported by Colonel A. C. Friedrichs.[66]

Linden near Hanover, 24 January 1825

... In the initial deployment of the troops at the beginning of the battle in the morning of 18 June 1815, the 2nd Dragoon Regiment stood in column (by troops), like the other cavalry regiments, so that, if necessary, it could form upon its front in battle array. The regiment of His Royal Highness, The Duke of Cumberland, was posted to its left, and the 1st Dragoon Regiment of the King's German Legion to its right. These regiments stood in the right angle formed by the highways from Mont St Jean to La Belle Alliance, and from the former to Nivelles, the latter highway to its rear. In front of this cavalry was (I believe) the infantry brigade [should be division] of Lieutenant General Count von Alten.

After we suffered some losses from the fire of the enemy artillery, notwithstanding the great distance, we received the order to move slightly to the right, and in particular behind the artillery emplaced to the left of the highway to Nivelles and opposite the enemy cavalry. It was probably around two or three o'clock in the afternoon that the 2nd Dragoon Regiment was ordered to march to Braine l'Alleud, so that it could charge from there at the left flank of the enemy position, where several lancer squadrons had been posted, and here stand by for the order to attack.

We found the village of Braine l'Alleud occupied by a company of Belgian infantry, we had arrived in that area through a hollow way, unseen by the enemy. Instead of an order to attack, we received an order to return to the battlefield, where we took up position behind the artillery on the right flank of the cavalry. A short time later, we were ordered to form up in front of the artillery and to charge the enemy cavalry, which expected our attack, standing quite a distance from us to the left of the Hougoumont farm. The 2nd Dragoon Regiment had hardly followed the order to form up when Lieutenant Colonel von Jonquières gave the signal to attack. Because of the great distance from the enemy at which the charge was commenced, and due to the soft, poor terrain, the charge could not be executed in the closed order normally adopted by the regiment. Deployed in the rear of lower ground, the enemy cavalry, which consisted of cuirassiers and chasseurs, nevertheless turned around after their second rank had fired off their carbines at us. That part of the enemy cavalry not in the path of our charge, wheeled in on our flanks as we pressed on in our pursuit, and we therefore were forced to fall back in our turn. We were closely pursued from our flanks and rear by the enemy, and, with our regiment completely dispersed, would have carried the enemy with us to our position. However, through my efforts to make a number of dragoons join me in opposing the enemy, I was able to gather the dispersed men of the regiment on my flanks. Although officers and men were intermingled, we nevertheless advanced in close order. In thus forcing the enemy to take flight, we saved those comrades killed and wounded in our first attack and, moreover, made the enemy abandon the guns that had fired their last canister rounds at us. We took many prisoners, among them a colonel of the Emperor Napoleon's General Staff, as he told us. While still on the battlefield, the Duke of Wellington expressed his satisfaction with the regiment's and my conduct through Lieutenant Streeruwitz[67] of the 2nd Hussars. The battle thus ended with a not very common feat: a completely dispersed regiment, pursued and surrounded by a superior enemy, and within range of his guns, forms up and advances again in closed order. While one of many, that feat certainly contributed to the greatness of the outcome

. . . . A. C. Friedrichs, colonel

6th Brigade of Major General Sir Hussey Vivian

1st Hussars, King's German Legion

No. 9 From *Belle-Alliance*

Pflugk-Harttung's letter no. 13. Report of the 1st Hussar Regiment of the [King's] German Legion on its participation in the action at Quatre Bras, letter of Major George von der Decken[68] to Colonel von Wissell,[69] commander of the 2nd Uhlan Regiment at Verden.

Letter no. 56. Report of the 1st Hussar Regiment of the [King's] German Legion on its participation in the Battle of Belle Alliance, reported by Major George von der Decken.

Hanover, 21 December 1824

. . . At Tournai, on 16 June at eleven o'clock in the morning, the regiment received the order to march off without delay. We left Tournai at one o'clock and marched without interruption until one o'clock at night to Braine le Comte. The regiment here fed for two hours and moved off again before daybreak.

At 12 noon [on 17 June], the regiment arrived at the position at

Quatre Bras without at all having rested or fed [that day]. After taking our place within the brigade in the first cavalry line on the extreme left flank, and, specifically, to the left of the British 10th and 18th Hussars, the regiment dismounted and rested for about two and a half hours, when masses of French cavalry moved up. While they showed signs of moving forward, our troops continued marching rearward, away from the position. As soon as the enemy cavalry began its advance, our brigade had to retreat on a side road, leaving the main highway to the left. When, at first, the enemy was pursuing us, the 1st Hussar Regiment formed the rearguard. But after the enemy turned to the main highway and advanced only along that road, we continued our march to the position at Waterloo without being disturbed.

Towards seven o'clock in the evening [17 June], our pickets, left behind at Tournai, joined us in the camp assigned to our brigade behind the infantry on the extreme left flank of the position.

We made contact with the Prussians through patrols detached from the pickets that our regiment had to post in the evening of the 17th on the extreme left wing. On the morning of the 18th, some of the regiment's officers were instructed, on orders from Lord Wellington, to transmit communications to the Prussian generals and obtain information on their approaching columns. Two of our officers succeeded in doing that, and Lord Wellington was then informed of the approach of the Prussian General von Bülow and his columns. Towards eleven or half past eleven at midday, the brigade was ordered to mount horses; after the brigade had formed line at various points, we moved quite close behind the left flank of our infantry. Covered from the enemy cannonade by a small ridge in front of us, we received the order to dismount horses.

Towards half past six o'clock in the afternoon, we mounted horses. Both General Vandeleur's and General Vivian's Brigades were ordered to move to the centre of the position. Our brigadier had us wheel right by divisions, and led our brigade masterfully in an appropriate way that, always protected by the ridges, our brigade was hardly ever exposed to enemy cannon fire or musketry. On arrival at the main highway, the greater part of our brigade passed beyond it, except for Nos 3 and 4 squadrons of the 1st Hussar Regiment, and formed line by wheeling left. The 1st Hussar Regiment was then formed up here on both sides of the highway and was considerably exposed to the enemy's small arms fire, as the enemy was strongly and continuously engaged with our infantry. Our brigade marched off forward by divisions from the right flank, forcing our Nos 3 and 4 squadrons to break off in threes to the right to pass the highway. The latter two had to move at a faster pace to be able to follow the column, by then formed on the other side of the highway by squadrons, who, moreover, also rode at the trot, if I remember correctly. Our regiment was ordered to form up several times, while part of the other regiments of our brigade were engaged with enemy infantry, and that with good success.

Several times, the regiments had to break up its squadrons into pairs and threes in order to pass through openings in hedges, and were then re-formed into squadrons. At times, the regiment was thereby exposed to enemy cannon fire, without, however, suffering significant losses. Towards a quarter to eight or quarter after eight o'clock, our regiment passed close to the highway, keeping it to its left, while on both sides our infantry advanced, sometimes in a hurry, always driving back the enemy infantry.

Since seven o'clock in the evening, columns of Prussian troops had linked up with our troops on the left flank and, about this time, had advanced with strong columns against the enemy's left flank. After nine o'clock in the evening, they by themselves, took over the pursuit of the enemy on the major highway. All other troops, including our brigade, were ordered to set up camp. Our brigade had been assigned to an area 1 to 2 English miles to the right of the highway; it was, perhaps, one hour from the actual battlefield. Several of the regiment's patrols, sent out for our security and patrolling to the right of the highway, brought in at a late hour many prisoners; they also gathered a number of wounded and took them to nearby houses.

George von der Decken, Major[70]

No. 10 From *Belle-Alliance*

Pflugk-Harttung's no. 54. Report on the activities of the 1st Hussar Regiment of the [King's] German Legion during the days from 16 to 19 June, 1815.

16 June
From one o'clock noon, the 1st Hussar Regiment marched to [from?] Tournai by way of Leuze, Chièvres, Soignies, and to Braine le Comte, where it arrived at one o'clock at night.

17 June
In the morning from half past three o'clock to Quatre Bras, where it arrived at nine o'clock. The skirmishers were engaged with the enemy. After four o'clock in the afternoon, we retreated to the area of Waterloo on the left flank of the position.

18 June
Battle. Bivouac at night near Vieux Genappe.[71]

19 June
To Houtain [le Val] near Nivelles.

7th Brigade of Colonel Sir F. Arentschildt[72]

3rd Hussars, King's German Legion

No. 11 From *Belle-Alliance*

Pflugk-Harttung's letter no. 58. Report of the 3rd Hussar[73] Regiment of the [King's] German Legion on its participation in the Battle of La Belle Alliance.

On 16 June, the regiment received the order to march to Enghien, but to leave those companies in their present position that were in charge of placing pickets etc. along the border. In accordance with this order, Major Krauchenberg[74] and three companies remained near Peruwiz. Lieutenant Colonel Meyer marched with the other seven companies to Enghien, where an order had arrived for the regiment to keep marching without delay and join the English Army. After the regiment had fed the horses on the highway on this side of Enghien, it set off again around one o'clock in the night from the 16th to the 17th and marched to Nivelles. This march at night was most arduous because of the poor condition of the roads and the bad weather, and the many obstructions from baggage trains and infantry columns that blocked the narrow country roads here and there and that had to be passed. The regiment arrived at Nivelles around ten o'clock in the morning and, after a short halt, continued its march to Waterloo. It arrived there at three o'clock in the afternoon at the area where the first troop contingents began to take up the positions assigned to them by Lord Wellington. After staying there for several hours, the commander of the regiment received an order from the Earl of Uxbridge to march to Brussels and there take up quarters,[75] which at this late hour was quite difficult an undertaking but was eventually accomplished. But as early as three o'clock on the morning of the eventful 18 June, the regiment assembled again (that is, the seven companies of the regiment) and marched to Waterloo, where at ten o'clock it took its position in the order of battle. The English cavalry stood at the centre of the line, drawn up by brigades in half closed columns behind a low ridge, which was occupied by squares of infantry. The 3rd Regiment was originally the last unit in this column and kept advancing as the leading regiments and brigades were directed to other points on the line of the position.

The battle began with a heavy cannonade which made our regiment suffer severely in its first position, losing in the first half hour several men and as many as twenty horses. In order to take the regiment somewhat out of the target range of the artillery, several movements to the left and right were performed, all of these in perfect order and with precision. The regiment nevertheless suffered heavily from the fire of the heavy guns; it also lost its brave leader and commander, Lieutenant Colonel Meyer, who had one of his legs smashed by a cannonball and had to be taken to the rear. Between two and three o'clock in the afternoon, the regiment had moved up to the head of the column, as the preceding cavalry had been posted to, and was engaged at, different points. Led by Captain von Kerssenbruch,[76] three companies made a very handsome charge against two squadrons of cuirassiers, rolled them over completely and pursued them for quite a distance. Before these three companies had returned, the two other squadrons [i.e. four companies] of the regiment were ordered by Major General von Arentschildt to charge two enemy cavalry regiments, one of these cuirassiers, the other dragoons, which were about to advance towards the English line. The attack was vigorously executed, and those of the enemy's sections that the two squadrons were able to charge were made to yield and were driven back. But since the enemy's front line was much wider, our squadrons were surrounded on both flanks and had significant losses in officers, men, and horses. Captain Janssen,[77] Lieutenant and Adjutant Bruggemann[78] and Cornet Deichmann[79] were killed; Lieutenants Oehlkers,[80] True[81] and Cornet von Dassel[82] were badly wounded and had to leave the battlefield. The regiment was reassembled and did not reform in squadrons, as this was not necessary due to the reduced number of men fit for battle; the entire complement of seven companies had shrunk to 60 *Rotten* [120 men]. It resumed its original position by the side of infantry squares, but soon found a new opportunity to charge; this was against the left flank of a cuirassier regiment, which was about to attack an infantry battalion that, with levelled bayonets, had attacked and thrown over an enemy battalion, our charge was a great success. The cuirassier regiment was partly rolled over, and its charge against the infantry was obstructed. However, several squadrons of lancers moved towards the rear of the regiment and forced it to give up its gains and to withdraw quickly behind the infantry squares. On that occasion, a Hanoverian field battalion displayed much cold-blooded courage, and through its fire caused great loss to the enemy. In this action, the regiment again had had considerable losses; Captain von Kerssenbruch was killed in that attack. Even later on, behind the infantry squares, the regiment suffered much from canister and small arms fire. Cornet Hans von Hardenberg[83] had his left arm smashed, and several men were wounded by a single canister shot. At this part of the position, the infantry had severely suffered and were unable to drive back the enemy skirmishers who had moved up quite close and were killing many men. A detachment of the 3rd [Hussar] Regiment under Captain George Meyer[84] was therefore sent forward to drive them back, and he succeeded completely by keeping them back at a safe distance. For the remaining short span of time, the regiment stayed at this position. Towards evening, as the Prussians attacked the right flank of the French, and as the entire English line went over to the final general attack, the regiment also advanced beyond the battlefield. Later on, it retired for a short distance and bivouacked on the battlefield.

The regiment manoeuvred all day under the direction and leadership of Major General von Arentschildt, who commanded the 7th Cavalry Brigade. After the death of Captain von Kerssenbruch, command of the regiment was taken over by Captain von Goeben,[85] the most senior officer then present

The 13th Light Dragoon Regiment, although part of the brigade, did not join the 3rd Regiment for the duration of the battle,[86] and the latter had by itself to hold the position assigned to the brigade. The regiment's losses in the battle were: killed, 4 officers (Captains von Kerssenbruch and Janssen, Lieutenant Bruggemann, and Cornet Deichmann), 2 sergeants, 1 bugler, 21 men,[87] and 69 horses; wounded: 8 officers (Lieutenant Colonel Meyer, who died in Brussels, Lieutenants Oehlkers, True, Cornets von Dassel and Hans von Hardenberg severely, Captains von Goeben, von Schnehen,[88] and Cornet Hoyer[89] lightly, 9 sergeants, 1 bugler, 103 men, and 74[90] horses. Several men died from their wounds during the following weeks, and a number of the wounded remained unfit for service.

On 19 June, that part of the regiment still fit for service marched with the entire English Army from the battlefield to Nivelles, where it set up its bivouac.

Hanoverian Cavalry Brigade of Colonel Baron Estorff[91]

Bremen & Verden Hussars

No. 12 From *Belle-Alliance*

Pflugk-Harttung's letter no. 61. Report of the Hanoverian Bremen Verden Hussar Regiment on its conduct on 17 and 18 June by Major General A. von der Bussche.[92]

Report on the position taken up by the Bremen and Verden Hussar Regiment on 18 June 1815.

For several weeks, the Bremen and Verden Hussar Regiment had maintained advance posts in front of Mons towards Valenciennes and [Le] Quesnoy. In the morning of the 16th, the advance posts received definite information about the assembling of large troop bodies near Philippeville. On orders from Major General Hill, the regiment marched in the evening to Lens, where the Luneburg Hussar Regiment had also arrived; both together formed the brigade of Colonel von Estorff. In the night of the 17th, the brigade marched to Halle by way of Enghien, and there joined the corps of Prince Frederick of the Netherlands.

On the morning of the 18th, the Bremen and Verden Hussar Regiment was assigned a position near Mussain[93] to cover the right flank; it detached a squadron to the far side of Bierghes on the highway to Enghien. An enemy cavalry detachment appeared here in the afternoon at three o'clock, but made off again in a hurry. At the same time, various small patrols were observed in the direction of Steenkerque. The regiment was thus unable to participate actively in the major events of this day.

August von der Bussche, Major General

THE ARTILLERY

Horse Artillery, King's German Legion

Major A Sympher's 2nd Troop

No. 13 From *Belle-Alliance*

Pflugk-Harttung's letter no. 14. Report of the 2nd Horse Artillery Battery of the [King's] German Legion on its participation in the action at Quatre Bras.

Letter no. 62. Report of the 2nd Horse Artillery Battery of the [King's] German Legion on its participation in the Battle of La Belle Alliance, Lieutenant Colonel H J. Kuhlmann.[94]

Stade, 1 December 1824

Relation on the participation of the 2nd Horse Artillery Battery of the King's German Legion in the Battle of Waterloo

In the evening of 15 June 1815, the 2nd Horse Battery of the German Legion, commanded by the undersigned and quartered at Ghislenghien (between Ath and Enghien), was ordered by the English Major General Cooke,[95] to whom the battery was subordinated, to be on stand by and be ready for an immediate departure. On the following morning at one o'clock we marched off, past Enghien, and joined the English Guards and a battery of English foot artillery,[96] all under Major General Cooke's command; the two batteries were put under the command of Lieutenant Colonel Adye[97] of the English artillery. This column arrived at Quatre Bras towards four o'clock in the afternoon. The Duke of Wellington immediately ordered the horse battery to move up front, two guns were positioned before the Quatre Bras farm, and the remaining four guns to the left of the farm behind the highway [Namur road], and we then opened fire on the enemy artillery, which was stationed about 1,200 paces before us on an elevation. Towards five o'clock several enemy squadrons launched a forceful attack against the two guns in front of the farm but were completely dispersed by our fire and that of the infantry posted near the guns on the highway. Those infantry men were Hanoverians and were commanded by Major General Best, if I am not mistaken.[98] Shortly thereafter, the two guns, together with a third gun of my battery, advanced still further and, on higher orders, fired until dark at the enemy guns which occupied the heights opposite from us.

As the army retreated to the Waterloo position on 17 June, I joined again the English battery of Lieutenant Colonel Adye. Even as the greater part of the army had arrived at that destination, the enemy still pressed our rearguard so forcefully that it was considered necessary for our two batteries to assist our troops with a few shots. These had the desired effect in that the enemy now let up on his determined pursuit. The fire of the enemy's guns, which was then directed against us, did very little damage. We afterwards set up our bivouac assigned to us in the vicinity.

At around eight o'clock in the morning of 18 June, the Hereditary Prince of Orange, who commanded the army division to which we belonged, assigned positions to the English brigade and to the 2nd Horse Artillery Battery, into which we moved instantly. The 2nd Horse Artillery Battery was posted at the right flank of the English foot artillery brigade. The terrain, on which we stood, was slightly elevated, sloping downward both in front and in back, thus forming a kind of plateau. The ground consisted of clayey soil and had been softened by the rainfalls lasting throughout the night to the extent that the 9-pounder cannon and the 5½-inch howitzers could hardly be moved by the men. This plateau extended somewhat both to the right and the left, but in the latter direction it turned inward towards the enemy in an obtuse angle. The troops to our left were posted on and behind this plateau. To the right of our emplacement, at a distance of about 600 paces, was Hougoumont. Behind us were the [Foot] Guards[99] who, however, were sent to Hougoumont as reinforcements during the enemy attack. Several cavalry regiments stood some 100 paces to our right rear, and, later, an English howitzer brigade moved up before the said cavalry.[100] The Duke of Wellington visited us several times and gave us the distinct order never to fire at the enemy artillery.

Several hours later, a strong column of enemy infantry moved towards Hougoumont. As soon as it was within effective firing range, our artillery covered it with such a powerful fire of ball and shrapnel that it fell into disorder several times and retreated. But it always formed up again and finally moved to its left, behind Hougoumont, where it could no longer be observed by us. It then renewed its attack against Hougoumont and was able to seize the area outside the walls of

Hougoumont. This area was covered with trees which protected the enemy; to have any effect, we were limited to firing shrapnel in its direction. The Hereditary Prince of Orange complimented in a loud voice the two artillery brigades involved, that is, the 2nd Horse Artillery Battery under my command, and the English brigade, for the well-aimed and effective fire.

While this happened, an enemy heavy battery with guns of large calibre had taken up position opposite us at a distance of about 1,200 paces and opened fire on us, to which we could not respond due to the Duke of Wellington's previously mentioned order. Later in the afternoon we noticed that, at quite a distance to our left, the enemy made a strong attack against our line. We were unable to ascertain its effect due to the distance and particularly due to the intervening bend of the plateau. It then turned out that our position had in effect been broken through because the enemy cavalry moved down behind the said plateau out of our sight. It unexpectedly fell on our left flank and forced us to retreat (the two artillery batteries under Lieutenant Colonel Adye's command). It was only at some distance to the rear that my battery was able to locate a somewhat empty space, free of retreating troops and wagons, where other batteries had already halted[101] and where it was possible to put everything in order to the extent that circumstances permitted, which was indeed a time consuming process.

It was at this time also that Lieutenant Colonel Adye joined us with his English battery, which had retreated still farther to the rear. Since on the 16th that battery had fired less than ours, it now had to let us have some of its ammunition. As soon as this had been accomplished, both batteries under Lieutenant Colonel Adye returned to their earlier positions, as was likewise done by the remainder of the artillery gathered at this location, to take part again in the battle. However, by the time of our arrival in the battle line, the fortunes of this day had already favoured our side, because the enemy was on the retreat.

The 2nd Horse Artillery Battery of the legion artillery did not take part in the pursuit of the enemy but bivouacked on the battlefield during the night.

The battery's losses in killed and wounded were: on 16 June, 1 man; on the 17th, 1 man; and on the 18th, 10 men and 18 horses.

On the morning of the 19th, we marched off with the Guards by way of Nivelles etc.; we saw no action later on. The lost horses as well as the damaged guns were replaced on the 19th and joined the battery on its march on the 21st. The Hereditary Prince of Orange, of whose army division the 2nd Horse Artillery Battery was a part, as well as General Cooke, had been wounded and had left the battlefield, which was all the more regrettable to me because we had fought under the very eyes of these generals and had received assurances of their satisfaction.

H. J. Kuhlmann, Lieutenant Colonel

Foot Artillery, King's German Legion

Captain von Rettberg's Battery

No. 14 From *Belle-Alliance*

Pflugk-Harttung's letter no. 16. Report of the Hanoverian 2nd 9-pounder Battery of von Rettberg on its participation in the Action at Quatre Bras.

Letter no. 66. Report of the Hanoverian 2nd 9-pounder Battery of von Rettberg on its participation in the Battle of La Belle Alliance by C. von Rettberg, Lieutenant Colonel in the artillery regiment.

Description of the participation of the Royal Hanoverian 9-pounder Battery under the command of the then Captain von Rettberg of the former artillery of the King's German Legion of Great Britain in the battles of Quatre Bras on 16 June and of Waterloo on 18 June 1815.

Following Napoleon's return from the Isle of Elba to France, two newly established batteries moved to the Netherlands in the Spring of 1815 as part of the Reserve Corps commanded by His Excellency the Lieutenant General von der Decken.[102] Of these, I was put in command of the so called 2nd Battery (at the end of February, I had just arrived at Ostend from Portugal with the 1st and 2nd companies of the King's German Legion artillery, and was then in charge of the 6th Company of said regiment, part of which was at Hanover, part on detached duty). This battery consisted of a small detachment from the 5th company of the legion artillery, of three detachments of the Landwehr artillery of the former Landwehr Battalion Northeim, Alfeld, and Salzgitter, and of newly inducted men, of whom a few had served in the Hanoverian Army, dissolved in 1803, and others who had served in the Westphalian army.

In May and in early June the battery had its cantonments near Brussels. On 3 June it was inspected by the Duke of Wellington, and was attached a few days later to the 4th English Division of Lieutenant General Sir Charles Colville. The commanders of the newly deployed batteries were told to report in writing to their divisional generals, but to remain in their present cantonments until further orders.

Such was the situation when in the night from 15 to 16 June the battery received an order from the Brussels headquarters to instantly go on stand by and be ready to march immediately. As late as seven o'clock on the next morning I received the order to follow the 5th Division, until then commanded by Major General Sir James Kempt (Sir Thomas Picton had not yet arrived), which had already marched off on the road to Charleroi by way of Waterloo, and to report to same, in that the 4th Division was still too far off at Oudenarde.

I caught up with the division on the far side of Waterloo, where it had halted. I was just given permission by the divisional commander to send the horses to a drinking place when the alarm was sounded and all troops were set in motion and advanced on the main road by way of La Belle Alliance and Genappe. We encountered many Belgian baggage carts, wounded soldiers, and refugees, and past Genappe, at about two o'clock in the afternoon, we heard some cannon fire before us. The Duke of Brunswick and his corps proceeded right behind my battery; he was riding by my side at the head of his troops when I received an order from a staff officer to hurry with my battery to Quatre Bras, as the French were about to attack that place in force. I hastened there with my battery in full trot. The French maintained a vigorous cannonade with their numerous artillery on the intersection of roads in order to impede our communications. I had the battery unlimber to the left of the farm of Quatre Bras in rear of the highway from Nivelles to Namur which continued through some lower ground, as our infantry before us was driven back and the French occupied the elevations in our front.

At about three o'clock the French cavalry launched an attack against the troops posted in front of Quatre Bras, which was repulsed. On that occasion the battery under my command helped greatly to throw the enemy cavalry into disorder by firing at its right flank, before it was driven back by our own cavalry. Towards five o'clock, His Excellency General Count Alten ordered the battery to move further to the left and to take up the same position on the other side of the highway that earlier had to be abandoned by an English battery.

The French had set up eighteen guns opposite this point, of which only five were out in the open. I had the ammunition wagons halt at a covered position on the highway; I posted our guns as far apart as possible and had them manned by the least number of gunners necessary for their operation. In this manner, I succeeded in maintaining the battery in this position until ten o'clock in the evening in spite of the enemy's very lively cannon fire, and to keep our losses to one NCO, one gunner and three horses killed and two gunners and one driver being wounded. The young inexperienced NCOs and men displayed a most laudable courage and endurance on this occasion.

Towards six o'clock in the evening, a second captain[103] of Major Lloyd's English battery arrived with a howitzer and expressed his desire to join ours, since the remaining guns of his battery had been lost, I then assigned him a position on our right wing. Posted to my right was the 4th Battery of the legion artillery, commanded by Captain Cleeves (now a lieutenant colonel). At around eleven o'clock at night, Lieutenant Colonel Heise of our artillery, who was also on hand, sent an adjutant to the artillery headquarters at Quatre Bras with a report on losses in dead and wounded and on the amount of ammunition used that day. To my request for an early replenishment of the latter, the commander of the English artillery, from where we received our supply, let me know that we would be re-supplied early on the next morning. Today, we had used more than half of the available ammunition. I was anxiously looking forward to the replenishment, but it was not to happen due to all the movement on the next day.

On 17 June, the entire allied army retreated from Quatre Bras to the position near Mont St Jean. Sir T. Picton had taken over the command of the 5th Division on the preceding afternoon and had even been wounded;[104] he nevertheless remained with the division which was at the head of the retiring army.

The battery marched at the head of the column (17 June) and failed to learn about the enemy pursuing us; only upon arriving at the sunken road near La Haye Sainte was our rearguard severely pressed by the enemy and it became most difficult for us to move out of the hollow way and to take up our assigned position. The battery was now posted on the left of the highway on the left wing of the combined army, as was the entire 5th Division. To our left stood only a small corps of Nassauers, part of whom formed a picket line in our front during the following night. We thus remained on stand by all night in the heaviest rains and in some very stormy weather.

The skies cleared a bit towards nine o'clock in the morning, and we observed the French army move up in large numbers, cross country from Plançenoit, and on the highway from Genappe. There was thus no doubt that we would be attacked. At daybreak I immediately sent for a replacement of the missing ammunition from the large artillery park, regrettably without result. As I learned later, the officer charged with this task was unable to make his way through the retreating baggage carts and did not find the ammunition depot.

The terrain was exceptionally favourable for the placement of the battery. It stood on a plateau which descended gradually towards the enemy, behind a ridge several feet high, lined with a hedge and a country road in front; it later being referred to in the enemy's reports as a field fortification. The hedge was chopped down to facilitate movements. There was a lower area behind the battery, where the battery's ammunition wagons were stationed and where they were relatively well protected. To the right was the position of the Scottish brigade consisting of one battalion, each, of the 1st, the 42nd, and the 92nd Regiments [he fails to mention the 44th], commanded by the English Major General Sir Denis Pack; to the left was a brigade of Belgian infantry, and behind the battery were the brigades of Generals von Fink [Vincke] and Best. To the rear in the valley and on the right of the previously mentioned ammunition wagons was the brigade of English cavalry under the command of General Sir E. [William] Ponsonby.

Beginning around twelve o'clock some vigorous musketry fire occurred on our right wing, which appeared to mask the intended attack against our left wing. Between one and two o'clock several columns of French infantry of Count d'Erlon's corps rushed out from behind a ridge, where they had been standing out of our direct view, and rapidly advanced against our left wing. The heavy rains had, however, softened the terrain; this and the effective fire of our artillery, and particularly that of the battery commanded by myself, which enfiladed the enemy columns on their right flank to good effect while ascending our plateau, broke up their formation before they reached our position. They thus proceeded in open order and became engaged with the Belgians[105] and part of the English infantry in a bayonet melee. This moment was used by the Scottish brigade to turn the enemy's right flank; at the same time the English cavalry under Sir Edward Ponsonby advanced and drove the French infantry back in complete disorder. Several thousand prisoners were made on this occasion.

After this failed assault, no further attack was attempted throughout the day against our left wing. The main attacks were now directed against our right wing and the centre at La Haye Sainte and Mont St Jean. The enemy then placed a numerous artillery opposite our position at a distance of some 900 to 1,000 paces, which maintained a continuous cannonade until evening, to which I could only respond at a slow rate because of the lack of ammunition. The battery suffered only relatively moderate losses due to its favourable position. Most of the enemy's balls passed over us or struck in the hedge-bordered ditch.

After seven o'clock in the evening a Belgian battery took up position on my left and resumed firing which I was unable to participate in due to my battery's lack of ammunition. Soon afterwards, shortly before sundown, the Prussian General von Ziethen arrived with numerous cavalry. A Prussian battery, part of this force, drew up next to the just mentioned Belgian battery. General von Ziethen proceeded to the highway with his

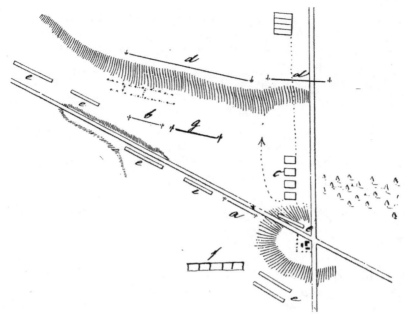

Positions of the 2nd Hanoverian 9-pounder Battery in the Battle of Quatre Bras. *a*, first position; *b*, second position, *c*, French cavalry attack, *d*, French artillery, *e*, Allied infantry on the left wing, *f*, Brunswick cavalry, *g*, Captain Cleeves's Foot Battery.

cavalry to be on hand, as he told me himself, for the enemy's soon to be expected retreat, judging by the disorder beginning in his rear. The expected retreat occurred in fact around eight o'clock, and by nine o'clock the enemy's entire army had disappeared from our sight.

The battery spent the next night on the battlefield. General Sir J. Kempt, who, upon General Sir T. Picton's death that day, succeeded him as commander of the 5th Division, expressed on the next day to the battery his full satisfaction as to its comportment on the two memorable days, his laudatory comment to be included later in the Divisional Report. An order was given me to classify the enemy guns and wagons which stood or were lying on the opposite side. Of the former I found 25, of the latter 40; some of the wagons blew up on the next morning due to the burning slow-matches left in them. On this day the battery's losses were one man killed, and one officer and ten men wounded. A further six horses killed and five dead from their wounds or having to be killed because of their wounds.

On the afternoon of the 19th the battery began its march with the 5th Division towards Paris by way of Nivelles and Mons, but at Montdidier joined the 4th Division, to which it belonged according to earlier orders. The battery arrived near Paris on 1 July and, following conclusion of the armistice, set up its bivouac in the Bois de Boulogne on 7 July.

C. von Rettberg
Lieutenant Colonel in the [Hanoverian] Artillery Regiment

Captain Braun's Battery

No. 15 From *Belle-Alliance*

Pflugk-Harttung's letter no. 64. Report of the Hanoverian 1st 9-pounder Battery Braun on its participation in the Battle of La Belle Alliance, by Major W. Braun.[106]

Description of the participation of the 1st Royal Hanoverian 9-pounder battery in the battle of 18 June, under the command of Captain W. Braun of the King's German Legion.

The main quarters of the 1st 9-pounder Battery, Hanoverian Artillery, were located at Wondelgem, one hour distant from Ghent,[107] where, in May 1815, I was appointed commander of the same and charged with its reorganisation. I there received for that purpose one half of the men and of the horses of a 6-pounder battery, which I had organised in Hanover and taken to Brussels. Until then, the Hanoverian battery in the Netherlands was equipped with guns and ammunition wagons of different national origin, and for that reason, and because of the poor condition of the vehicles, was unusable for field service. On 8 and 9 June I received the complete equipment of a 9-pounder battery with all necessary reserves from the English arsenal in Ghent. The crew assignments and the proper use of the ordnance entrusted to me in so short a time period was made possible only through the extraordinary dedication of Lieutenant von Schulzen[108] and of a number of artillery NCOs of the King's German Legion who had been transferred to me by Lieutenant Colonel Sir J. Hartmann[109] of that corps.

At eight o'clock in the morning on 16 June I received the order from the Brussels Headquarters to proceed by the most direct route to Quatre Bras and to report to the brigade of Major General Sir J. Lambert,[110] cantoned near Ghent, who had received a similar order. During the night of the 16th, the battery bivouacked with Lambert's infantry Brigade on the major highway from Ghent to Brussels and received the order during the night not to march towards Quatre Bras but, instead, to proceed to Waterloo by way of Brussels. On the 17th the battery bivouacked in the Soignes Forest, three hours away from Waterloo, and arrived at 12 noon of the 18th at the plateau on the far

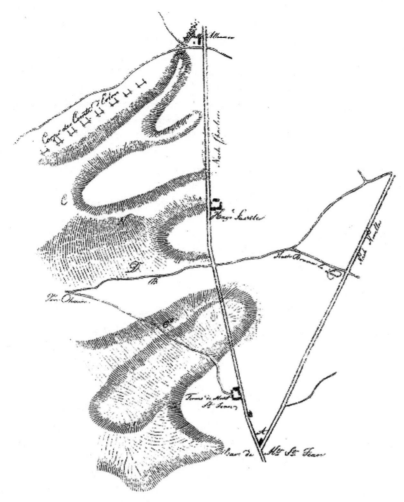

Positions of the 1st Hanoverian 9-pounder Battery in the Battle of La Belle Alliance. *a*, position of the battery at noon; *b*, second position, *c*, attack position of five enemy battalions, *d*, third position at 2.30 p.m., *e*, position of the ammunition wagons during the third position; limbers were at *b*; *n*, position of three enemy guns at 6.30 p.m.

side of Waterloo. Together with the infantry brigade of Sir J. Lambert, the battery here drew up in close column by the side of the Genappe highway, in line with the cavalry of the right centre. The battery remained at this location until 3 p.m., apart from minor movements caused by enemy fire and its tightly compressed formation. On higher orders, I had investigated during this time the terrain to the left of the

Genappe highway for a suitable emplacement for the battery. At three o'clock, Lambert's Brigade and my battery were ordered to move towards the 5th Division to the left of the Genappe road, in order to assist in repelling the attack of the 1st and 2nd French Corps under Marshal Ney. We moved to the previously selected position about 200 paces to the right [left, see preceding sentence] of the Genappe highway. During this movement I was wounded in my left thigh by an enemy cannon ball, which also killed my horse. The battery participated during the remainder of the battle in this position without any further lateral movements. Its severe losses on this day truly attest to its deportment and best military character.

Wounded, Captain Wilhelm Braun; killed First Lieutenant Detlev von Schulzen, 2 gun captains; killed or wounded 43 bombardiers, gunners, and drivers.

W. Braun, Major, Royal Hanoverian Artillery

Captain A. Cleeves's Battery

No. 16 From *Belle-Alliance*

Pflugk-Harttung's letter no. 15. Report of the 4th Battery of the [King's] German Legion on its participation in the Action at Quatre Bras (Events on 16 and 17 June 1815).

Letter no. 63. Report of the 4th Battery of the [King's] German Legion on its participation in the Battle of La Belle Alliance by Lieutenant Colonel Andrew Cleeves,[111] commander of the horse artillery.

Wunstorf, 25 November 1824

In the spring of 1815, the battery was assigned to the 3rd Infantry Division of General Karl von Alten, KCB, as part of the reorganisation of the Royal Army of Great Britain under the supreme command of Field Marshal the Duke of Wellington. On 15 June, it consisted of one captain, Andrew Cleeves, the lieutenants Robert Manners, Royal Artillery, who on the 17th joined the battery as a volunteer, Wilhelm von Goeben,[112] Heinrich Hartmann[113] and 2nd Lieutenant C. H. Ludowieg,[114] 13 artillery NCOs, 79 gunners, 95 Train NCOs, buglers, artisans, and drivers, 157 Royal horses, and one assistant surgeon, one heavy 5½-inch howitzer and five 9-pounder guns.

Until 15 June, the headquarters of the division was located at Soignies in Flanders, where the division was assembled that day from its widely dispersed cantonments.

It began its march towards Nivelles on 16 June at 2 a.m., where it arrived around eight o'clock [a.m.], and kept marching towards Quatre Bras until ten o'clock when it halted and prepared everything for the battle. Around twelve o'clock the division marched off again, with my battery at its head. Between 2 and 3 p.m. the division arrived at the houses of Quatre Bras. The Duke of Wellington and his staff were gathered there before the large house. I reported my presence to Colonel Sir George Wood, Royal Artillery, who was in command of the army's artillery. On his orders, the battery was temporarily stationed in reserve behind the houses to remain protected from the enemy's vigorous cannonade; the battery nevertheless lost several men and horses. This short halt was well used to familiarise ourselves with the lay of the land and with the course of the action; we also provided infantry ammunition to troops who had already been in battle.

The roads from Charleroi to Brussels and from Nivelles to Namur intersect here at almost right angles, therefore the name Quatre Bras. The main house is located on a moderate elevation, and offers an unlimited view to the left and to the front; ahead to its right is a dense wood in which a fierce battle was raging. The terrain to the left of the front is quite wavy; it is apparently superbly tilled and bears a rich harvest, the seed grains having almost reached the harvesting stage. The road to Namur, which passes by the front of the house, becomes somewhat of a sunken road. The terrain rearward of this road is completely crossed by thick, impenetrable hedges and enclosures.

The enemy troops in our front were mostly cavalry. A strong battery had been drawn up by the enemy at a distance of about 1,000 paces from the front of the house, and another one on the right wing, which caused much damage by its enfilading fire. After a halt of half an hour, Sir George Wood ordered me to drive away that battery, if at all possible. We had a problem entering the sunken road and went at the trot for about 500 paces along the road, and unlimbered to the left of Quatre Bras in an open field, near another battery, which I soon recognised as the Hanoverian one commanded by Major Heise.[115] He was much delighted to have his former legion battery come to his assistance. Together, we soon succeeded in demolishing and chasing off the French artillery, which never again showed up this day. But we brought down upon us several assaults by their cavalry, which were, however, repulsed at great loss to the attackers. The 68th English infantry regiment,[116] formed in square, covered my left flank, and Major von Ramdohr's Luneburg [Landwehr] Battalion was on my right. Those various attacks resulted in the loss to our battery of Lieutenants von Goeben and Hartmann, severely wounded, and of several men. The battery maintained this position throughout the night.

On our arrival at Quatre Bras we learned of the glorious demise of the Most Serene Duke of Brunswick. Our cavalry arrived late at night.

All afternoon we heard some terrible cannonading near Ligny, and towards evening that area was brightly lit.

17 June
The enemy opposing us remained quiet, apart from occasional skirmishes. The morning was spent by the battery in making all necessary repairs. General von Alten took me along on a visit of the position; I afterwards accompanied Colonel von Ompteda to inspect the roads and to determine to what extent the route in the rear had to be cleared in preparation of the retreat. The division broke camp around twelve o'clock and retreated in column formation towards Genappe, my battery marched at the tail end. It was an exceptionally hot day, and an extremely fatiguing one for the infantry. The division halted in front of Genappe for quite a while, not being urged on, and observed to our left our rearguard, composed of cavalry and artillery, as it was pursued by the enemy. Towards five o'clock in the afternoon we were caught in a severe thunderstorm and downpour; the division then resumed its march and passed through Genappe.

In the evening between seven and eight o'clock (17 June), the division arrived on the heights of Mont St Jean, where the army was rallying and taking up the positions that were defended on the next day. On our march we saw several cavalry engagements to our left, and stayed here during the night which happened to turn out very stormy and showery.

18 June, Battle of Waterloo
The morning from daybreak until about ten o'clock passed quietly without any skirmishing as an introduction to the battle. The infantry busied itself primarily with cleaning and repairing their weapons. The [3rd] Division was posted between the Charleroi road and the very inviting and handsome Hougoumont farm. It formed the right centre, with battalion or two battalion squares standing *en échiquier* behind the plateau of Mont St Jean. Being part [of the division], the two 9-pounder batteries of Major Lloyd, Royal Artillery, and mine were positioned in front of the same. To my left at about 100 paces distance was a light 6-pounder and rocket battery, Royal Artillery.[117] The Duke of Wellington in person sited these batteries, with the injunction not to ever become engaged with the enemy artillery, except in critical circumstances, and only to target enemy infantry on the move with our full power, and to conserve our ammunition. To my knowledge, the division held on to this position without any significant changes throughout the battle until the [final] advance.

The ridge rose slightly towards the plateau at the left centre. The terrain in front of us was quite undulating and most suitable for veiling, and keeping out of sight, the position and movements of the enemy. Located to the right was the Hougoumont farm with gardens and a fairly extensive wood towards the enemy; in front, to our left was the La Haye Sainte farm; behind us a gentle slope towards the Nivelles highway, which joins the Brussels highway at the village of Mont St Jean. That village is situated on the highway, directly behind the centre of the position. Farther to the rear, behind our right flank, two small towns, in open country, and the Forest of Soignes could be seen. It is traversed by the highway, at which the village of Waterloo was located and the headquarters and, on the 19th [18th?], the ammunition depot. I am unable to say anything specific about the enemy order of battle opposite us, nor about the various kinds of troops. The distance from us was about 2,000 to 3,000 paces.

The 1st and 3rd Divisions formed the right army corps under the command of His Royal Highness, The Hereditary Prince of Orange. It is impossible for me to pinpoint the exact time of the various phases of the battle. I was too much involved with the operational details of the battery to pay any attention. Neither Lieutenant Manners, although capable and active officer that he was, nor 2nd Lieutenant Ludowieg still very young and inexperienced, albeit very willing, were familiar with the battery's gunners. The former had the misfortune of having his left leg shot off at a time when the battle raged at its greatest violence.

At about eleven o'clock we espied a compact column of enemy infantry, certainly 3,000 to 4,000 men, which advanced through the meandering depressions and the fields of high corn towards the wood of Hougoumont. As soon as they approached to within 700 to 800 paces, I opened fire on them (the first cannon shots of the battle). The firing was joined with great effect by Majors Lloyd and Kuhlmann and resulted in the total dispersion of the enemy column. Both the Prince of Orange and General Alten witnessed this opening cannonade. It was at least an ominously favourable overture which elicited much applause.

In the meantime, the enemy had come appreciably closer; his massed artillery opened up a vigorous and well directed fire at the wood of Hougoumont as well as at our own positions. My neighbour to the left became too noisy with his light 6-pounders, disregarding the Duke's injunction. Soon enough, he was to feel the effect of the enemy 12- and 8-pounders. Lloyd's and Kuhlmann's batteries also suffered considerably; Major Lloyd, a truly brave officer, was killed. From now on the battle raged on without interruption. Between twelve and one o'clock, the enemy made a forceful attack on our left wing which, however, was repulsed, and our cavalry made many prisoners.

Repeated cavalry attacks by the enemy, mostly in column formation, were intended to break up the right centre, but were repulsed with losses. Our squares had suffered severe casualties and had been much reduced. My battery was about to run out of ammunition, and before five o'clock I was told that all ammunition wagons were empty; I ordered them to go to Brussels. (I procured a small keg of cognac from the reserve and had it distributed among the men, who badly needed this little refreshment). The Hougoumont farm had erupted in flames; the smoke billowed before us in the valley. At about six to seven o'clock we observed about 800 to 1,000 paces away a strong column of enemy artillery moving to the enemy's right flank, and I believe that at this time the enemy was made to feel the arrival of the Prussians. Some enemy guns had also moved quite close to our left; we were entirely out of ammunition, which I duly reported. Lieutenant Manners had the left half battery limber up to be ready to retreat; he told me this had been at the order of the Prince of Orange. I ordered him to halt behind the squares; but shortly afterwards he was fatally wounded.

Meanwhile, the enemy cavalry made a ferocious attack against our division; it was quite unexpected because its approach had been hidden by the depressions of the terrain, by gun smoke, and the smoke from the burning Hougoumont farm.[118] This attack caused the gravest confusion among our artillery posted in front, part of which had suffered severe losses and had been shot to pieces. Major Sympher, commander of a 9-pounder horse battery of the legion which had been held in reserve, filled the gap.[119] His fire against the enemy cavalry was most effective, as witnessed by Lieutenant Colonel Hartmann and myself. He ordered me to reform my battery and join Major Sympher's battery. With the exception of No. 4 gun, which remained where it had been left and was manned again later, I managed to haul my guns out of the chaos as we had the limbers with us, and reformed on a field close to Mont St Jean and had the empty limbers filled again without delay (the ammunition was supplied by Captain Sandham, Royal Artillery[120]). I then led the battery, now joined by several unattached English guns, back to the position. The brigade major, Captain Baynes, Royal Artillery and Lieutenant Mielmann[121] of our regiment made every effort to reassemble the scattered artillery; they succeeded to a large extent. We had hardly arrived when I received an order, I believe from the aide de camp Captain Heise, to draw up to the foot of the hill and await further orders. At the same time, Captain Sinclair, Royal Artillery,[122] and Lieutenant Ludowieg were directed to advance, which they did immediately. We met our badly wounded divisional commander, the highly respected General von Alten, as we moved to the right of the division, and of the column which was in attack formation. We opened a brisk cannonade on the advancing enemy and his artillery.

After the end of the victorious advance on the centre of the enemy, who yielded everywhere in great confusion, Major Sympher[123] followed to the enemy position, where he remained during the night. Lieutenant Colonel Hartmann gave me permission to stay where I was since I was out of powder.

By virtue of the most persistent exertions during the night and into the morning of the next day, I and my exhausted men succeeded in returning the battery into an operational condition. I had the satisfaction to be able to follow the much reduced division in the afternoon of the 19th to Nivelles, fully supplied with all necessities. Our loss in horses was amply made up for by enemy ones which had been captured in the battle.

Andrew Cleeves, Lieutenant Colonel, Commander, [Hanoverian] Horse Artillery

THE INFANTRY

2nd Division of Lieutenant General Sir H. Clinton
1st King's German Legion Brigade of Colonel du Plat

1st Line Battalion, King's German Legion

No. 17 From *Belle-Alliance*

Pflugk-Harttung's letter no. 31 Report of the 1st Line Battalion of the [King's] German Legion on its participation in the Battle of La Belle Alliance.

16 June

At half past eight o'clock[124] in the morning, the battalion was ordered to break camp immediately. It arrived one hour later at the designated assembly point. General Clinton gave the orders to continue our march without waiting for this day's provisions, which were already en route. Around four o'clock in the afternoon we first heard the sound of gun fire; we continued our march and arrived near Braine le Comte around nine o'clock. Our march was resumed after a halt of one hour.

17 June

In the morning at seven o'clock we passed through Nivelles, on the way to support the troops positioned at Quatre Bras. After [marching] two hours past this location there was a halt; upon receipt of an order, we set off on our march back. Since the men had not had anything to eat all of yesterday nor today, General Clinton agreed to let the men cook their meat at a suitable location. The men had hardly put down their things in order to go for water, when a new order arrived to hurry towards Waterloo at the greatest speed. A few hours later, General Hill met the column and gave the order to immediately attack the enemy with the bayonet should he arrive before us at Waterloo, and to do our utmost to drive him back. Should this not be possible, we were to retire upon Halle.

Towards four o'clock in the afternoon we saw a column to our right. The light companies were told off to reconnoitre; they determined that these were Nassau troops. At five o'clock we arrived at the position; at six o'clock there commenced a heavy cannonade and small arms fire, accompanied by a heavy thunderstorm which lasted until dark. At our campsite the soil was so softened by the heavy rains that it gave way under one's feet.

18 June

All was quiet during the night. The grenadier company was detached on outpost duty. At eleven o'clock in the morning, the battalions stood to arms, and the brigade formed in columns right to the front. At exactly twelve o'clock, the first cannon shot was fired from our flank, and the cannonade continued uninterruptedly. At four o'clock we were ordered to form square and to advance. On our advance, we attacked and dispersed an enemy square. Our cavalry was unable to further harm them because enemy cavalry moved up to charge us. This attack was repelled. In the meantime, the remnants of the square had taken up position in a garden to our right and in a ditch in front of us [at Hougoumont], and were so close that their fire caused us to lose several officers and men. Their fire was mainly directed at the artillery placed in front of our squares, forcing their crews to leave their guns and to join us. The square of the 95th Regiment to our left therefore changed from square to skirmish order and drove off the enemy skirmishers. At the same time, the 2nd Line Battalion was ordered to drive the enemy out of the garden, which was then successfully done. From now on, the enemy moved his numerous cavalry into battle, and we were attacked seven times, always by fresh cavalry, cuirassiers, lancers and dragoons, but they were driven off each time and suffered losses. Towards eight o'clock, the Duke of Wellington rode up and ordered the squares to form line of four ranks and advance in line against the enemy Guards; these, too, were beaten, and victory had been won. The enormous exertions, the men had eaten little or nothing during the past three days, made it impossible to take part in the pursuit of the enemy, and camp was set up one hour away from the battlefield. The Prussians, who had just arrived, now pursued the defeated enemy.

The battalion's losses were: Captain von Saffe,[125] Captain von Holle,[126] Ensign von Lucken,[127] 2 sergeants, 1 drummer, 16 rank and file killed;[128] Major von Robertson,[129] Captain Schlutter Junior,[130] Adjutant Schnath,[131] Lieutenant Muller,[132] Lieutenant Wilding Junior,[133] Ensign von der Hellen,[134] 9 sergeants, 80 rank and file wounded;[135] 1 drummer, 23 rank and file missing.[136] The missing soldiers fell behind on the march from Nivelles and were taken prisoner by the enemy.

2nd Line Battalion, King's German Legion

No. 18 From *Belle-Alliance*

Pflugk-Harttung's letter no. 33 Report of the 2nd Line Battalion of the [King's] German Legion on its participation in the Battle of La Belle Alliance by Lieutenant Colonel G. von Muller.[137]

Munden, 23 November 1824

Historical account of the participation of the 2nd Line Battalion of the King's German Legion in the Battle of Waterloo on 18 June 1815, to the best of what, without having a map, I have retained in my memory.

The 2nd Line Battalion was part of the division of Lieutenant General Sir Henry Clinton and of the brigade of Colonel du Plat, who was killed in the battle. [The brigade] consisted of the 1st, 2nd, 3rd, and 4th Line Battalions of the King's German Legion. The battalions were under strength and may have numbered 400 men each, on the average. The division, with its headquarters at Ath and cantonments in the surrounding region, broke camp on 16 June and arrived at the battlefield on the evening of 17 June at around five to six o'clock. The terrain was somewhat undulating in its contours, but otherwise quite open. The battalions were assigned campsites for the night in one of the low areas of the rolling terrain. Between six and seven o'clock on the morning of 18 June, the brigade advanced a short distance and took position on one of the ridges in front in the first line of the order of battle. The 2nd Battalion had the Brussels highway about half of a musket shot to its left; at the beginning there were no troops on the other side of the highway; to the right of the brigade stood an English brigade of Clinton's division.

After several changes in our position, the line advanced a little in the previous direction, we observed at around eight o'clock some movements in the line of enemy infantry on the opposite ridge; but it was mainly the enemy artillery which moved into position. The brigade of Major General von Fink[138] deployed at this time to the left of the brigade (if I am not mistaken), so that it had the highway to its right. It seemed to be after nine o'clock that the enemy began the cannonade from the opposite ridge and, at the same time, had a battery of about four pieces cover the highway. Before the brigade, somewhat to its right and almost in front of the 2nd and 4th Line Battalions, some heavy musketry fire was developing in two small woods (or enclosures) in the lower terrain fronting us. The enemy's cannonade became noticeably more vigorous as more of our artillery went into action. It was primarily the left flank of Colonel du Plat's Brigade which suffered from the enemy battery drawn up on the highway.

We remained at this site until we were ordered, between twelve and one o'clock, to form squares and advance. The 1st and 2nd Line Battalions formed separate squares, the 3rd and 4th Battalions were combined in a single square. After we had advanced in squares some 1,000 paces, enemy infantry (about 1,000 to 1,200 men in my opinion) appeared diagonally to our left on a wave like eminence. They were in line and 400 to 600 paces from us. The brigade manoeuvred its squares so that the 2nd Battalion became its right flank, and then halted. There was a brief exchange of musketry fire. Soon, however, Colonel du Plat gave the order to advance and attack the enemy with levelled bayonets, who did not expect this attack. As soon as we advanced, he retreated and took cover on our right flank in an old oak wood, which was surrounded by a fairly deep ditch and an earth mound. (I believe Colonel du Plat fell here during the advance, as I did not see him again afterwards). On our arrival on the elevation we observed a well spread out line of infantry 800 to 1,000 paces from us. In front of it stood a line of French cuirassiers, 600 to 800 men. They were attacked, I believe, by the 2nd Dragoon Regiment of the King's German Legion, but it was repulsed by the fire of the French infantry in the wood and driven back by the enemy cuirassiers as far as the rear of our squares. Since those were now held up by the fire from our squares, it was our dragoons' turn to pursue the fleeing enemy, and this was repeated two to three times.

A part of the enemy's infantry, which had taken the previously mentioned oak wood [at Hougoumont], caused the brigade severe losses with his fire, as he was now on our right flank due to the advance of our line, and less than a musket shot away. The 2nd Battalion received an order from one of General Clinton's ADCs to take and occupy this wood, and, after the battalion had deployed from square, this was done without significant enemy resistance. That copse must have been one of the woods before us where the sound of vigorous musketry fire could be heard to come from at the beginning of the battle, because among the dead we found, apart from a number of Frenchmen (they wore blue with red), several men of the light infantry of the English Guards and some Brunswickers.[139] The other battalions of the brigade remained in squares.

After about half an hour, the enemy had turned round the wood, which apparently had had its rear section unoccupied, and attacked us in our right flank with several hundred men, if my estimate is correct. This he combined with an assault in open order on our front. The wood was then abandoned. Since the other battalions had held their position, our battalion immediately reformed outside the wood, renewed its attack, and was fortunate enough to be able to take it and remain in its possession during the fighting later on. The battalion lost a number of soldiers and officers during the second attack. Captain Thiele[140] was killed; Captain Claus von der Decken[141] was badly wounded in his chest; Captain Purgold[142] suffered a minor wound on his side; Captain von Wenckstern[143] similarly on one of his ears.

Between seven and eight o'clock, several battalions marched by the rear of, and through, the wood; I noticed Major General Hugh Halkett among them. I believe they went to the area of La Belle Alliance, which appeared to be located a little more than a quarter of an hour to the left of us. The fighting soon ended in our area, and between eight and nine o'clock I was ordered to advance. The brigade had moved to the right; the battalion advanced without meeting an enemy straight ahead through cornfields, where there were a number of dead enemies. It was already quite dark when the battalion arrived at the N. N. village[144] and met a strong Prussian column. This was the site where the English Dragoon Guards fought their last action against the enemy cuirassiers. Since there was no way to pass through at this point, I was ordered by General Sir Henry Clinton to remain here during the night and join the division in the morning. The battalion's losses on that day were, I believe, 101 wounded or killed.[145]

> G. von Muller Lieutenant Colonel, formerly Commander,
> 2nd Line Battalion, KGL

3rd Line Battalion, King's German Legion

No. 19 From *Belle-Alliance*
Pflugk-Harttung's letter no. 34 Report of the 3rd Line Battalion of the [King's] German Legion on its participation in the Battle of La Belle Alliance.[146]

16 June
The battalion had just returned from its exercises on this morning when it received an order to march off at once and to join the brigade[147] on the highway from Ath to Enghien, near the village of Meslin l'Eveque. We therefore left Lens at eleven o'clock, marched through the villages of Cambron[148] and Gibecq and met the brigade at the assigned destination in the afternoon, where we already found General Clinton's division fully assembled. After getting some rest, we marched to Enghien where we believed we would find our next quarters. Around five o'clock we arrived before this town, but received an unexpected order to march past it and immediately straight on to Braine le Comte.

Once past Enghien, we left the highway and then followed a country road in poor condition. Towards evening, we heard the sounds of a cannonade coming from not too far away. A rumour was also spreading that the French had attacked our advance posts, which was gaining credibility from the fact that there was a major converging of troops of all kinds on this road. These hurried on in forced marches and thus made the road nearly impassable. At eight o'clock we halted at a small village, about half an hour from Braine le Comte, and were led to a small field of clover, where the brigade had hardly space enough for its closely crowded columns to rest up. Here we remained until half past ten o'clock. We then broke camp and marched through Braine le Comte in extremely bad weather, with rain coming down in sheets. Not very far away from this town, we came to a large forest (Forest of Soignes[149]), where the roads were hardly passable for man or beast because of the bad weather and heavy travel of artillery and cavalry units and the many wagons that had bogged down and got stuck.

17 June
We had passed this forest by about one o'clock. We now halted and bivouacked on an open field. At daybreak, we broke camp and marched to Nivelles, where we did not stop but marched straight through town. On the far side, we encountered a large number of wounded of the army, and only now did we learn with certainty that on this road, at Quatre Bras, a superior French force had yesterday attacked our advance posts. They were nevertheless thrown back by the 1st and the 3rd Divisions and some other troops under the command of Prince William of Orange, after very heavy fighting, in which our losses had been quite substantial. After we had passed through town, we encountered the Prince of Orange who rode on with us, and we therefore firmly believed that now we would see some fighting. After we had marched for one hour, we halted and rested on this road. We remained here until the afternoon when we suddenly received the order to march back to Nivelles. However, we had hardly arrived at this town when we received orders to at once march on to Halle. As soon as we had passed Nivelles we noticed that ours was not the only brigade marching back but that the entire army was retiring; the highway and the byways were full of troops as far as the eyes could see. We now learned also that the Prussians under Blücher had been thoroughly beaten and driven back by Bonaparte. Thus, the reason for our retiring was probably to keep our armies from becoming separated, and to keep Brussels covered.

As we had come up to within about half an hour from the large village of Waterloo, a halt was called, and the army took up positions at this location. The French also advanced, and we heard some skirmishing going on in the evening. During the remainder of the day, there was some reconnoitring for the general, and issuing of dispositions for the troops. Very heavy rains set in, in the evening and continued through the night; the bivouac was most uncomfortable as a result, the more so since we had not had anything to eat or drink since the morning of the 16th. Things remained quiet otherwise.

18 June

Early this morning we observed some movement both on our and the French side. Finally, at ten o'clock, the army moved forward towards Nivelles. As soon as we had taken up our new position, at about eleven o'clock, both sides started a violent cannonade. Our division (the 2nd) was posted at the centre and more to the right flank. Although we were not going into action any time soon, we were, however, exposed to the gun fire all the time. It steadily closed in on us in the afternoon. Still, our battalion was extremely lucky, we had no significant losses, even though masses of balls and shells were flying in our direction.

We remained under this kind of fire until about half past two o'clock when we received an order to advance. We moved slightly to the left and crossed the highway from Waterloo to Nivelles. We passed over a ridge from which we could survey a plain (fields of wheat in front) and were surprised to see our cavalry overrun and pursued by French cuirassiers (who belonged to the Imperial Guard, as we learned later). At the same time, from what we could see, our infantry advanced in squares in order to support our cavalry. The squares of our brigade also quickly marched down the hillside. Our cavalry now reformed behind us. Although the French cuirassiers charged our squares, they were soon driven back by our vigorous musketry and two artillery batteries posted behind us on a ridge. During this period we suffered severely from the heavy skirmish fire of French tirailleurs who were located in a wood to our right. They could not be overcome by the light companies of our brigade, who had earlier been detached; the French certainly were several battalions strong. There were tirailleurs also in front of us who were covered by a square of French infantry slightly to our left.

The cuirassiers reformed and made another attempt to break through our centre. They charged the squares of our brigade but were received with such murderous fire that they fell into disorder and took to flight. We shouted 'Hurrah!' and pursued them with levelled bayonets for some distance, which upset them so much that they never stopped. Soon thereafter, our brigadier, Colonel du Plat,[150] was badly wounded; Lieutenant Colonel Wissell[151] then assumed command of the brigade, and Major Luttermann[152] that of the battalion.

We now remained here, still exposed to a heavy cannonade, until the Duke of Wellington rode up and ordered the brigade to advance in line.

The outcome of the battle now seemed to have been decided. Accompanied by our cavalry, we advanced towards the French batteries which kept up their heavy fire, but their guns then were abandoned, one by one, and were left standing where they were. All firing ceased as darkness set in. Our brigade advanced to a place near where the French camp had been, and there bivouacked for the night.

The battalion's losses on this murderous, but glorious day had been: Captain Didel killed;[153] Major Boden,[154] Lieutenants Jeinsen,[155] Leschew,[156] Kuckuck Senior,[157] Kuckuck Junior[158] wounded; 1 sergeant and 16 rank and file killed; 2 sergeants, 1 drummer, 90 rank and file wounded, and 33 rank and file missing.[159]

It was said that 150 guns had been captured, not counting 60 that had been seized by the Prussians. They had arrived in the evening on our left flank and had supported the attack against the French right flank, thereby frightening the terror stricken French even more.

19 June

On this morning, the Prussian army passed our camp and pursued the beaten French. We broke camp at ten o'clock in the morning, marched through Nivelles and halted one hour beyond this city and set up our camp.

20 June

We broke camp in the morning and marched towards Binche; near this town we turned off the road towards the right, and the brigade stayed in a small village, Maurage,[160] where the 1st Battalion was assigned quarters, while the others spent the night in a garden under their blankets.

4th Line Battalion, King's German Legion

No. 20 From *Belle-Alliance*

Pflugk-Harttung's letter no. 35, Report of the 4th Line Battalion of the [King's] German Legion on its activities from 16 to 19 June.

[On] 16 June 1815, the battalion (in Ellignies St Anne[161]) received the order to march off, as the French had attacked the Prussian Army. It marched through Enghien to Nivelles[162] and in the evening of 17 June occupied a position near Waterloo. On 18 June, towards twelve o'clock noon, the Battle of Waterloo began and lasted until about nine o'clock in the evening. After the Prussians had driven back the right wing of the French Army, the enemy troops retreated, and the battalion took part in pursuing them until Maison du Roi. The battalion belonged to the

2nd Brigade (under command of Colonel du Plat, who was badly wounded, the command then being transferred to Colonel Wissel) of the 2nd Division under Sir Henry Clinton. [On] 19 June, the battalion marched past Nivelles to Iverness.[163]

3rd Hanoverian Brigade of Colonel Halkett

Bremervorde Landwehr

No. 21 From *Belle-Alliance*

Pflugk-Harttung's letter no. 43, Report of the Hanoverian Landwehr Battalion Bremervorde on its participation in the Battle of La Belle Alliance by Captain F. Scheuch.

Verden, 9 November 1824

... In the campaign of 1815 the Bremervorde Landwehr Battalion, then commanded by Lieutenant Colonel von der Schulenburg, now deceased, formed, together with the Osnabrück, Salzgitter, and Quackenbruck Battalions, a brigade under the command of Major General Halkett. This brigade was part of General Clinton's division.

In the month of June the brigade was cantoned near Ath, and the Bremervorde Battalion in the village of Isières.[164] On 16 June at eight o'clock in the morning, we received the order to break camp. By ten o'clock we were already marching and, after the brigade's other battalions had joined us, we marched without interruption until the evening of the 17th, when we took position behind a ridge near Waterloo. It was already occupied in strength by English and allied troops. We there spent the night from the 17th to the 18th. On the 18th, we moved closer to the just mentioned ridge. I believe we were part of the reserve of the right flank. Our brigade was posted in a line of columns. We occupied a terrain that rose gradually forward from us to a crest, on which the first line was positioned. To our rear were tilled cornfields, meadows and swampland, traversed by a country road which was bordered by a few lowly shrubs. By the way, there were one or two houses close to our rear, to which, later on, the battalion was to bring its wounded.

Towards 12 noon on 18 June the enemy began the battle with a vigorous attack at the right flank on the Hougoumont farm and its small wood. Around two o'clock our brigade was ordered to advance in deployment column, but after moving forward about 300 to 400 paces, it had to return to its previous position. Apparently a dangerous situation involving our forward lines had been brought under control without our assistance. At about half past three o'clock, our cavalry posted on the left flank of the main line had been driven back, and our brigade was therefore forced to immediately form square. When soon thereafter our cavalry had reformed and taken up its former position, we stood again in line, the apparent danger having been averted.

At around five o'clock[165] the vanguard of the Prussians arrived and, as it seemed, drove into the enemy's right flank. After six o'clock the Prussians received reinforcements, and now the entire line of the English army advanced in pursuit of the fleeing enemy. The brigadier, Major General Halkett, now took the Osnabrück and Salzgitter Battalions under his personal command, and put the remaining two battalions to the disposition of Lieutenant Colonel von der Schulenburg, (now deceased). The Bremervorde and Quackenbruck Battalions were then separated from the two already mentioned ones and advanced to the height of the Hougoumont farm without meeting an enemy. During the night from 18 to 19 June, they camped on the battlefield near the border of the small wood at Hougoumont. On the next morning they united again with the other two battalions.

Since we were part of the reserve, we did not become involved in a fire fight. But during 18 June our brigade was exposed to an almost continuous heavy cannonade, from which our battalion lost two officers and, I believe, sixteen men, most of whom from my own company, namely one officer and ten men.[166]

Without doubt, the number of killed and wounded would have been much higher, had not the earlier rainy weather softened the soil, so that the canon balls etc had lost much of their lethal force that these could have kept by bouncing off a hard soil surface.

F. Scheuch, Captain

Osnabrück Landwehr

No. 22 From *Belle-Alliance*

Pflugk-Harttung's letter no. 42 Report of the Hanoverian Landwehr Battalion Osnabrück, 2nd Battalion, Duke of York Regiment,[167] on its participation in the Battle of La Belle Alliance by Major L. von Dreves.[168]

Osnabrück, 3 January 1825

Report on the Participation of the 2nd Battalion, Duke of York Regiment, in the Battle of Waterloo.

The 2nd Battalion, the Duke of York Regiment, commanded by the former major, now deceased, Lieutenant Colonel Count von Munster, was part of the 3rd Hanoverian [Landwehr] Brigade, commanded by the former colonel, now Major General Halkett, in the 2nd Division under the command of the English Lieutenant General Sir Henry Clinton.

On 16 June 1815, the battalion was cantoned in the villages of Rebaix and Ostiches[169] near Ath, and received marching orders on the morning of the 16th, to march that day with the brigade to Braine le Comte. It arrived there towards eleven o'clock at night, and marched off from there at half past one o'clock in the morning of the 17th passed Nivelles on the Brussels road to the area of Braine l'Alleud. It here set up bivouac with the other battalions of the brigade in a location circumscribed by the acute angle of the Nivelles to Brussels highway in front, the village of Braine l'Alleud to the right rear, and the village of Merbe directly in the rear. Merbe Braine was occupied by a detachment of Brunswick lancers; two battalions of line infantry and the artillery of that corps had occupied the ridge, with the village to their right. To the left of our position were some battalions of the King's German Legion; no troops could be seen to our right. The enemy's dispositions could not be determined from this location. The generally open terrain was, however, quite uneven, with elevations alternating with depressions. It was rising in our front up to the highway; after several hundred paces the ridge dropped off on its far side and then rose to another elevation in the direction of La Belle Alliance. Behind our line, the terrain became lower towards the village of Merbe Braine, to rise again to a plateau on its far side.

The battalion remained in this position with the brigade until about eleven o'clock at midday of the 18th. Around that time, a horse battery of the King's German Legion, commanded by the former major, now Lieutenant Colonel Sympher, had taken up position before us on the elevation on this side of the highway. It was joined on the same ridge and at some distance to the right by several guns of the Brunswick artillery. The brigade then advanced several hundred paces by battalion columns and took up a new position to the left of the previous one, near the highway.

The enemy began firing at our column. At about two o'clock in the afternoon a strong formation of enemy cuirassiers appeared some distance away and moved up from the area between Hougoumont and La Haye Sainte, whereupon the brigade formed square. The enemy cavalry retired, however, without carrying out an attack. Towards about four o'clock in the afternoon, the battalion advanced in column formation across the highway, with Hougoumont to its right, through the first depression formed by the terrain, and up to the opposite ridge, where it took position in the first line. (The brigade's other battalions apparently were assigned different destinations, because from then on the battalion was by itself).

The Brunswick 3rd Light Battalion stood on the same plateau in square in front of the battalion at a distance of 60 paces. To the forward right, a very strong English battery had its position on the elevation; to the forward left were English infantry at a distance of several hundred paces. The battalion remained here until the French Guard attacked later on. Although protected by a ridge in front, it suffered considerably from the enemy artillery fire. To the left one could see English infantry advancing, although its further moves could not be observed from the battalion's position.

At about half past six o'clock, the battalion moved up to the crest of the ridge and was assigned a position to the right of the battery mentioned earlier.[170] To the left of the battery were battalions of the brigade of the English Colonel Adams;[171] no troops could be observed to the right of the battalion. Opposite our position, very strong enemy columns stood in the background, of which four battalions of the French Guard were nearest to us. These then attacked in columns, while their skirmishers moved up to within a short distance from us. After the skirmishers had been driven back by the English and the battalion's riflemen, the battalion attacked in column in coordination with the English to the left, who advanced in line, against the French columns approaching through a depression in the terrain. After putting up a strong resistance, they began to retreat.

As the French Guard retired in some disorder, a French general (whose name, I believe, was Cambronne) was energetically engaged in attempting to halt and reform the battalions. He succeeded several times; but their retiring continued, however, as they were forcefully driven back by our pursuing battalions. Our brigadier, the then Colonel Halkett, had observed that action and, with unequalled intrepidity, rode through the French skirmishers, who covered the retreating columns, to that general and, with great luck, brought him back before the entire line, through the enemy skirmishers, and made him his prisoner, notwithstanding [the man's] forceful resistance.[172]

The retiring Guard still halted several times after that general had been taken prisoner and, by taking every advantage of the terrain, attempted by their fire to stop their pursuers. They eventually had to yield to the forceful advance of the pursuing troops and dissolved into a disorderly mob.

In its pursuit of the enemy, the battalion drove in on four French batteries, one by one, of which two kept on firing. After several rounds of fire from the head of the battalion and from our riflemen, they were seized in our subsequent attack. The third battery was about to retreat and was then taken, and, upon the approach of our battalion, the artillerymen of the fourth battery left their cannon, which were then captured. The battalion pursued the enemy jointly with English and Prussian troops, eventually intermingled with them, on and along the side of the Genappe highway, until about ten o'clock at night. The remnants of the battalion gathered near some houses, probably Maison du Roi or Le Caillou.

The battalion was unable to continue its advance further, due to the extraordinary exertions on this day. Having thus become separated somewhat from the other troops, I was charged at eleven o'clock at night by the brigadier, the then Colonel Halkett, with a reconnoitring assignment, with as many of the battalion's men as I was able to put on the road. I undertook this with the greater part of the remnants of the battalion in the direction of Genappe. While faced with great difficulties due to the extreme exhaustion of the troops and the darkness of night, I executed this assignment to the satisfaction of the brigadier.

On the morning of 19 June, the battalion reformed in the area on this side of Genappe and marched to Nivelles, rejoining the other battalions of the brigade on the march.

Following are the losses of the battalion during the battle, according to a report of 25 June 1815 (the losses shown in the existing *Report Book*, which was not properly maintained, does not separately list those killed): killed, 1 lieutenant, 1 ensign 1 NCO;[173] wounded, 2 captains (of whom one died from his wounds), 1 lieutenant, 2 ensigns, 1 NCO, 1 drummer, 68 corporals and soldiers.[174] prisoners, 18 corporals and soldiers.[175]

L. Von Dreves, Major

Salzgitter Landwehr

No. 23 From *Belle-Alliance*

Pflugk-Harttung's letter no. 45 Report of the Hanoverian Landwehr Battalion Salzgitter on its conduct in the Battle of La Belle Alliance. Letter of Major von Hammerstein, Battalion Commander, to the Brigadier, Colonel Hugh Halkett.

Bivouac, Le Cateau, 24 June 1815

Report of the Salzgitter Battalion at the Battle of 18 June.

The Salzgitter Battalion, which had arrived with the brigade between Waterloo and Braine l'Alleud at six o'clock on the previous evening, and there had set up its bivouac, received the order from you, my dear colonel,[176] to stand ready in front of the bivouac at four o'clock in the morning. We then immediately marched to the position adjoining the centre, where we formed the right wing. We formed in divisions at half distance and now received an order to let the men lie down and rest up. The position was favourably located in a slight depression but our men were within range of enemy fire right from the beginning of the battle. Unfortunately, my battalion suffered significant losses in this first position, in which the brigade remained for three hours until two o'clock in the afternoon. At this time, the enemy seemed to have the intention to turn the left flank, and we therefore left the position we had held until now, formed into column and, with the entire brigade, made up a square in close column formation.

The two battalions of the right wing (Bremervorde and Quackenbruck) were soon ordered to march off to the right, whereupon the Salzgitter and Osnabrück Battalions individually formed squares four ranks deep. Two howitzer shells fell into my square on that occasion and killed several ranks; but each time the ranks were calmly closed again. Our two squares now marched forward, more to the right and up an elevation at battalion distance apart, and deployed while under a severe cannonade: a deployment which redounds a particular honour to the battalion in having it executed in outstanding order while exposed to heavy fire. Here we stood in line for a short time only, because the enemy seemed to have made some gains on his left wing; also, we had to reform in squares because of the enemy cavalry. The assigned position was on the far side of a deep hollow way, from which the men could climb up only singly and under heavy fire of case shot. They reformed calmly, as always, and marched in close column far enough under the gun range that their fire became almost ineffective. It was now necessary to seize the wood and the Chateau [Hougoumont], for the possession of which a battalion of English Guards, the 2nd line Battalion [KGL], and two battalions of Brunswickers had fought all day in vain. Only small detachments of these battalions were still in the wood; as to the enemy, there were skirmishers of different corps in the wood, particularly of the [Imperial] Guards, whose strong solid columns to the left [of the wood] seemed to threaten our flank. My battalion was assigned this challenging task at around seven o'clock in the evening. The Osnabrück Battalion and the 95th English regiment faced the [French] columns, and we thus protected each other. Massed columns of enemy infantry and cavalry also stood to our right. The enemy held on most tenaciously. We moved forward by companies; my men had also run out of ammunition and began using the enemy's cartridges.[177] The small Brunswick detachments remained behind. Our advance was made extremely difficult by the enemy who had protective ditches on both of his flanks. Under these circumstances, and because dusk was setting in, nothing seemed to be more effective than an attack with the bayonet. Shouting 'Hurrah!', we were quick enough and fortunate to gain possession of the wood, certainly a most important position. The battalion rallied immediately upon leaving the wood and advanced up the elevation in closed column. It was night by this time. We were followed by the 2nd Line Battalion, and were later joined by a battery of horse artillery.

Everything was quiet now, and camp fires were being lit. I was in doubt as to which direction to follow to find the brigade, took a left turn, and at ten o'clock at night came up to Maison Rouge [Roi?] on the highway to Genappe. Two battalions of Vincke's Brigade had already gathered here, and that was where I set up bivouac as ordered by General Maitland.

I cannot praise enough the good conduct of my officers and men on this day. The following have excelled in particular by their calm intrepidity:

1 Major Rudorff,[178]
2 my brother, Captain von Hammerstein,[179]
3 the rifle officer, Ensign Mull,
4 the two Sergeants Werner and Brand of the 1st Light Battalion,
5 the soldiers NCO Fritze of No. 1 Company, Franz Lierat of No. 2, Corporal Schulze of No. 3, NCO Beker of No. 4 Company.

My battalion had to deplore the following losses on this day: 2 wounded officers: my brother, Captain von Hammerstein and Lieutenant von Spangenberg; and of the men, killed, 1 sergeant and 22 privates;[180] wounded, 2 sergeants and 63 privates.[181]

Finally, I regret to have to add that Lieutenant Tospau of my battalion had absented himself on the day before the expected battle, and returned on the following morning. With your permission, my dear colonel, I had to separate him immediately from the battalion before the battle for that reason, and because none of his fellow officers would serve any longer in his presence.

Hammerstein, Major and Commander of the Salzgitter Battalion

3rd Division of Lieutenant General Baron Karl von Alten[182]

No. 24 From *Belle-Alliance*

Pflugk-Harttung's letter no. 5 Report of Lieutenant General von Alten to the Duke of Cambridge on the conduct of the Hanoverian troops in the action at Quatre Bras.

Letter no. 20 Report of Lieutenant General von Alten to the Duke of Cambridge on the conduct of the Hanoverian troops in the Battle of La Belle Alliance.

To His Royal Highness, Field Marshal and General Military Governor, The Duke of Cambridge, Knight of the Order of the Garter, etc.

Brussels, 20 June 1815

Your Royal Highness will already have been informed by Lieutenant General von der Decken of the favourable outcome of the two actions that we have fought against Bonaparte's army on the 16th and the 18th; I nevertheless feel obligated to send Your Royal Highness a detailed report on these. Lieutenant Wiegmann, my senior adjutant, who is bringing you this report, has participated in both battles and may be able to inform you on whatever might have been overlooked by myself. I commend this very gifted officer to Your Royal Highness's gracious consideration.

In the evening of the 15th, the entire army broke camp at its different widely scattered cantonments and directed its marches towards Nivelles. On the 16th, about 3 infantry divisions and some cavalry regiments reached that location and moved on to Quatre Bras, where there is a crossing of the roads from Mons to Namur and from Brussels to Charleroi. The French had split their army and attacked at the same time Field Marshal Blücher and the Duke of Wellington's corps that had been brought up against them. Our troops took their position along the Namur highway between Quatre Bras and Sart Dames Avelines, with the right wing occupying the former village, and the left wing the latter. This deployment occurred under the heaviest enemy cannon fire, which, however, made not a single man flinch. The enemy had taken hold of a wood to the right of Quatre Bras. This was attacked by our army and taken and lost by turns. Both sides now engaged in a heavy cannonade, and the enemy tried several times to overrun the left flank which consisted of my division. I sent the 1st Luneburg Battalion to drive him again out of the village of Pireaumont before us, which the Brunswick infantry had been forced to leave. Lieutenant Colonel von Klencke carried out this task with great determination, and he succeeded not only in retaking the village, but also in throwing the enemy back into a wood on the far side of the village and then resisting his repeated attacks. The enemy infantry advanced in several columns, against which I detached the Grubenhagen, Duke of York and Bremen Battalions. These drove the columns back, with artillery support from Captain Cleeves of the [King's German] Legion. The enemy cavalry attempted several times to charge our right flank, but the steadfastness of the troops kept it from breaking through. In this situation, the Luneburg

Landwehr Battalion under Lieutenant Colonel von Ramdohr distinguished itself in particular. He let the enemy approach to within 30 paces and then ordered a salvo which threw back the cavalry with great loss. We were fortunate in being able to remain master of our position, but since the Prussian army, which stood on our left flank, had suffered a rather severe reverse, we were forced to retreat at noon on the 17th.

My division formed the rearguard up to Genappe. We rested there for several hours, but, as the enemy was pursuing us, we continued marching on the Brussels highway to Mont St Jean. The Duke of Wellington's entire army assembled here and took up position on the heights before that village, such that the left flank leaned on the village of Frischermont, and the right flank on the highway from Nivelles to Brussels. The highway from Genappe to Brussels crossed the centre of the army, where my division was positioned. The attached map,[183] prepared in a hurry by Major Kuntze, will provide your Royal Highness with an approximate view of our position and of the enemy's attacks. I had the 2nd Light Battalion of the King's German Legion, commanded by Major Baring, occupy the farm next to the highway and located in front of, and close to, the left flank of my division. A company of the Hanoverian Jäger and two light companies of the British Guards were posted in the farmstead and wood in front of the right wing [Hougoumont]. It will not be possible for me to give your Royal Highness as detailed a report of this battle as of the previous one [Quatre Bras], because the army was widely spread out and I could not see all of the left wing. Therefore, except for some general aspects, I must limit myself primarily to what concerns my division.

The infantry of the army corps commanded by His Royal Highness, The Prince of Orange, of which my division was a part, stood in columns in a chequerboard pattern drawn up at ¼ distance. These consisted, each, of two battalions side by side, with the right one in left in front, and the left one in right in front formation, so that deployment in line or squares could be quickly executed. The distance between columns was sufficiently large to permit the passage of the cavalry posted in the third line and of any advancing artillery. The corps of General Lord Hill stood in reserve near Braine l'Alleud, and also covered the highway from Nivelles to Brussels. Some cavalry was posted beyond that highway to keep the enemy's movements under observation.

At noon, around one o'clock, the enemy sent tirailleurs towards the wood in front of our right wing, whose possession was very important for us; otherwise the enemy might seize an elevation and from there might threaten our right wing. He gradually had strong infantry columns march up, which were supported by artillery. We also had our artillery move up and fire at these columns, which, however, were not deterred from advancing. They seized this wood several times but it was always retaken by us. The division of Guards who stood at the extreme right wing kept defending this outpost with intrepid tenacity. Meanwhile, the enemy emplaced numerous artillery pieces against us, which began a heavy cannonade. Thus covered, a column of several thousand men moved straight up on the Genappe highway; these were thrown back, however, by the two light battalions and the 8th Line Battalion of the King's German Legion and the Luneburg Field Battalion. Our battalions now formed squares. From behind this [enemy] infantry, a numerous cavalry force moved up with such impetuosity that it overthrew the skirmishing infantry and advanced up to the plateau between the squares that stood in a chequerboard pattern. They imperturbably stood their ground till the British cavalry drove forward and threw the enemy back. The squares exposed the most were commanded by Lieutenant Colonel von Wurmb and Major von Skopp.[184] Lieutenant Colonel von Langrehr had already been wounded and been taken to the rear. By now, the fire from the enemy artillery became ever more violent, and the cannonade from both sides increased to such a force, the likes of which perhaps only very few of the oldest veterans might have experienced. More than 200 cannon took part in this action.

The attacks of the enemy infantry and cavalry were repeated several times and at various points. Buonaparte was intent on rupturing the centre by all means, and thus opening the way to Brussels. One of the columns was driven back by a battalion, which was led by Colonel von Ompteda. The enemy nevertheless moved ever closer and with fresh troops, and his artillery fired canister at our squares from a distance of 150 paces. But there was no yielding; the dead were pushed to the side and the ranks were closed again. The squares moved towards the enemy cavalry that had already taken part of our position, and, with their steady firing, forced it to leave the plateau. Some of these had been reduced to almost nothing and had to yield, but they retired in good order and advanced again when given the order. At all times, the Duke of Wellington was an eyewitness to these happenings. This hero was always present at the points of greatest danger, and the Prince of Orange displayed a degree of courage that was worthy of his great ancestor.[185] It was his corps against which the enemy's main force, led by Bonaparte in person, was directed.

Eventually, when we were in the greatest need and could hardly resist anymore the attackers' advancing forces, General von Bülow struck at the enemy's right flank with 30,000 men that had come to our support in forced marches. Now, victory was ours; the enemy was fleeing in all directions and abandoned the greatest part of his artillery. Close to 200 cannon and several eagles have been captured. The number of prisoners is not yet known, but there must be many thousands. Our army has advanced to Binche, and that of the Prussians to Charleroi.

These two days have cost us very much, and it is with deep regret that I must inform your Royal Highness that the greatest part of our most distinguished officers has not survived. Among these were, in particular, the Colonels von Ompteda and du Plat, the Lieutenant Colonels von Wurmb and von Langrehr. Our consolation will be that the graves of these men are crowned with glory, and that the Hanoverians are now renowned for their bravery. As an eyewitness, I can testify only in regard to the Field Battalions Bremen, Luneburg, Verden, Grubenhagen, and Duke of York that they have proven themselves worthy to be entered in the annals of our military. Very favourable reports have also reached me from several brigade commanders whose Landwehr brigades have taken part in the fighting. Colonel Halkett praised the Osnabrück Battalion in particular. Of our cavalry, only the Duke of Cumberland Regiment was present in the battle, but did not advance to a charge.[186] It had been exposed to the cannonade for some time that caused considerable losses.[187]

Although every officer and soldier that I was able to observe did his duty, I nevertheless feel an obligation to name some of them who have exceptionally distinguished themselves on these hot days. It is my hope that, since your Royal Highness is disposed to give rewards to the deserving, you will be pleased to bestow tokens of your satisfaction and approval on these men, for whom these will be supreme incentives. With his bravery and intrepidity, Major General Count von Kielmansegge gave his brigade a most splendid example; he always supported me with all his might.[188] The conduct of Lieutenant Colonels von Klencke, von Wurmb, and von Langrehr, of Majors von Skopp, von Bülow, and von Stockhausen deserves the highest respect. According to the attached report from Colonel Halkett, I may be justified to commend Major Count von Munster to your Royal Highness's consideration. I shall not fail in my gratitude to the officers of my staff, and in particular to Colonel von Berger who, as Chief of the General Staff, always stayed by my side on the 16th and also on the 18th and who, through his advice and deeds, has been of exceptional assistance to me. Your Royal Highness is familiar with the meritorious talents of this officer, and, on my part being severely wounded, I would not have been able to continue in my command of the Hanoverian troops if Colonel von Berger had not handled its major affairs, although having suffered a contusion himself.

To Major Heise, of the King's German Legion, whom your Royal Highness has assigned to me as Military Secretary, I must accord the well earned praise for having, on these two days, displayed an eagerness and a performance that redound to his greatest honour. Majors Kuntze and von Schlutter have used every opportunity to be of assistance to me, although they had no specific assignment, due to myself being restricted to the command of the division; I therefore cannot fail to mention them in this report. Lieutenant Count von Kielmansegge has also been of great help to me.

At this time, I cannot name all the officers who distinguished themselves on these days because I have not yet received the brigade commanders' reports. I will collect these, however, and send a summary to your Royal Highness to bring their names to your attention as best as possible. Neither have all the listings been received of the killed, wounded, and missing, as the army immediately began to move off again. I hope to have these transmitted in a few days. A list of the names of those fallen shall also follow shortly.

Since public recognition is every officer's supreme prize, I dare proposing to your Royal Highness that it may please you to graciously grant a promotion to those who served meritoriously on these days, as it is done in the British Army, and as this government has no orders to confer. I am convinced that this will have the most beneficial effect for the army's morale, from which will follow the most handsome results. Provided that Your Highness will concur with this proposal, I will name for you in a special report those who I am convinced deserve this kind of recognition. I also feel obligated to invite Your Royal Highness's attention in regard to the widows of the fallen officers, non-commissioned officers and soldiers. A good many are certainly in need of support, and in my view, our country can, in this way, best honour the memory of those who have fallen for their fatherland and for their sovereign.

As to the internal organisation of the corps after the losses it had suffered, I intend to submit at the earliest my proposals in this regard to Your Royal Highness. It will be most difficult to bring all battalions up to strength again, and it might be advisable to combine some of them. There will be a particular need of suitable men for the rank of staff officer. I still need to advise your Royal Highness that the wound I had suffered near the end of the battle will not hinder me to remain in command of the Hanoverians, if Your Highness will continue to entrust me therewith under these circumstances. It is my hope to be fully restored again in a few weeks. By the way, I will not fail to assure your Royal Highness how deeply I feel about the loss your own family has suffered through the death of the Duke of Brunswick. He has fallen near the Duke of Wellington, and every German will certainly mourn with me over the loss of this noble prince who has done so much, he fought and gave his life for a good cause.

K. von Alten, Lieutenant General

On 8 July a second report followed this one from Brussels about the brigades of Colonels von Vincke, Best and Halkett in which these and individual officers were praised in a similar manner.

2nd King's German Legion Brigade of Colonel Ompteda

It is surprising to note that there is no correspondence from the 1st Light Battalion KGL in Pflugk-Harttung's book nor have any others come to light in my searches. However, a large number of letters from this battalion were sent to William Siborne and published in the editor's *Letters from the Battle of Waterloo* (Nos 147–162).

2nd Light Battalion, King's German Legion

No. 25 Account of Rifleman Lindau

Extracted from Reminiscences of a Soldier of the Campaigns of the King's German Legion, *by Friedrich Lindau,*[189] *former Rifleman in the 2nd Light Battalion. Bearer of the Guelphic Medal, the Waterloo Medal, and the Medal of Merit in Bronze.*

The Defence of the farmstead of La Haye Sainte during the Battle of Waterloo (18 June 1815).

During this winter from 1814 to 1815 and in the spring of 1815 we had been cantoned in several Belgian cities and led a merry life; because every day we were paid more than 16 Mariengroschen[190] per day. This lasted until the middle of June.

On the afternoon of 16 June we received the order to stand ready; we were to march off immediately. Towards evening we heard the rumbling of cannon in the distance and were surprised because we had not heard of the closeness of the enemy. We broke camp at dusk and marched throughout the night.

At dawn of the next morning, a sutler woman from Hamelin came to us; her name was Ehlers Wieschen and she had married a man named Pieper.[191] She inquired about her husband; I was unable to tell her where he was, but I asked her to measure some rum into my canteen. She would not take any payment from me, her compatriot and, thus, a friend.

At daybreak we were posted in a hollow way from where we soon moved to the left and came upon the battlefield where the Brunswickers had severely suffered the day before. It was a horrible field strewn with corpses; in the true sense of the word it was bathed in blood that rose above our ankles with every step. We then moved around a wood that was said to be occupied by the enemy and spread out for skirmishing, but then received orders to retire.

Half an hour later, probably around four o'clock, the skies suddenly became as dark as night, lightning lit up the darkness, and the crash of the thunder claps was accompanied by the roar of the cannon. As the rain poured down on us we pressed together so tightly that we might have fitted into a large room; it was so heavy that soon the water was up to our knees.

After the terrible downpour had let up a bit, we moved along a highway, on which our cavalry passed us on its advance against the enemy. Within the space of one hour, our horsemen charged three times and returned three times as well. They were so covered with mud that no longer could we make out the colour of their uniforms and were in doubt whether they were friend or enemy.

Towards evening we marched through a field of high corn that we trampled into the mud, making it look as if it had been mown, and then arrived at the farmstead of La Haye Sainte, which borders directly on the highway. Two companies were immediately sent into the orchard, which did not please me at all because I could not find a single dry spot. I therefore went into the courtyard in a search for some straw; here I met my brother[192] who was unable to give me any, either, as there was nothing left in the barns.

It was then that Major Baring came out of the house and gave an order to butcher the livestock that was still left in the stables. The meat was distributed, and also to the men of the line battalions outside who had shown up to find some straw. In the meantime, I had discovered some peas in the loft of the house, which I gathered in a cloth; with these and a large piece of meat I hurried back to my comrades and asked them to light a fire. Since it was still raining and the ground in the garden was just mud, nobody was in the mood. One of them was leaning against a tree, another against a wall; others again had sat down on their knapsack and were staring at nothing in particular; nobody was willing to lay down.

I therefore went back to the courtyard where I had heard that there still was wine in the cellar. I sneaked in there, found a cask that was half full and filled my canteen. With this I went on a search for my youngest brother who I knew was with a battery nearby.[193] He was the one that at

Rohrsen had been chased back [home] with a good beating from me; we had not seen each other again since that time.[194]

In front of the gate of the barn I happened to bump into men from our 1st Battalion; they almost emptied my canteen. I then went off in the darkness and was soon challenged by a patrol. The corporal who led the patrol I recognised to be a fellow countryman named Meyer. He was with the Bremen Field Battalion, was severely wounded on the next day and became a prisoner of the French. I asked him about my brother but he had no information. I shared my wine with him, and marched with the patrol back to the farm. Once again I went down into the cellar and returned with mine and Corporal Meyer's canteen well filled. The men of the patrol emptied my canteen, and Meyer went off with his. Later on, I returned several times to the cellar and brought wine to my comrades in the orchard. At midnight I was posted as a sentry at the tip of the orchard which faced the enemy; I then sat down on my knapsack and fell asleep. As morning dawned, my backup man whose name was Harz and who was also born at the Harz,[195] awakened me and said: 'Get up and give me some wine! Today will be a hot day, and I will be killed, because I just had a dream that I was hit by a shot in my body; it did not hurt at all, and I fell peacefully asleep again.' 'Dreams don't mean anything,' was my reply, and 'Come on now, they are working on a barricade. We will help, to make us warm up; there is no wine left'. We pushed the remaining half of a wagon onto the roadway where the orchard adjoined the buildings; others brought ladders and farming tools; three spiked French cannon were also moved there.[196]

The roaring of French artillery fire reached us as late as midday. We stood behind the hedge ready to fire and looked out for the enemy. Before long, a swarm of enemy skirmishers came up. The crash of a thousand [French] rifles filled our ears, and a jubilant *'En avant!'* could be heard. They were backed up by two columns of enemy troops of the line that marched at so rapid a pace that we said to each other: 'The French are in such a hurry because they want to have their meals in Brussels today.' Only until the enemy came close to our hedge did we open fire; it was so murderous that the ground was covered at once with a mass of wounded and dead.

The French halted for a moment; they then opened a fire that did us great harm. My friend Harz fell down by my side from a ball through his body. Captain Schaumann of the 2nd [Light] Battalion[197] was also killed; my brother had carried him on his back to the farm where he laid him down, but by then he was already dead.

We still did not give up our position. But as soon as the column on the right advanced to the gate of the barn and threatened to cut off our retreat to its entrance, we slowly fell back, firing all the time. Meanwhile our Major Bosewiel[198] had also been wounded. I saw him lying on the ground; he raised himself one more time, but then fell on his face and expired.

The enemy stood already at the entrance of the barn. But we drove him back and were able to enter, although at heavy loss. We then loosed off such a violent fire down the barn towards the open entrance, where the French stood in a dense crowd that they did not dare to enter. I had been at this spot for about half an hour. Then I went to a loophole next to the locked gate that faced the highway. Here, the French were so tightly packed that I often saw three to four enemies felled by a single bullet.

A short time later, our Captain Graeme[199] had the gate opened, and we stormed with levelled bayonets against the tightly packed enemy. He did not resist because we pushed ahead with irresistible fury. I stabbed and hit into that mass like a blind man in a rage. We pursued the enemy beyond the barricade, when English hussars suddenly appeared close to us. They cut so mercilessly into the enemy that a large crowd returned without arms to us and asked for pardon. Upon the hussars' return from the pursuit, they led the prisoners away.

Posted behind the barricade, we stood by now for a renewed attack, which was hardly half an hour in coming. We easily fought back the skirmishers. But as new columns drove in on us, we retired into the doorway, which I locked up on Captain Graeme's order. I and several others took position at the loopholes next to the doorway, from where we fired at the enemy wherever he was most tightly packed. We quickly stepped back to reload and let the others take our place. But the French also stuck their muskets in the openings and felled several comrades next to me. Quite a few of ours fell off the scaffolds above us from where they had fired over the wall. But this only enraged us all the more, and I could hardly wait to loose off another shot, and I eagerly reloaded my rifle, so that I must have fired off several hundred cartridges that day.

Ever more [French] regiments were brought up, but they were repulsed each time. One particular enemy officer caught my eye, who rode back and forth on the field in front of us and was giving directions to the advancing columns. I already had my sight on him for quite a while; finally, as he was just bringing on fresh troops, I had him lined up and fired. His horse made a leap, reared up, and crashed down with its rider.

A short time later we made a sortie. I opened the gate; the nearest enemies were bayoneted, the others took to flight. We followed them for a distance and then halted. I now noticed not far away from me the officer that I had shot at. I hurried towards him and grabbed his golden watch chain. But I hardly had it in my hand when he reached for his sabre, shouting abuse at me. I then hit his head with the butt of the rifle that made him fall back and stretch out, and I then noticed a golden ring on his finger. But I first cut a small portmanteau off his horse, and was about to pull off the officer's ring when my comrades shouted: 'Better get going; the cavalry is upon us!' I saw some thirty horsemen charge towards us, and with my booty I ran as fast as I could to join my comrades who, with a volley, forced the enemy to retire.

We then stayed for a while on the highway, and the pile of dead enemies made me feel good; they were already lying several feet high, next to the barricade. I saw a grenadier next to the wall who had been shot in the body. He tried to pierce his chest with his sabre but was too weak to do so. I grabbed the sabre by the hand guard in my attempt to throw it away. The Frenchman immediately let go, apparently afraid I might hurt his hands on pulling it off.

Next to the barricade a wounded soldier was lying in a puddle of water who had been shot in the leg. His pain made him cry out loud as he was trying to roll out of the water. I grabbed him by the arms, another man got hold of his legs, and so we laid him next to the wall, with his head bedded on a dead comrade.

Some 20 to 30 English horses were running around nearby; most were wounded. I called one which stayed put and then let me lead it into the courtyard where I brought it to Major Baring. He, however, ordered me to chase it out of the farm. I then showed him a pouch with gold coins that I had found in my recent booty, the portmanteau, and asked him if I could leave it in his safekeeping. He refused to take it with the words: 'Who knows what will yet happen to us today; you have to see yourself how best to safeguard the money.'

A short time later there was another attack on the farm, and my captain ordered me to stay at the gate. But at this time the fighting lasted longer, with ever new columns moving up; we soon ran out of cartridges. As soon as one of ours fell, we immediately emptied the contents of his pouch. Major Baring, who was riding about the court–yard, consoled us with the news that we would soon receive more ammunition.

At that moment I was shot through the back of my head, which I reported to my captain who stood above me on the scaffold. He ordered me to go to the rear. 'No', was my answer, 'as long as I can stand upright I will stay at my post.' I then took off my neckerchief, wetted it with rum and asked a comrade to pour rum on the wound and wrap the cloth around my head. I tied my shako to the knapsack and reloaded my rifle.

My captain above me, whom I could see whenever I reloaded, often bent himself over the wall, commanding and cursing and hitting into the French. I cautioned him not to bend too far over the wall or else he might get shot. 'That does not matter', was his answer, 'just let those dogs shoot!' Shortly thereafter I noticed that his hand was bleeding and that he wrapped it with a handkerchief. I then shouted: 'Captain, Sir, now it is your turn to go to the rear!'

'Ah, nonsense', he replied, 'there is no going to the rear; it is nothing!' He took his sword with his left hand and kept cutting at the flood of enemies that were rushing up.

Soon thereafter I heard some shouting coming from the barn door: 'The enemy's trying to break in!' I went there, and hardly had I fired a few shots down the barn when I noticed heavy smoke appear from under the beams. In no time at all did Major Baring, Sergeant Reese, from Tundern, and Poppe[200] come running to extinguish the fire with field kettles full of water they had filled at the pond.

As the loopholes behind us were not fully manned, the French vigorously fired at us through these. I and some comrades posted ourselves at the loopholes whereupon the enemies' fire became weaker. Just as I had fired a shot, a Frenchman grabbed my rifle to tear it away from me. I said to my neighbour: 'Look here, that dog is pulling at my rifle.' 'Wait,' he said, 'I have a shot loaded,' and the Frenchman fell right away. At the same moment another grabbed at my rifle, but my neighbour to the right stabbed him in his face.

Now as I was about to retract my rifle to reload it, a mass of balls came flying by me. They rattled at the stones of the wall; one of them ripped off one of my woollen shoulder rolls, another smashed the cock of my rifle. To obtain another one, I went to the pond, where Sergeant Reese was about to expire; he could not talk anymore. But when I tried to take his rifle; I knew it was a good one, he made a grim face at me. I took another one, there were many lying about, and returned to my loophole. But soon I had fired off all of my cartridges, and before I could keep up firing I searched the pouches of my fallen comrades, most of which were already empty.

So our firing became weaker, and the pressure of the French more forceful. Fire broke out again in our barn, and it was extinguished again. I then searched the cartridge pouches of the dead in the courtyard. Major Baring rode up to me and said: 'You must go back!' To him I replied the same that I had already told Captain Graeme; 'He is a scoundrel who deserts you, as long as there still is a head on one's shoulder!'

Soon afterwards I heard a general shouting throughout the farm: 'Defend yourselves! Defend yourselves! They are coming in everywhere; let us draw together!' Our men had left the scaffold. I observed several Frenchmen on top of the wall. One of them jumped down off the scaffold; but at the same moment I drove my sword bayonet into his chest. He fell down on me and I flung him to the side; but my sword bayonet had been bent and I had to throw it away.

I saw my captain in a hand to hand fight with the French at the entrance of the house. One of them was about to shoot at Ensign Frank,[201] but Captain Graeme pierced him with his sword; another one he struck in his face. I tried to run there to help, but all of a sudden I was surrounded by the French. I now made good use of the butt of my rifle. I thrashed around me until only the barrel of my rifle was left, and freed myself.

Behind me I heard curses and abusive language: '*Couyons Hanovriens*' and '*Anglais*', [Hanoverian and English scoundrels] and noticed how two Frenchmen brought Captain Holtzermann into the barn. I was going to free him when suddenly a Frenchman gripped me by my chest from the side. I seized him, too; but then another one stabbed at me with a bayonet. I threw the Frenchman sideways whom I was holding so that he became the one to be stabbed; he let go of me and, shouting: '*Mon Dieu, mon Dieu!*', fell to the ground.

Now I hurried to the barn through which I hoped to escape. When I found its entrance blocked by a crowd, I leapt over a small partition to where some of my comrades and Captain Holtzermann were standing. Soon a great many Frenchmen moved in on us and shouted: '*En avant, couyons!*' [Get going, scoundrels!].We were driven out of the corner where we stood and forced to jump over the partition. One of ours who was unable to jump because of his wound was stabbed in his lower body. We were outraged. We cursed the French and were going to go for them; but Captain Holtzermann[202] managed to calm us, even though inside we were seething with rage about such disgraceful treatment that no captured Frenchman had ever received from us.

We were then taken from the barn through the courtyard and doorway to the highway, where many Frenchmen pressed against us, felt us up and pillaged us. One of them tore off my haversack and found the pouch with gold coins inside. Another one immediately grabbed at it, but the first one held on to it, and thus erupted a violent fight. Then my knapsack was torn off my shoulders; others pulled at my uniform, groped for watches and found them; I had two silver ones and a golden watch. After everything had been taken from me I got into a fit of rage and with my fist hit another Frenchman in the face who still hoped to find more loot on me.

Then two cannon shots were fired from our side that felled many Frenchmen but also struck some of our men. Our enemies were startled for only a moment, and then they tore off Captain Holtzermann's sash and sword scabbard. We picked up some rock and wanted to revenge ourselves on the hated enemies for such despicable treatment. But our captain calmed us and turned to a French officer whom we remembered to have been our prisoner at the Jewish cemetery of Bayonne. He attempted to protect us and forbade any more plundering but was cursed and laughed at.

We still hoped for the English cavalry to make a charge; we would then have joined in the attack on the enemy. However, all that appeared were French cuirassiers, almost all with bandages on their heads, who led us along on the highway. They forced us to run as fast their horses, and then killed one man from the 1st Battalion by stabbing him through the body, because he could not run fast enough.

We might have gone for an hour in between French infantry, which stood in line to our right and left, when the French army followed us in complete disorder, artillery, cavalry, and infantry all intermingled. Even in our sad situation we could not feel anything but immense delight. I whispered to my neighbour: 'If here we had just one hundred men with our arms, we could make prisoners of all of them.'

After about three hours, we were taken into a completely dark barn, where we met other prisoners. We had hardly gone in there when French infantrymen, stragglers out of control and order, broke the gate open and began plundering. In the confusion, I and some of my comrades pushed outside. It was a moonlit night, and I noticed that fleeing Frenchmen were all about us.

For a long time now I had suffered a terrible thirst; I therefore hurried over to a well that I had noticed nearby, without a thought to my safety. I there ran into a few French guardsmen and asked one of them in French for water. 'You are not a Frenchman', he said in German, 'where are you from?' 'I am a Hanoverian.' 'And from what area?' 'From Hamelin on the Weser River.' 'I was posted in that city', he continued, 'When we were sold off by our general.' 'Then why are you now with the French?' I asked him. 'Because I could not stand being a prisoner', he replied; 'That is why I preferred active service.' He then gave me a pot of water and a piece of bread.

Corporal Fastermann[203] now joined us; he had also escaped from the barn, and was also given a drink of water and a piece of bread. The Guardsman advised us to keep to the right where the Prussians were; the retreating French army would be on the left. 'In one hour', he added, 'we will all be in the hands of the English.'

I thanked the man, shook his hand, and I and Corporal Fastermann hurried off to the right. We arrived this way unhindered at a wood of young trees where we sat down in a small hollow because I was dead tired. It must have been about midnight and it was very cold; my limbs were shaking and my teeth kept chattering in my mouth. Things were all quiet to our right, but from the left we heard some irregular firing by the French and shouts of '*Vive l'Empereur!*' all the time.

After half an hour, the chill drove us on again, and we warily continued our march through the wood. We soon were at its end and walked for a stretch over open fields where everything was quiet; only from some distance came the noise made by the French on their retreat. We then turned into a hollow way to be better protected. But we immediately heard some noise in front of us, and somebody shouted: '*Halt là, qui vit?* [Stop, who is there?]' 'A friend!' Fastermann answered. The other man levelled his bayonet. 'Take care, Fastermann', I said; but he leapt at the Frenchman, grabbed him by the throat and pressed him against the wall of the hollow way. I tried to get hold of his musket, but did not succeed. I then pulled off the bayonet and ran two stabs into the Frenchman's body. Fastermann picked up the musket, and we both of us were now armed in a fashion.

We now listened closely for any noise, even pressed our ears to the ground, but everything was quiet; we therefore kept going along the hollow way. At its end we happened upon a large barn, with its door slightly open. I carefully crept up to it, heard some cursing in French and returned at once to my comrade. What were we to do now? It was near dawn already, there was heavy fog all around us, and we did not know in which direction to turn.

We decided to hide in a small barn nearby, and where, we hoped, nobody would look for us. We had hardly been in there for a few minutes when we heard a rustling and flapping noise above us and loud shrieks. We sank down for sheer fright; my knees were shaking. But at that very moment we laughed at each other because a rooster had saluted the new morning, and we happened to be in a chicken coop.

We did not like it here, and so we hurried on. Hardly had we been out on an open field when a farmer ran past us. Fastermann ordered him to stop; but the farmer would not listen. Fastermann threatened to shoot him; the man then stood still. He told us that he was about to call some Prussians who were standing a quarter hour away on a ridge, because the French were plundering his village and intended to set it on fire.

We hurried along with the farmer and soon happened upon a Prussian picket of two uhlans. They challenged us and we told them where we came from and who we were. Meanwhile, an officer approached with his squadron and let the farmer give him directions to his village, and dashed off; the farmer hurried after him.

We were then taken by one of the uhlans to a neighbouring village that was filled up with Prussians. On the highway that led through the village they were searching in the mud for valuables because at this place Napoleon's coach had been plundered during the night. We were shown that coach in the gateway of the nearest house; its doors were open, in the interior that was lined with velvet stood a bedstead, and a kitchen was located in the rear.[204] We were led to a house where we were provided with bread and meat, and a cellar was shown us where we could help ourselves to some wine. We went down there with a bucket but found the floor covered with a foot of water so that we had to draw the wine while still standing on the stairs.

Now that we finally had some peace and quiet, we became aware how tired to death we were. The wound in my head also caused me severe pain. A surgeon was called who washed the dried blood from my head and neck and covered the wound with a dressing pad.

After a few hours we were taken on a wagon for some distance to an inn where our troops were expected to pass by. We then lay down at a ditch by the roadside and waited. A few Dutch came by but were unable to give us any information. An officer eventually showed us the direction we would have to follow to find our people.

We took off again and soon were overjoyed to see our men; but what condition were they in? In all, they might have numbered one hundred men. I went to Major Baring and saluted him. He enquired about our fate and asked how many of us had gained their freedom.

I marched with the battalion for half an hour until it set up camp. It was then that Adjutant Riefkugel[205] brought me an order to go back to Brussels. I refused and claimed that nothing was wrong with me, and expressed my wish not to be taken to a military hospital. It must have been three times that I addressed the major in the same way, but all in vain. A wagon had already been brought on, but I did not want to get up on it until the adjutant gave me a direct order, and I had to obey. 'You come back to us when you are cured', were the parting words that sent me off on the road to Brussels. Until now I had remained in good spirits and had repressed my pains, but now I felt lonely and sad, the day's heat was insufferable, I could not sleep and wished for my death.

Suddenly somebody shouted: 'Halt!' A Belgian major, Twent[206] by name, who had served with our battalion in Spain and now rode at the head of his battalion, came to me and asked: 'Are you not Lindau?' I then had to tell him what had happened to me so far; he then had me poured some wine from his canteen, gave me a piece of white bread and a five franc coin out of his pouch, shook my hand and told me not to forget him. I could never remember without deep emotion his friendly gesture that gave me so much comfort in my lonely and painful situation.

On arrival at Brussels, I was quartered in a private house because the hospitals were full up. My hosts treated me very well, but particularly at first, I suffered much pain and felt bored all the time. Only during the last eight days I had the pleasure to live in the same house as my Captain Graeme.

After about four weeks, the doctor allowed me to join my battalion and I marched off to Paris with a detachment of three hundred men. Only then did I meet my brother again who was assigned to my company. He would not believe his eyes when he first saw me. 'Where do you come from, Friedrich?' were his words; 'I thought you were dead. I had searched for you on the battlefield, and found and buried you.' 'Oh no,' I said 'Who knows whom you have buried!' A few days later I also met my other brother, the gunner, who had also believed me dead.

Due to my wound I was unable to perform regular duties and was therefore assigned to the storehouse. I was in charge of sending for bread, corn, wood, and straw and thus led a more agreeable life than my comrades in the camp. I enjoyed doing these tasks, except that the wound in my head caused me some trouble. My sight was not all that it should have been, and all objects seemed larger than they actually were, and once in a while I did not really know what I was doing.

Being in that condition, I applied for my discharge. Major Baring rejected my application because discharging me would have been to my disadvantage. But I had firmly made up my mind and would not listen to well reasoned and well intentioned advice. The major refused to agree to my request several times. But when I would not give up on my demand, I eventually received my discharge paper and marched off to my home country with the battery in which my youngest brother was serving.

5th Line Battalion, King's German Legion

No. 26 From *Belle-Alliance*

Pflugk-Harttung's letter no. 36 Report of the 5th Line Battalion of the [King's] German Legion on its participation in the Battle of La Belle Alliance.

(On) 16 (June) at daybreak, we took off for Nivelles, where we arrived at noon and halted for half an hour with the brigade. Between Nivelles and Mons a position was then taken up in front of a gorge. We remained there undisturbed, and after dusk marched again through Nivelles. We arrived at the battlefield of Quatre Bras at the time of the last cannon shots, joined the division and bivouacked here for the night.

PS The Duke of Brunswick Oels was killed today at Quatre Bras. The Prussians were driven from their positions at Charleroi etc.

17 June
Marched off at noon. Our battalion and the 8th Line Battalion together made lateral movements beyond the Brussels highway. Now and then we were fired at by a pursuing enemy battery, but without effect. The weather was terrible. At seven o'clock in the evening we moved with the division into the Waterloo position near the La Haye Sainte farm. An enemy battery moved up against us. The battery attached to our division also came on and soon silenced the enemy battery. The rains continued all night. At Lord Wellington's order, the grenadier company of our battalion was detached to keep the Brussels highway under control.

18 June
Two hours before daybreak [came the order to] stand to arms; since the rain still came down in sheets, both armies kept quiet until noon, and we cooked our meals. Some reconnoitring was going on by both sides and Napoleon could be discerned on his grey horse. At noon the battle began, the strength of the battalion was as follows (excluding the grenadier company detached the day before, and the light company sent during the fighting in a hurry to La Haye Sainte in support of the 2nd Light Battalion): 1 lieutenant colonel, 2 captains, 12 officers, 14 sergeants, 227 bayonets. The enemy launched many cavalry attacks against the division's position, causing our battalions to form squares. Only the 5th Battalion had to remain flexible due to the terrain on which it was posted, deploy in line, or form square, because it was exposed to both kinds of troop bodies [infantry and cavalry]. The battalion repulsed three attacks of the enemy cavalry; in one of these our square was not yet fully formed, and the enemy had moved up to 8 paces from us. Before us was also enemy infantry, which was supported by artillery. Colonel von Ompteda, the commander of our brigade (and also of our battalion), remained with us, realising the seriousness of our situation. At half past five o'clock we had formed square, the Prince of Orange in person gave the order to deploy [to form line] and to drive the enemy infantry out of La Haye Sainte. Our colonel alerted the prince to the fact that enemy cavalry was hidden behind some bushes and that therefore, we ought to be provided with cavalry support. The prince then rode off; but a short time later the prince's ADC, Lord Somerset,[207] came at full gallop with the same order. We then deployed, leapt over a ditch before us with a cheerful 'Hurrah!'; the enemy infantry gave way, but as we were still driving that infantry before us, our little troop was attacked in flank and rear in no time at all

by an enemy cuirassier regiment. The carnage was terrible, until we were rescued by our cavalry. At first, only Lieutenant Colonel von Linsingen,[208] 6 officers, and 18 men retreated unscathed; our strength increased after one hour, however, when the lightly wounded rejoined us, and by then the battle had been decided in our favour. Absent from our attack were 65 grenadiers and the light company who had been detached.

The battalion's losses were as follows: killed, 3 officers, 1 sergeant, 40 men; wounded, 8 officers, 10 sergeants, 1 drummer, 77 men;[209] missing,1 officer, 1 sergeant, 11 men.[210] Total: 12 officers, 12 sergeants, 1 drummer, 128 men. Officers killed: Colonel von Ompteda, Captain von Wurmb,[211] and Adjutant Schuck.[212] Wounded: Captain Sander,[213] Lieutenant Berger,[214] Lieutenant Bothmer,[215] Lieutenant Klingsohr,[216] Lieutenants Witte[217] and Meyer,[218] Ensigns Walter[219] and Winkler.[220] Prisoner: Lieutenant Wheatley.[221] The enemy took flight in all directions.

19 June
Near Nivelles

8th Line Battalion, King's German Legion

No. 27 From *Belle-Alliance*
Pflugk-Harttung's letter no. 38 Report of the 8th Line Battalion of the [King's] German Legion on its participation in the Battle of La Belle Alliance.

15 June
The battalion marched from Mignault[222] to Escaussines [d'Enghien].

16 June
Also from Escaussines to Nivelles, where it set up camp. At five o'clock in the afternoon, it was ordered to advance and arrived at eleven o'clock in the evening at its bivouac before Arquennes.[223]

17 June
At two o'clock in the morning the battalion was put in readiness for an attack. The enemy attacked at daybreak, and the battalion received the order to retreat. Starting at three o'clock in the afternoon, the battalion was retired in the most perfect order to the Waterloo heights, where it arrived at eight o'clock in the evening and took up its new position. Throughout the night, the rain came down in sheets. Since the battalion had no protective cover, the muskets had become totally wet and unusable, and all the barrels had to be cleared.

18 June

At daybreak in the morning, the battalion was ready for an attack; towards eight o'clock, the enemy attacked the right flank, and at ten o'clock, the battalion stood under heavy fire. The battalion had formed square, but a short time later was ordered to deploy and charge the enemy infantry, which it did in perfect order. The enemy infantry retired and his cuirassiers drove in on the battalion in a violent charge. Unfortunately, the battalion lost its Royal Colours because the bearer, Ensign Moreau,[224] was badly wounded, and so was Sergeant Stuart,[225] who picked them up afterwards, both left lying on the battlefield. Lieutenant-Colonel Schroder[226] was fatally wounded in this charge, and command of the battalion was taken over by Major Petersdorff.[227] The battalion had been severely cut down and completely dispersed by the cuirassiers from its assigned position. However, it soon reassembled and formed square at the same location, although it turned out to be very small due to the many losses in killed and wounded.

All out efforts were made by the cuirassiers and the violent cannon and howitzer fire to break up our centre, at which the 8th Battalion was also posted. But these designs came to naught as the 8th Battalion steadfastly held on to its position throughout the battle, At six o'clock in the evening there was a general advance by our side, which caused the enemy to retreat, and in which as, part of the line, the 8th Battalion kept pursuing the enemy as far as Genappe.

The following Officers, NCOs, and soldiers were among the losses on this day of battle: Captains Werterhagen[228] and Voigt[229] and Lieutenant Marenholz,[230] the Sergeants Adam[231] and Waldmann,[232] Drummer Hentze,[233] and 28 rank and file killed;[234] Adjutant Brinkmann,[235] Captain Rougemont,[236] Lieutenant Sattler[237] and Ensign Moreau, as well as 4 sergeants and 57[238] rank and file wounded; 2 sergeants,[239] 2 drummers and 13 rank and file missing.

19 June

The battalion advanced to Arquennes, where it set up camp.

1st Hanoverian Brigade of Major General Kielmansegge

No. 28 From *Belle-Alliance*

Pflugk-Harttung's letter no. 6 Report on the participation of the 1st Hanoverian Infantry Brigade (Kielmansegge) in the action at Quatre Bras.

Letter no. 21 Report of the 1st Hanoverian Infantry Brigade on its participation in the Battle of La Belle Alliance.

My fellow countrymen's strong interest in the performance of Hanoverians in the last war, during the eventful days from the 16–18 June 1815, makes me expect that not a single fragment of accounts by eyewitnesses will be received with mere equanimity. Perhaps, this induces more [participants] to offer similar contributions whereby a comprehensive whole, truthfully told, should come into being, and be of no little significance in regard to the history of the events of the last war.

In those days, this writer was associated with the following Hanoverian battalions, about whom he can offer reliable information:

1 the Feldjägers,
2 Bremen Field Battalion,
3 Luneburg Field Battalion,
4 Verden Field Battalion,
5 Duke of York Field Battalion and
6 Grubenhagen Field Battalion.

They formed the 1st Hanoverian Brigade, which was assigned to the 3rd Division of the 1st Corps.

On 15 June, these were cantoned in villages on both sides of the highway between Mons and Soignies in a way that the brigade could be assembled within four hours. At three o'clock on the afternoon of 15 June, an order arrived that the division was to rally immediately before Soignies.[240] Upon assembling in front of Soignies, advance posts were placed at once towards Mons and Charleroi; the battalions were quartered in churches and large buildings. The troops' late arrival during the night kept them from receiving provisions; on breaking up camp afterwards, most of the battalions were without foodstuffs which could not be brought up even later. At two o'clock at night [early hours of 16 June] the division was ordered to move off. It arrived at Nivelles at ten o'clock in the morning after a very fatiguing march by way of Braine le Comte and Bornival. The 2nd Brigade of the King's German Legion was detached towards Charleroi;[241] the 5th English Brigade was to rest near Nivelles, both of these parts of the 3rd Division, and the 1st Hanoverian Brigade was to rest on the road to Quatre Bras.

Hardly had the designated location been reached, when the order was received to break camp immediately and to advance on the highway to Quatre Bras from where we had been hearing heavy cannon fire for some time and from where crowds of wounded and stragglers, Belgians in particular, had been coming. As we approached Quatre Bras, the enemy had taken a wood to the right. The brigade was therefore ordered to deploy on both sides of the highway and to send skirmishers against the wood. Upon our advancing in line some distance, the enemy abandoned the wood. The brigade reformed in column and proceeded past the crossroads of Quatre Bras on the Namur highway. We met the Duke of Wellington at Quatre Bras from where he directed the troop movements for the remainder of the day. Shortly before our arrival, the Duke of Brunswick had fallen. After passing Quatre Bras, the brigade was exposed to a heavy cannonade and lost a number of men. Upon the head of the column reaching the village of Pireaumont to the right of the highway, [the column] wheeled, and the men were ordered to lie down to lessen their exposure to the enemy artillery fire. The Luneburg Field Battalion was now at the fore, upon marching off by the left, and was ordered to throw back the enemy who was advancing from the village of Pireaumont. It did this with great determination, took the village, and would have seized two enemy cannon which had been run up on our flank, if the signal to halt had not been given by a Brunswick hornist on our left flank. Repeated by our buglers, it also caused the two companies to halt which were almost in the rear of the cannon, and the enemy thus gained enough time to retire. The enemy tried several times to retake the village of Pireaumont, although without success. Not giving up on his objective, the enemy now advanced with a stronger column. The Luneburg Battalion was therefore reinforced by the Grubenhagen Battalion; two companies of the Duke of York Battalion were posted in the village of Pireaumont, and two companies of the same battalion behind the village in reserve. All attacks were thus repulsed and the enemy was pursued into a nearby wood. In order to support a major attack, the enemy had a mass of skirmishers advance to the right of the village towards the highway. In response, a Jäger company and several sections of the Bremen Battalion were sent against them. Their attack was so vigorous that [their opponents were] thrown back several thousand paces; they even abandoned a favourable position behind ditches and hedges, where the Jägers now took hold and killed many of the enemy who were forced to retire over a plain. In the evening, the Verden Battalion relieved the Luneburg and Grubenhagen Battalions at their position and, together with the Jägers and parts of the Bremen and Duke of York Battalions, set up a line of advance posts. Losses of the battalions on that day were:

1 Feldjäger: 2 killed and 14 wounded;
2 Bremen Field Battalion: Captain Bazoldo severely wounded, 2 sergeants and 14 men wounded; 3 men missing;
3 Luneburg Field Battalion: missing (probably killed in a field of tall corn) Captain Korfus, 7 men; killed: 1 NCO, 1 hornist; wounded:

Lieutenants Volger and von Weyhe severely; Lieutenant von Plato and Ensign Sachs lightly, 1 NCO and 51 privates;

4 Verden Field Battalion: 10 men killed or wounded;

5 Duke of York Field Battalion: killed 1 hornist, 5 men; wounded: Lieutenant von Marenholz, Ensign Rabius, 1 corporal, 23 men; missing 6 men;

6 Grubenhagen Field Battalion: killed 4 men; severely wounded: Lieutenant Westphal, Ensign Ernst, 3 NCOs, 24 privates, lightly wounded 2 officers and a number of soldiers.

At two o'clock in the morning of the 17th, the enemy attacked our line of advance posts and continued these attacks uninterruptedly in varying strengths until ten o'clock in the morning, without breaking through at any one point.[242] On the 16th and 17th, the previously deployed reserves had supported those positions which had been attacked by a superior force. On both days, our Jägers and riflemen displayed their superb shooting skills and their intrepidity in their quick charges, even when faced by an enemy superior in number, while their officers led the men in an exemplary, and most praiseworthy manner.

The enemy's fire eased off after ten o'clock in the morning, and the division was ordered to rally its battalions, without being noticed by the enemy. Only at this time had the Duke of Wellington learned of Field Marshal Blücher's retreat and decided to retire to the Mont St Jean position. Towards eleven o'clock, the division marched off by way of Sart Dames Aveline. The rearguard pulled in the advance posts one hour after the division's departure, and joined it, without a determined enemy pursuit. A terrible rain shower rendered the country roads almost impassable, along which the division was marching. The enemy's cavalry made a forceful charge at the army's rearguard on the Brussels highway past Genappe. After moving into the Mont St Jean position, a cannonade commenced which lasted until darkness set in. The division's men spent the night hungry and without shelter from the unending rains.

The losses of the 1st Light Brigade on the 17th were:

1 Bremen Field Battalion: killed: 1 corporal, 5 men; wounded: Captain von Lepel, Ensign Bruel, 2 sergeants, 1 corporal, 2 hornists, 45 men;

2 Verden Field Battalion: killed or wounded: 20 men;

3 Duke of York Field Battalion: killed: 1 man; wounded: Major von Bülow, 10 men.

On the 16th, the entire baggage had been sent from Soignies to the rear on the Brussels highway; on the 18th, on its overly hasty retreat from Brussels, the major part had been lost so that many officers had nothing left except whatever they had on their bodies; the tents had also been lost. During the continuous bivouacking throughout the campaign, the division thus had to suffer the direst deprivations.

On 18 June around 9 a.m. it stopped raining, and the occasional ray of sunshine seemed to want to warm our limbs. Everybody was already busy putting their wet weapons back into working condition. The endurance and the good will of the men despite all privations cannot be praised enough. They were joking about the hardships of the past days and nights, and there were no complaints about the hunger and thirst they had suffered. To them, the eleven o'clock order to break camp came as a pleasant relief. The movements of the enemy army had been observed from early in the morning. The brigade advanced in columns at ¼ distance to the crest of the plateau which was about 500 paces forward of the site of the bivouac, and then formed in line; the enemy also deployed his columns. Our artillery immediately started a cannonade, which led to a vigorous response from the enemy.

In front of the English Guards Division, which was at the right of the 3rd Division, was the Hougoumont country house. Keeping it in our hands was important for holding our position. To make up for the Guards Division's lack of light infantry, the 1st Feldjäger Company as well as 100 men, each, from the Luneburg and Grubenhagen Battalions were detached to that location. The enemy directed his first attack against this post, with many more to follow. It was taken three times by the enemy, but each time our men drove him out again. Our Jägers and riflemen killed a good many of his men since these attacks were always launched in close columns.

The La Haye Sainte farm, located in front of, and close to, the 2nd Brigade of the [King's] German Legion, was occupied by its 2nd Light Battalion. When an enemy column advanced towards that post, the 1st Light Battalion [of the Legion] and the Luneburg Field Battalion were ordered to reinforce the position, which controlled the highway. The enemy had already penetrated the garden before the arrival of the Luneburg Battalion. During our unit's attempt to regain possession of the garden, several enemy battalions by-passed the walls and moved to its rear. Our men failed in their efforts to enter the farm buildings. Coming from behind the infantry column, enemy cavalry now cut down most of the battalion, dispersed it, and made several prisoners. Because of its heavy losses and the counter attack of the 5th and 8th Battalions of the 2nd KGL Brigade and their cross fire, the enemy column was kept from pressing ahead any further. In pursuing his intention of a breakthrough, the enemy used the open terrain at our centre, where the 1st [Hanoverian] Brigade was posted, and now advanced with masses of cuirassiers against this part [of the line]. The 2nd Jäger Company, which had been skirmishing in front of the brigade, retired, and the battalions forming the square on the right and the Herzog von York and Grubenhagen that on the left. These movements were hardly completed when a large force of cuirassiers attacked the two squares on their front and on the left flank. The enemy cavalry was received with the utmost calm, and, in accordance with orders, fire was not opened until the riders had approached to within 30 to 40 paces, who then took to flight in the greatest hurry while leaving behind many dead and wounded. A good number of cuirassiers whose horses had been killed were taken prisoner, among them a colonel, a staff officer and other officers. Our own cavalry had been too far to the rear to take advantage of the enemy's confusion in his hurried retreat; it was only after the cuirassiers had reformed between us and the enemy infantry that our cavalry did go over to the attack.

During the cuirassiers' attacks, the gunners of the batteries posted on our flanks had to take refuge in the squares, but hurried back to service their guns upon the retreat of the cavalry. In the case of an overly swift attack of the cavalry, the artillerymen saved themselves by lying under their guns and letting the riders rush by, only to service their pieces again immediately afterwards.

After the battalions of the 1st Brigade had again been deployed and had made some lateral movements by battalions in support of the neighbouring brigades, the enemy renewed his attack with masses of cuirassiers, and this time en echelon. After this charge was also repulsed, the enemy cavalry reformed outside musket range and attempted to break through the squares in a renewed attack on three flanks. Having become more cautious after the failed assaults, the cavalry still attempted isolated charges, which were conducted with considerable circumspection. Our soldiers, on the other hand, had learned to trust their own resilience from their defeat of the earlier attacks, and repelled these last ones with the greatest steadiness. Their high spirits from having turned back all of the enemy's onslaughts became still greater upon hearing their generals and senior officers praise their battalions for their intrepid and brave conduct. The commander of the 1st Corps, the Prince of Orange, even went so far, in an outburst of his satisfaction, to say before their front:

'I thank you and these brave battalions; you have decided the battle!'

The enemy cavalry reformed again after some time and sent a mass of skirmishers ahead to lure us into firing our weapons; they cost us some losses in our squares. The enemy then advanced two light artillery pieces to several 100 paces before the front of the left square, under the cover of infantry and cuirassiers. We had no means to defend ourselves against the murderous fire of case shot because our artillery had been out of ammunition for some time and was therefore sent to the rear.[243] An attack against the enemy formation with two weak battalions was all the less possible as a very strong infantry column was advancing against the square on the right. Our two battalions on the right, reinforced by some Nassau battalions, were ordered to advance in squares. They forced the enemy cavalry to yield, but were then exposed to the severe case shot and musketry fire of the approaching column, and this led to the wounding of the commanding general of the 1st Corps [Prince of Orange][244] and of the remaining staff officers of the two battalions.

The retreat of the Nassau squares[245] made it impossible to retain the area just gained and necessitated taking up a position further to the rear. A renewed cavalry attack during this movement was repelled, even though the heavy case shot and musketry fire had almost completely overthrown one of the flanks of the square and had changed it into a triangle. While not yet out of the range of the enemy fire, the battalions were halted and, to the extent that circumstances allowed their reforming, were once again led against the enemy in the desire to quickly regain the lost terrain. The enemy right then made his last and boldest charge; the fire from a strong column forced the battalions to retreat again, which was less orderly than the previous one due to the severe losses in officers and men. The remaining officers were all the less able to restore order as there was a large number of troops of all arms retreating towards that point and thereby causing their efforts to fail.

By eight o'clock in the evening, the enemy made such a powerful attack against the battalions of the right wing that the remaining officer in charge of the square was forced to order its retreat since his battalions and those of the right wing had run out of ammunition. At that time, the general in command of the 3rd Division, as also the lieutenant colonel commanding the square, the brigade major and many officers and men, had been killed or wounded. These battalions and others of the 3rd Division were reassembled and reformed close behind the line, whereupon they returned to their former position that no longer was contended by the enemy. The division was ordered not to participate in the pursuit, and spent the night on the battlefield.

At eleven o'clock on the morning of the 19th, the army again broke camp. The 3rd Division now formed the vanguard of the rapidly advancing infantry and was first to occupy Montmartre and the Paris gates.

The losses on 18 June of the 1st Hanoverian Brigade were:

Feldjäger Corps: killed 15 Jäger, wounded Captain von Rheden,

Lieutenants Grote and Schulze, 3 corporals, 32 Jäger;

Bremen Field Battalion: killed Lieutenant Colonel von Langrehr, 1 sergeant, 1 rifleman, 9 privates; wounded Major Muller, Lieutenants von Quistorp senior, von Quistorp junior, Wehner, 2 sergeants, 2 corporals, 1 bugler, 4 riflemen, 54 privates; missing, presumed dead: 1 bugler, 25 privates;

Verden Field Battalion: killed 3 sergeants, 53 privates; wounded: Major von Schckopp, Captains von Bandemer and Jacobi, Lieutenants Seelig, von Brandes senior, von Brandes junior, Suffenplan, Ensign and Adjutant Gerhardt, 6 sergeants and 86 privates; missing 14 privates;

Duke of York Field Battalion: killed: 2 corporals, 12 privates; wounded: Captain Pavel, Lieutenant Molt and Ensign Müller (died from their wounds), 2 sergeants, 4 corporals, 4 buglers, 35 privates; lightly wounded: Major von Bülow, 2 sergeants, 3 corporals, 17 privates;

Grubenhagen Field Battalion: killed: Lieutenant Colonel von Wurmb, 12 privates; wounded 54 privates.

Luneburg Field Battalion: killed: Captain von Bobart, Ensign von Plato and 18 privates; wounded: Lieutenant Colonel von Klencke, 3 sergeants, 1 bugler, 84 privates; missing: Major von Dachenhausen, 1 bugler and 80 privates, of whom many are presumed dead.

During 16, 17, and 18 June the brigade lost in killed, wounded and missing 38 officers and 939 NCOs and privates.[246] It moved into the field on 16 June with 94 officers and 2,200 rank and file, and in the three days was thus reduced to almost half of its former strength. Most of the mounted officers had lost their horses; two of the brigade commander's had been killed, and nine in one square alone. The number of men who died of their wounds is unfortunately very large.

Bremen Field Battalion

No. 29 From *Belle-Alliance*

Pflugk-Harttung's letter no. 12 Report of the Hanoverian Field Battalion Bremen on its participation in the action at Quatre Bras.

Letter no. 41 Report of the Hanoverian Field Battalion Bremen on its participation in the Battle of La Belle Alliance by Captain C. von Scriba.

Stade, 4 December 1824

Description of the participation of the Bremen Light Battalion under the command of Lieutenant Colonel von Langrehr in the brigade of Major General Count von Kielmansegge and in the division of His Excellency

Lieutenant General von Alten in the Battle of Quatre Bras on 16 and 17 June 1815.

15 June

On 15 June 1815, the Bremen Light Battalion was quartered in the village of Neufvilles[247] near the town of Soignies. On this day in the afternoon at four o'clock the alarm was sounded, and at half past five o'clock the battalion was on its way to Soignies in spite of its widely spread cantonments. It arrived there at seven o'clock after several delays caused by other troops and their baggage and was quartered in the church of the town, together with the 33rd English Infantry Regiment and part of what then was the Verden Field Battalion. Sleeping there was impossible because of the terrible dust and the unavoidably loud noise; moreover, meals could not be prepared in a suitable manner due to the tight space and lack of time. Everybody was therefore quite relieved when camp was broken up the next morning.

16 June

It was almost dawn when the brigade of Major General Count von Kielmansegge, of which this battalion was a part, set out from Soignies on 16 June. Immediately outside this town, the brigade took its place, in right-marched off column, in the division of Lieutenant General von Alten. The division now marched in fairly closed order on the highway leading to Brussels, followed in the same direction by the heavy train, which was left behind at Braine le Comte. The division, however, took the direction to the right on country roads to Nivelles. The air was very warm, while the marching, very slow in the beginning, now became faster, and soon some men were left behind. But the marching order was never disrupted, and all officers marched by the side of their units. The entire road from Soignies to Nivelles runs over undulating terrain. The division crossed paths with other troops in Nivelles and halted there for a brief stop. The division then moved on to the highway, directly outside Nivelles, which leads from this place to Quatre Bras. About half an hour from Nivelles, there was a halt, and camp was set up directly by the side of the highway. Most of the stragglers arrived with the rearguard. Foodstuffs were provided, and cooking was started but could not be finished. It was already three o'clock when the English Major General Sir Colin Halkett, who had ridden ahead on the highway, brought the order to move off quickly. Some soldiers took their half cooked meat with them, others threw it away and made do with bread and brandy.

Immediately after breaking up we encountered cartloads of wounded, primarily Nassauers and Belgians. The division was in left-marched off column. Shortly before Quatre Bras the formation was changed from column to line to the right of the highway, and muskets were loaded. But this took only a few minutes. A few stragglers from the Brunswick Hussars made a great noise about the enemy having occupied the wood in front and to the right of Quatre Bras; some musketry nearby lent their claim some credibility. The [3rd] Division then marched on through Quatre Bras. The firing from guns and muskets was quite heavy just past that locality. The time might have been about five o'clock. We continued our march on the Namur highway for only another half hour. The battalions in front [Light Battalions Luneburg and Grubenhagen] took part in the fire fight; our battalion and the two Feldjäger companies halted after less than half an hour and lay down in the ditches on the side of the highway as ordered by the commander of the division, who remained on horseback near us on the highway most of the time.

Near here, the highway runs nearly parallel with the enemy's position, and descends somewhat on the downward slope of several hills towards Dames Avelines. The terrain falls off gradually towards the enemy, but after 1,000 paces it rises again towards the highway from Quatre Bras to Charleroi. It is crossed by many ditches and hedges and does not lend itself to fighting in close formations. The two aforementioned highways form an acute angle at Quatre Bras.

At about six o'clock the enemy skirmishers moved to within 60 paces of our position, and several men were wounded by their fire, both in our battalion as well as among the artillerymen of the two guns that had drawn up to our right. The two Feldjäger companies advanced in skirmish order, followed soon afterwards by the No. 1 and No. 8 divisions [platoons] of our battalion, as ordered by our commander. They quickly, and in good order, drove off the enemy, whose retiring eventually ended in outright flight. All of the battalion's officers were overcome with joy over the brave conduct of the soldiers, and were justifiably in good hope about the impending major events. The remainder of the battalion soon advanced in support of the two divisions. It was almost eight o'clock when our battalion was assembled some 1,000 paces away from our earlier position, and it immediately set up camp. There were dead and wounded near our place, mostly French and Scottish highlanders. The night was cool and dry. No. 3 company was sent 180 paces forward on picket duty. Setting up fires was not allowed. Towards eleven o'clock in the evening, Lieutenant Muller of the Hanoverian artillery joined us with two guns; upon receiving orders he left us before the hour was over.

The enemy bivouacked not far away from us. There was much bustle and noise at his numerous watch fires; we could distinctly hear the challenge calls of his pickets and patrols, and their chopping wood, etc.

With our own patrols we remained in continuous contact with the Feldjäger to the right and the Duke of York Battalion to our left. Our campsite was on a moderately high elevation. Before its front ran, in a somewhat oblique direction, a shallow and not very wide water filled ditch, bordered by a hedge, towards a swamp near the village of Sart Dames Avelines. Traversing the middle of the battalion was a little used country road which passed over a wooden bridge in poor condition and ran straight towards the enemy. The terrain bearing away from our position ascended gradually such that the just mentioned water filled ditch formed a little ravine. The village of Sart Dames Avelines was situated half an hour away to our left rear, and at almost the same distance was Quatre Bras to our right rear. More than a quarter of an hour to the left was a forest [Bois Delhutte] which extended almost all the way to the village of Frasnes on the Charleroi highway. In, and in front of that village, about three quarters of an hour away from us, was the enemy's main force. Their wounded told me that they were 25,000 men strong and were commanded by Marshal Ney. Our men were able to have four hours of undisturbed sleep, notwithstanding a few musket shots somewhere in the distance.

Strength of the battalion on the morning of 16 June 1815: 1 lieutenant colonel, 1 major, 4 captains, 8 lieutenants, 1 adjutant, 6 ensigns, 17 NCOs, 8 buglers, 405 rank and file.[248]

Deducting the losses: wounded: 1 captain, 12 rank and file; missing: 4 rank and file.

Remaining strength of the battalion in the evening of 16 June 1815: 1 lieutenant colonel, 1 major, 3 captains, 8 lieutenants, 1 adjutant, 6 ensigns, 17 NCOs, 8 buglers, 389 rank and file.

The battalion's losses on this day were: 1 captain (von Bazoldo) severely wounded, 12 men wounded and 4 men missing.

17 June

At daybreak the enemy rushed out of the wood [Bois Delhutte] and vigorously attacked the Light Battalion Grubenhagen, which was posted near there, but he was repulsed after half an hour of heavy musketry. I assumed that this isolated attack was to be accompanied at the same time by a general assault on our line, and we were, indeed, attacked less than a quarter of an hour after the initial attack by a much superior force. Our company on picket duty was recalled to the battalion. The time may have been almost four o'clock. We had the advantage of a favourable position, which we were able to defend tenaciously and with the best success. The enemy retreated after three quarters of an hour of heavy skirmish fire, apparently also because of a threat to his flank from a detachment of the

Duke of York Battalion led by, I believe, Lieutenant von Wrede.[249] This attack was followed by more of the same at short intervals, often by superior numbers, and at other times by a weaker force. I assumed therefore that it was the enemy's desire to entice us to leave our position and pursue him, which might have turned into a disadvantage for us. Our commander was therefore content with occasionally ordering small detachments to follow the enemy for 400 to 500 paces. But we lost many men in these useless attacks. Our ammunition had to be replenished several times; it was sent to us in small barrels. At about half past ten o'clock, the greater number of muskets had become overheated and the barrels choked by grime. No. 1 and No. 2 companies were therefore ordered back to the highway near Quatre Bras under Major Muller's command, and to clean their muskets and put them in a serviceable condition. The enemy refrained from any action against the two remaining companies. Around half past eleven o'clock, the former two companies were ordered to join the brigade, and marched off with it on a country road. Until Genappe, that road runs almost parallel to the highway from Quatre Bras to Brussels.

Some movement was observed on the enemy's side, and also that his columns at Frasnes and on this side of the village had received reinforcements. The [1st Hanoverian] Brigade marched past Genappe and at half past two o'clock joined the [3rd] Division some 1,000 paces beyond this town on a slight eminence. The two companies that had been left behind now also joined the brigade. Our troops camped for one and a half hours under a scorching sun. The division resumed its march at four o'clock. Upon breaking camp there was an extremely heavy downpour, which almost enveloped the enemy in darkness as he was following us. The country roads under our feet soon were full of water, in some deeper places it was more than knee deep. At five o'clock, the division entered the Brussels highway before the farm of Caillou, and here we saw our entire army in full retreat. The troops marched on this broad highway in two columns side by side. The retreat proceeded quite fast but nowhere did I observe the least bit of disorder. From time to time the enemy's energetic pursuit was driven back by the English cavalry and some guns of the horse artillery; the latter unlimbered for that purpose next to the highway at every 1,000 paces on their retreat. Most obvious on this occasion was the splendid bearing of the English cavalry which filled us with admiration and confidence, notwithstanding several adverse situations. After having passed the La Haye Sainte farm by some 250 paces at around half past six o'clock, we made a left turn from the highway and marched up a slight elevation to a plateau, on which the division took its place in the army's line. Several men had been left behind on this retreat, exhausted from slogging through the mud of the country roads, and became prisoners; they rejoined us from their captivity before our reaching Paris. The enemy ended his pursuit and took up a position opposite us at a distance of some 1,800 paces on a row of hills on both sides of the highway, with the centre near Maison du Roi. He loosed off 50 to 60 cannon shots, which left our battalion unharmed, and both armies then set up camp. The battalion had not received any foodstuffs during the entire day. Lieutenant Buttner, 2 NCOs and 40 privates were detached on picket duty.

Strength of the battalion on the morning of 17 June 1815: 1 lieutenant colonel, 1 major, 3 captains, 8 lieutenants, 1 adjutant, 6 ensigns, 17 NCOs, 8 buglers, 389 rank and file.

Losses: wounded, 1 captain, 2 ensigns, 1 NCO, 36 rank and file; killed, 4 rank and file; missing: 18 rank and file.

Remaining strength of the battalion on the evening of 17 June 1815: 1 lieutenant colonel, 1 major, 2 captains, 8 lieutenants, 1 adjutant, 4 ensigns, 16 NCOs, 8 buglers, 331 rank and file.

Note: The missing are believed to have been wounded or killed and to have remained undetected in the tall corn fields. Among them were a number of men who were well known for their reliability and were believed incapable of cowardly desertion.

C. von Scriba Captain, 6th [Hanoverian] Infantry Regiment

No. 30 From the same

Stade, 4 December 1824

Description of the participation of the Bremen Light or Field Battalion under the command of Lieutenant Colonel von Langrehr in the brigade of Major General Count von Kielmansegge and in the division of His Excellency Lieutenant General von Alten in the Battle of Waterloo on 18 June 1815.

The night of 17–18 June was extremely uncomfortable. Heavy rains lasted throughout the night with only short interruptions and brought markedly low temperatures, which felt like late October. The softened clayey soil had turned into mud, and nowhere was there a dry spot. There was no wood for lighting a fire, and only a few would benefit if here and there somebody found a piece of wood or a bundle of straw. Most of the men remained standing up during the terrible night, a circumstance that certainly would worsen the state of the wounded next day. Although spirits were low under these conditions, I can nevertheless attest to the fact that our fine men good naturedly put up with the inevitable and, at most, loudly expressed their displeasure with the terrible weather.

It was only by eight o'clock on the morning of 18 June that the sun's rays did their charitable work and enlivened the faces that had been marked by the chill, by hunger, wetness and exhaustion. A moderate breeze kept going until eleven o'clock and dried the ground for the day's heavy work. There was no thought of obtaining provisions, although one or the other were lucky to get something for their money.

The battalion stood on a plateau formed by a series of hills, and about 900 paces to the right of the Mont St Jean farm, and slightly forward towards the enemy. At the same distance to the left forward from the battalion was the farm of La Haye Sainte. The plateau, about 350 paces wide, descended towards the enemy into a small valley. It was similarly sloping towards the rear, although less so as it neared beside the [Mont] St Jean village, from where the terrain ascended again towards Waterloo. The Hougoumont chateau or farm was situated at a good quarter of an hour's distance; it was occupied by our army and prepared for defence as long as time would permit. The area was quite open over a wide expanse and was very well suited for a set piece battle. This is the terrain which was held by the battalion during the battle.

Immediately after nine o'clock, the battalion received orders to have their weapons cleaned and put in serviceable condition. Shortly after ten o'clock, various movements could be observed on the enemy's side. Some troop bodies crossed each other, single horsemen galloped back and forth, and infantry and cavalry could be almost clearly discerned. At eleven o'clock, our army also stood to arms. The battalion was formed by divisions in left in front closed column, about 200 paces to the left rear of our campsite, and next to the Verden Battalion, in its turn in right in front column. Lieutenant Colonel von Langrehr assumed the command over both battalions without, however, yielding that over his own battalion. Around half past eleven o'clock, the artillery, which was emplaced about 150 paces before us, began to fire at the enemy who advanced towards the Hougoumont chateau or farm. There was no response from the enemy for about ten minutes. We often lost sight of the enemy for several minutes because of the powder smoke. According to prisoners, this strong column had been commanded by Jerome Napoleon himself. As confirmed by several reports, the Emperor had given him this command with the words: 'This is the way to Cassel.'[250] At a quarter to twelve o'clock, there began before us a heavy, almost uninterrupted skirmish fire. At half past twelve o'clock, the Duke of Wellington and his suite passed by the battalion. Immediately afterwards, the battalion advanced about 100 paces and deployed; at this position the men lay down while keeping their weapons in their arms. The Duke of Wellington returned a short time later and slowly rode past our front. The Prussian General von Muffling[251] followed slowly a few paces behind the suite and shouted a few encouraging words at the battalions. Both the outward appearance of this highly respected troop commander, and the words, as they came from a well known allied general, made a visibly deep impression on our men. His Royal Highness, The Crown Prince of the Netherlands, was also often in our area.

To the right of us were Nassau troops[252] (800 men in my estimate). Throughout the battle, they stood in closed column. They never formed square. To our left, the Duke of York and Grubenhagen Field Battalions were posted together; they had gone through almost the same movements as we had. About one o'clock, we formed square together with the Verden Battalion. The enemy cavalry, cuirassiers, came on at a moderate trot, were received by fire by files at 40 to 50 paces from the flank facing them, and at once turned around without any further attempt at breaking through our flanks. They were sent off with a loud 'Hurrah!'. Everybody was gladdened by the calm, laudable conduct of our men. When shortly thereafter, His Royal Highness, the Crown Prince of the Netherlands, rode up to the square, shook hands with our lieutenant colonel and addressed a few flattering remarks at the two battalions, our commander had tears in his eyes.

All later descriptions of the battle have amply shown that the enemy's main attacks were directed at the centre, a manoeuvre that Napoleon was well known for. Because our position was very close to it, we had to continuously fight off most forceful attacks. Our square had severe losses from the shot directed at, and flying over, the artillery in front of us. Major von Schkopp (of the Verden Battalion) therefore induced (around two o'clock) Lieutenant Colonel von Langrehr to move us slightly to the right, which was done immediately. This movement no doubt saved us many men because shortly afterwards two powder wagons exploded, which had been standing 30 to 40 paces in front of us. Our battalion had no losses due to this, but the Verden Battalion lost a number of men. The Hougoumont farm and its outbuildings now were afire, and the musketry fire was very heavy both at this and at La Haye Sainte farm.

Soon thereafter we were again deployed but not for very long as the enemy cavalry advanced once more. We formed square quickly and in good order. The attacking force was quite large; I counted six very wide troops, which followed each other at about a quarter distance. They were cuirassiers as before. I estimated their strength at 700 sabres. All officers in the square made the greatest efforts to keep the men from prematurely firing single shots; the commander threatened to shoot with his pistol any violator. It was now a quarter past two. The cavalry

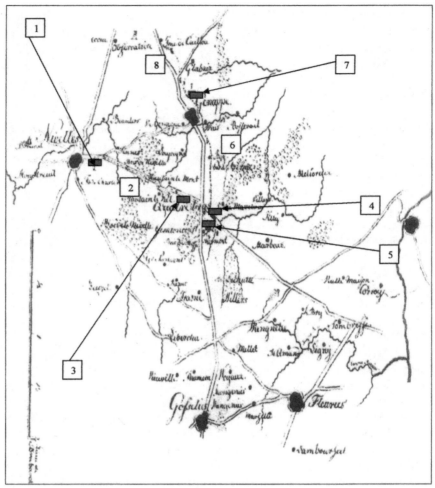

Captain von Scriba's map with its key, attached to letter no. 30

Plan of the Positions of the Bremen Field Battalion in the Battle of Quatre Bras.
Explanation.
1 Campsite of the battalion on 16 June at 1 p.m. on the Quatre Bras highway, one half hour outside Nivelles.
2 March to Quatre Bras between 3:00 and 4:45 p.m.
3 The battalion formed line and loaded muskets at this location.
4 Position on the Namur highway from 5:00 to 6:00 pm.
5 Site of the battalion's bivouac during the night from 16 June to 17 June.
6 March of the battalion on 17 June from 12:00 to 2:30 p.m.
7 Campsite of the battalion from 2:30 to 4:00 p.m. on an eminence near Genappe.
Assembly point of the division of His Excellency, Lieutenant General von Alten.
8 March from this campsite to the Waterloo battlefield between 4:00 and 6:30 p.m.

came on at a trot and halted at 70 to 80 paces away as if to catch their breath. The temptation to shoot was great, but the entire square stood motionless with cocked weapons. I saw the square to our left doing the same. The French cavalrymen were brave but too slow; instead of covering the short distance to us at the charge, they eventually trotted to the left corner of the square, wheeled left around it, passed the next side and finally the right flank. From all these sides they received a controlled fire and that at very close range. At most, it was at 6 paces distance from the flank which I commanded that the cavalry passed. It was led by a brigade general. I mention this trivial incident only because I and several of my comrades observed that he lay flat on his horse when the right flank was ordered to take aim. But we noticed also that he got away from the danger.

The cavalry suffered some losses from this attack, but not as heavy as could be expected from the close range. I believed that our men were aiming too high, which is why our officers often reminded our men of this.[253] There were, however, many riderless horses running around, and dead and wounded were lying around the square. We soon regarded the cavalry attacks as a time of rest for us, because afterwards the devastating artillery fire began once more with increasing violence. Our cavalry, standing about 300 paces in our rear, pursued the enemy cavalry, leading to a short but furious engagement. The crews of the guns in front of us sheltered themselves during the cavalry attack by crawling under the cannon. When the [enemy] artillery fire began again, we saw to our great consternation our neighbours on our right, the Nassauers, begin to yield in disorder. However, by virtue of their brave officers' efforts, who gave their men an outstanding example, the men were brought to a halt and were returned to their former position. This misfortune recurred, later, one or two times under similar circumstances. Their heavy losses were clear to see for, as mentioned earlier, they stood in a very close column. Around half past two o'clock, our brave commander lost his horse to a cannon ball. He immediately mounted Major Muller's horse. A few minutes later, he had a riderless horse caught and gave the major his own horse back. Less than a quarter of an hour later, the highly popular lieutenant colonel had his right leg shattered by a cannon ball. He stayed on his horse. With a few touching words, he took leave of us, and passed the command of the square to Major von Schkopp.

At three o'clock, we deployed for the third time, but stayed in line for less than half an hour. Just before forming square for the third time (half past three o'clock), Major Muller was thrown from his horse by a cannon ball and wounded, whereupon command of the battalion went to the undersigned [von Scriba] from then on until the 19th July in the camp outside Paris. Before the two battles, I had been the fifth officer in seniority in the battalion. The following third cavalry attack (cuirassiers again) was as vigorous and forceful as the second one. Like the first two, it was repulsed with fortitude and great success. Nothing could take away from our firm belief that it would be impossible for the enemy to break through our ranks. Everybody was in good spirits which seemed to rise even more yet. At this time we had, as earlier on, the great pleasure of often seeing near us our highly respected divisional commander, His Excellency Lieutenant General von Alten; his presence contributed to the general good spirits. From now on, however, the enemy cavalry stayed close to us, and we had to remain in square. At half past four o'clock, Major von Schkopp led the square forward towards the enemy, on to the slope of the ridge. The Crown Prince of the Netherlands followed this movement in person. I believe that our forward move was part of a general advance of the army,[254] but I cannot be sure as the powder smoke, at times hardly seeming to move, greatly limited visibility. Our advance and effective fire drove off the nearby cavalry. But we then came under heavy fire of case shot. This, and the retiring of the Nassau troops which caused a large gap in our line, forced our commander to fall back to our former position, a move performed in good order. A short time later, at about five o'clock, Major von Schkopp was wounded and left to go to the rear. Command of the square then went to Captain von Bothmer, of the Verden Battalion, and Captain von Bandemer became commander of that battalion.

We lost many men from the artillery fire, particularly from howitzer shells, and we strove all the time to fill the gaps. I must remark, by the way, that for transporting each wounded man, one, sometimes two, left the ranks. This circumstance reduced our strength considerably. At first, the bearers ended at the nearest houses of St Jean, but, later on, always farther to the rear to a point that the majority of the bearers did not return until after the battle had ended.[255] Also at that time, several wounded officers were carried to the rear. We now noticed with grave concern that the artillery in front of us had suffered severely from the cannonade. Although often replaced, it was eventually overwhelmed and had to leave the line. A Belgian horse artillery battery was almost completely demolished within 25 minutes, and retired with only three of its cannon. In spite of these ominous prospects, every battalion seemed to match its neighbouring one in courage and endurance. At six o'clock occurred the fourth cavalry attack, which, like the earlier ones, was bravely repulsed. We were kept idle until a quarter to seven o'clock, when there was the fifth and last attack as always only by cuirassiers. It was considerably less forceful than the four earlier ones and gave proof of the enemy's flagging spirits.

At this time, we heard a growing amount of artillery and small arms fire on the left flank of the army which indicated the arrival of Blücher's army. Our square, under artillery fire again, was losing its original shape; at first it became an irregular triangle, then only a mass closed on all sides without a distinct shape. Not far from us, I saw a strong column of enemy infantry moving at the *pas de charge* and with beating drums towards the English brigade of Major General Sir Colin Halkett. General Halkett advanced against them and very calmly met them with levelled bayonets and brought them into such disorder that they made off singly in full flight. During this time period (half past seven o'clock), as a decision was nearing, a strong square of French Guards with several guns also advanced towards us, and immediately started firing at a heavy rate. Our small troop could not withstand this strong assault for very long. At first, our men, full of fury, returned the fire but, unfortunately, were running short of ammunition. Ensign Kleinhanns was sent off to procure some; he returned much later to the battalion after having had no success. Individual volunteers were now sent against the enemy and moved up to his square with outstanding courage, but all efforts were in vain. Several of these brave volunteers were rewarded with the Guelphic Order. The gallant battalions [Bremen and Verden] yielded, but slowly and calmly. The officers' efforts and encouraging words brought the men to halt some 300 paces, at most, behind the original position, and still before the cavalry columns in the rear. We just were in the process of reforming and had succeeded to some extent when His Royal Highness, the Crown Prince of the Netherlands came up to us, praised the battalions' conduct and promised to remember us, but at the same time insisted on a quick advance. He would not even allow the completion of our reforming because, as he said, the enemy was already in disorder and had been beaten. Our brave troops, unformed although compact, advanced again, with the prince at its head, shouting 'Long live the Prince of Orange!' At our former position we were received with case shot from not more than 200 paces away. The men bravely stood fast as before, but all resistance ceased due to lack of ammunition. For a time, the men helped themselves to that of the dead that were lying about. The remnants of both battalions retreated slowly. In response to some officers' remonstrations they pointed out the lack of ammunition, even urgently asking them for fresh ammunition, and that they would willingly fight to the last. Both the officers and the men of the two battalions continued to be inspired by the best of will. Most were physically exhausted, but this did not diminish their morale. Although the memory of this inevitable retreat blemishes somewhat my and my stalwart comrades in arms' many pleasant reminiscences that we owed to the extraordinary courage of our brave soldiers, this day will remain a day of glory in the annals of the Bremen and Verden Battalions. Our highly revered brigadier, under whose command we had variously been in the campaign of 1813 and 1814, approached us on our retreat and gave the order to assemble at the village of [Mont] St Jean, where the remnants of the Duke of York and Grubenhagen Battalions and a company of Feldjäger were to unite with us. The time was eight o'clock. Only with great efforts could the men be kept together in the turmoil that prevailed on the highway. Reforming the troops was most energetically carried out, and after one hour, at nine o'clock, the division, now commanded by Major General Count von Kielmansegge, advanced again to the battlefield. The command of the brigade was passed on to Major von Stockhausen who at that time was the only remaining staff officer of the entire brigade, if I am not mistaken. The men struggled back to the battlefield, some were half carried. On our arrival at the battlefield we saw in the distance only the last of the fleeing enemy. A large column of prisoners, primarily French Guards, escorted by our cavalry, passed by us already at the Mont St Jean farm. After a brief roll call had been held, the battalion encamped some 400 to 500 paces to the right of La Haye Sainte farm, among countless dead and wounded. The time must have been about ten o'clock, it was already dark when a column of Prussians arrived next to our bivouac, and I learned that this was the brigade of General von Pirch, whose name was loudly called up shortly thereafter. The Prussian column remained for only half an hour and then took off in pursuit of the enemy. On the next morning, the arms were put in order, and the dead Hanoverian officers were gathered and interred. Some of our men even succeeded in obtaining something edible. Foodstuffs were not yet delivered; the first distribution of provisions did not happen until noon on 21 June at the bivouac near Bavay. The only exception was an ample quantity of biscuits, which we received on the morning of the 20th, thanks to the good offices of our new divisional commander, and the night quarters of 20 June in Binche. We left the battlefield as late as four o'clock in the afternoon and then marched to Nivelles, where we bivouacked for about a quarter hour before that town.

Strength of the battalion on the morning of 18 June 1815: 1 lieutenant colonel, 1 major, 2 captains, 8 lieutenants, 1 adjutant, 4 ensigns, 16 NCOs, 8 buglers, 331 rank and file.

Losses: killed, 1 lieutenant colonel, 1 ensign, 35 rank and file; wounded, 1 major, 2 lieutenants, 1 adjutant, 1 ensign, 4 NCOs, 2 buglers, 53 rank and file; missing: 3 rank and file.

Remaining strength of the battalion on the evening of 18 June 1815: 2 captains, 6 lieutenants, 2 ensigns, 12 NCOs, 6 buglers, 240 rank and file. Dead, Lieutenant Colonel von Langrehr[256] (died during the battle) and Ensign Oldendorff; wounded: Major Muller, Lieutenant von Quistorp I, Lieutenant von Quistorp II, Lieutenant and Adjutant Wehner, and Ensign Hartmann.[257]

C. v. Scriba Captain, 6th Infantry Regiment

5th Division of Lieutenant General Sir Thomas Picton
5th Hanoverian Brigade of Colonel Vincke

No. 31 From *Belle-Alliance*

Pflugk-Harttung's letter no. 25 Report of the 5th Hanoverian Infantry Brigade on its participation in the Battle of La Belle Alliance.

To Colonel von Berger, Chief of the General Staff

[Le] Roeulx, 20 June 1815

The report given below I beg your honour to submit to His Excellency, Lieutenant General von Alten. It is about the events of the recent memorable days, as they involved the 5th Hanoverian [Landwehr] Infantry Brigade.

During the night from the 15th to the 16th, I received orders to rally the Brigade at Halle, and in the morning of the 16th at eleven o'clock, to march to Waterloo. The brigade was widely dispersed, and it became impossible to march off before 12 noon; the roads were indescribably bad. I arrived in the evening at six o'clock, but there was nobody to give me further instructions. Since the sound of an uninterrupted heavy cannonade indicated some action in our front, I broke camp as soon as my men had had some rest, and arrived towards eleven o'clock before Genappe. Here, I received an order from His Grace, the Duke of Wellington, to bivouac in front of Genappe and to march off to Quatre Bras at dawn the next morning and there take up position. Only insignificant skirmishing happened there; we were only briefly under fire, but had no losses. In the afternoon, the army moved into the position at Mont St Jean, and I was assigned to the extreme left flank. During the night, an alarm was sounded due to a false rumour that the French had come. The brigade had formed up in a few minutes and was ready for battle. Towards 12 noon on the 18th, the enemy attacked the advance posts on our left flank, part of whom were sharpshooters of the 5th Brigade. It soon turned out that this was only to hide his actual plans, and that the enemy's real assault was directed at our centre. However, a fairly large cavalry force stood opposite us; it was covered by a heavy cannonade towards us and Major Heise's [Rettberg's] battery posted on the side. Except for a cavalry brigade, there were no troops on my left flank; Colonel Best's Brigade stood to my right. As the cavalry force started to move and advance directly towards us, I formed a large square with Colonel Best's Brigade and mine. My sharpshooters were posted at Major Heise's battery, which was emplaced slightly to the right in front. We had a very favourable position: before us was a moderate slope; in the rear of it a hollow way and the space between that and us covered by many obstructions, as that was where we had camped.

Unfortunately for us [preventing us from gaining any glory], the attack directed against these 8 battalions was prevented by that of the British cavalry, that had amassed in the meantime on our left flank, and I was ordered to have my brigade move to the Brussels highway.

In the first position, only a few men were wounded, but we had considerable losses on the march to the new position assigned to me, primarily due to the many contradictory instructions, at first to halt, then to march by files, and then again to march by companies, and eventually again by files. Even so, there was not the slightest sign of disorder, and the conduct of our men left nothing to be desired. At the new position, we were constantly exposed to cannon fire, to musketry, and finally to canister shots, to the extent that we lost quite a number of men. All my attempts to protect us were in vain.

My British neighbours formed double squares as the enemy cavalry was threatening to charge us. I did the same.

The Hildesheim and Peine Battalions were ordered farther to the rear of the highway to take up position and to detain the very numerous fugitives. The Hameln Battalion was placed forward and left of the little house on the highway. The Gifhorn Battalion, the only one still left to me, was posted on the right wing between the 1st Hussar Regiment of the [King's German] Legion and the Brunswick infantry.[258] We were here exposed to violent small arms fire, and Major von Hammerstein, unwilling to lie down, received severe, but fortunately not life-threatening, wounds. Several times, we had to retire and advance, in front with the line, until the final attack was made against the enemy's left wing; only now, our firearms were used, while I joined up again with the Hameln Battalion. After the end of the battle, I arrived at Gros Fromage[259] where I had to bivouac. This was the place where the enemy sent all his wounded during the battle, without having a single surgeon stay with them. To the extent possible, I had them provided with

Plate 1 *The Battle of Waterloo* by Andrieux, depicting the French cavalry charges against the British infantry squares at around 3–4 p.m. La Haye Sainte stands in the background on the right

Plate 2 French cuirassiers charge a square of Nassau infantry at around 3–4 p.m. Although spectacular as a representation, it is certain that the French cavalry attacked at little more than a steady canter, rather than hell-for-leather

Plate 3 The Duke of Brunswick receiving his mortal wound when charging French infantry with the Brunswick cavalry at Quatre Bras

Plate 4 The Prince of Orange views Belgian troops in line in a firefight with massed French infantry at Waterloo. The original description in the Anne S. K. Brown file says it depicts the Battle of Quatre Bras, but the observatory seen in the background on the right confirms that it is depicting Waterloo

Plate 5 Riflemen of the King's German Legion snipe at the French cavalry as a regiment of King's German Legion Hussars charge the French Red Lancers

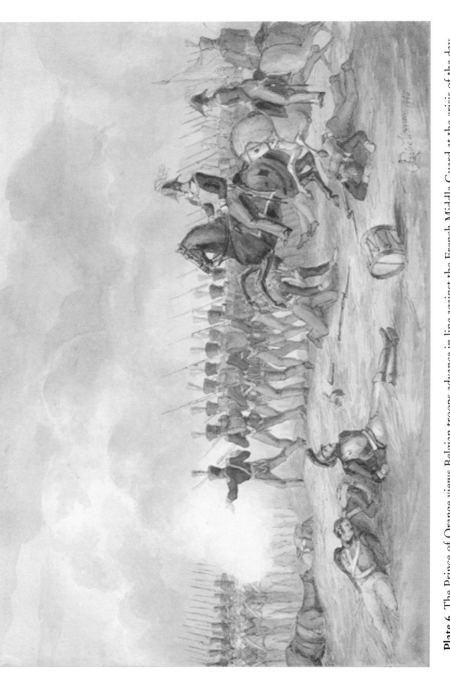

Plate 6 The Prince of Orange views Belgian troops advance in line against the French Middle Guard at the crisis of the day, around 8 p.m.

Plate 7 Prussian Grenadiers in column drive into the French Young Guard defending Plançenoit village

Plate 8 Prussian cavalry mercilessly pursue the fleeing French army throughout the night after the Battle of Waterloo

dressings. Among those found dead at this place was also General van Damme, according to the assertions of the other Frenchmen.[260] For the moment, I was under the command of General Maitland, and then under that of General Byng. In the morning of the 19th, the Hildesheim and Peine Battalions rejoined the brigade. We marched to Monstreux near Nivelles, where we camped together with the other brigades of the 5th Division. Lieutenant General Picton had lost his life on the 18th; in him we lost the divisional commander to whom we just had been subordinated. Major General Kempt has taken the command in his place while we are at rest in camp, whereas General Pack is in command on the march, because the former has also been wounded.

Today, at seven o'clock in the morning, the division moved out of its camp at Monstreux to this place [Roeulx] with its cramped cantonments. I cannot praise enough the excellent conduct of officers and men during the battle. The oldest veterans could not have faced the fire with greater calm than that shown by our young men. As soon as one of theirs had fallen or was wounded, another stepped up in his place, without the least commotion. Only the surgeons, musicians, and drummers ran away at the first cannon shot, but slowly turn up again. I have had the musicians and drummers remove their side arms until they have made up again for their disgraceful misbehaviour.[261]

In response to the order transmitted to me by Captain von Schluter, I have sent the list of killed, wounded, and missing to Major General Count Kielmansegge. Since then I have learned to my greatest regret that Major Leue is among the dead. Many of the missing also turn up again. However, a number of the wounded have already died.

E. Vincke, colonel and brigadier

Hameln Landwehr

No. 32 From *Belle Alliance*
Pflugk-Harttung's letter no. 44 Report of the Hanoverian Landwehr Battalion Hameln on its participation in the Battle of La Belle Alliance by Lieutenant Colonel von Strube.[262]

Hameln, 10 November 1824

Report of Lieutenant-Colonel von Strube, 2nd Infantry Regiment, formerly commander of the Hameln Landwehr Battalion; about the Battle of Waterloo on 18 June 1815 in regard to the involvement of the former Hameln Landwehr Battalion.

The Hameln Landwehr Battalion was part of the 5th [Landwehr] Infantry Brigade under the command of the then colonel, now Major

General, von Vincke, and belonged to the army's 5th Division commanded by the English General Picton. Before the beginning of the battle, the 5th Brigade was ordered to march to the left flank, where, together with the 3rd Hanoverian Brigade[263] under the command of colonel, now Major General Best, it formed a single square in the first line. This square stood on an open elevation and was covered on its left rear by cavalry of the legion, and on its right rear by English cavalry. To the right, Hanoverian artillery was in place, commanded by the then major, now Lieutenant Colonel, Heise [actually Rettberg's].

The battle began at ten o'clock in the morning.[264] Immediately at its onset, French cuirassier regiments moved against the square en echelon, but were charged and driven back by the just mentioned English cavalry. At about half past twelve o'clock, the 5th Brigade was ordered to reinforce the centre as quickly as possible, whereupon the Hameln Battalion was posted in line to the left of the Brussels to Genappe highway. Around half past one o'clock, the battalion had to form square in 4 ranks jointly with the Gifhorn Battalion, directly off the same side of the highway. This part of the terrain was slightly lower and the ground was very soft from the heavy rains on the 17th.

At around three o'clock General Picton, commander of our division, was killed, and command of the division went to General Kempt. The battalion remained in this position until about half past five o'clock.

I then received an order to have the battalion advance and occupy an elevation to the right of the highway. The Duke of Wellington, who had halted there, ordered me to deploy on this elevation. The Nassau Contingent was to the right of the battalion, and to the left were English regiments of the 5th Division, and the 8th Battalion of the [King's German] Legion. After taking up this position, the battalion's men fired off about 30 cartridges each, as the enemy infantry, in particular the Old Guard, launched their last attack. By waving his hat, the Duke of Wellington then gave the sign for the line to advance. The battalion, together with the Gifhorn Battalion, now pursued the enemy until half past ten o'clock in the evening, when it had arrived at the Gros Fromage Farm and thee spent the night in its bivouac. All of that farm's buildings and its yard were crowded with wounded, as the French had been using it as a hospital.

On the 18th, the Hameln Battalion brought about 400 men to the battlefield. Its losses were: 9 killed and 64 wounded, of whom several died soon after from their wounds.

At half past three o'clock in the afternoon of the 19th, the brigade broke camp, marched past Nivelles, and arrived at eight o'clock in the evening at its bivouac near Montroeul.[265]

W. von Strube, Lieutenant Colonel, 2nd Infantry Regiment

Hildesheim Landwehr and Peine Landwehr

No. 33 From *Belle-Alliance*

The Matter of the Hanoverian Peine and Hildesheim Battalions.

Pflugk-Harttung's letter no. 89 Major Count von Westphalen to Colonel von Vincke regarding his conduct during the battle.[266]

[1 July 1815?]

On the 18th an English officer brought me an order to retire. I do not know that officer, nor the commander of the division. Bad weather had kept the latter from visiting his brigade, stationed in and near Halle and soon to be led to face the enemy, and from familiarising it with his person and his adjutants.

The order was given to me in an overly hurried and awkward manner. The officer addressed me in English. When I gave him to understand that I did not speak English, he shouted at me from a distance of about 40 paces, '*Retirez-vous*', and pointed at the highway, whereupon he hurried off. I would have liked to ask him who had issued that order and how far I was to retire with the Hildesheim and Peine Battalions. But the bearer of this order must have been more concerned about another matter than this order, since he rode off in such a hurry.

I had no reservations about following the order since not much earlier your Excellency had advised me to no longer ask for operational instructions as these would be given me by an English adjutant. I sent my adjutant Courgelon to inform your Excellency of the retreat; however, he was unable to find you. While on the highway in the forest, I received a written order, signed by Lieutenant Colonel Scovell, Assistant Quartermaster General. The order stated that my retiring was caused by an error and, upon his own responsibility, I was to stay where I was and hold up any stragglers as they came up.[267] This was done, and they were turned over for the most part to different officers who were gathering their fugitives. In the morning of the 19th, an officer brought me an order from General Count von Kielmansegge to join [his corps], this being the intention of the Duke of Wellington. I had unclaimed biscuit distributed in a hurry [from carts] that stood on the highway, and marched off, at the latest 20 minutes after receipt of the order. When I approached the Duke's headquarters, I was ordered to detach 60 men, with officers, as escorts for the prisoners, and to continue marching on the highway without delay, where I was to join 5th Division, and no other troops; in which way our rejoining your Excellency then took place.

Count von Westphalen, Major

No. 34 From *Belle-Alliance*

Pflugk-Harttung's letter no. 90 Order from Lieutenant Colonel Scovell to Count von Westphalen.

Headquarters, 18 June 1815

To the Officer commanding the Battalion of Germans in retreat

Sir,

I am convinced it is a mistake, the Hanoverian battalion retiring. You will therefore halt your men on each side of the road where this shall reach you, and the only way you can repair the harm you are doing, is to stop all stragglers and form them with you in the wood. I promise to take all the responsibility to this order on myself, and to give you timely notice, should the army retreat.

> Your obedient servant, G. Scovell, Lieutenant Colonel,
> Assistant Quarter Master General

No. 35 From *Belle-Alliance*

Pflugk-Harttung's letter no. 91 Certification by Lieutenant Collmann that on 18 June he did not deliver to Count von Westphalen an order to return to the battlefield.

[Beginning of July 1815]

At the request of Major Count von Westphalen, I, the undersigned, certify that, while he retreated on the highway to Waterloo on 18 June, I did not deliver to him an order to return to the battlefield. I only inquired regarding the reason why he was retreating, and to convey to him the consternation expressed by Generals von Alten and also by General Count von Kielmansegge. It was only in the morning of the 19th that I delivered to Major Count von Westphalen the specific order to advance.[268]

> Collmann, Lieutenant, Orderly Officer

No. 36 From *Belle-Alliance*

Pflugk-Harttung's letter no. 92 Colonel von Vincke to Colonel and Chief of the General Staff von Berger regarding the conduct of Major Count von Westphalen and conflicting orders during the battle.

Camp near Arnouville, 3 July 1815

Your honour will herewith receive the report of Major Count Westphalen about the retiring of the two battalions that he commanded. At the time that this happened, the brigade had formed two squares. I myself was in that of the Hameln and Gifhorn Battalions, but noticed that an English adjutant had given different orders to the other two battalions [Peine and Hildesheim]. I immediately sent off an officer to obtain information about these for me, but, not being mounted, he was unable to return right away. Besides, Count von Westphalen's assertions are correct to the extent that I was able to determine; it is entirely impossible to know all the persons who deliver orders, since some were not even in uniform. On that day, I received several completely contradictory orders, one immediately after another, and I followed always those which appeared to me the most appropriate for the situation. I, moreover, need to testify on behalf of Count von Westphalen that on that day he displayed the greatest calmness and presence of mind while under heavy fire. Other units were also said to have received orders to retire to the second line. That was definitely the case with the artillery of Major Heise. Part of it did in fact retire,[269] and the remainder would have done the same if Major Heise had not considered the sending back of everything all at once as most calamitous. The situation did in fact change within a short time thereafter.

E. Vincke, Colonel and Brigadier

No. 37 From *Belle-Alliance*

Pflugk-Harttung's letter no. 93 Major Ludewig to Lieutenant General von Alten regarding the conduct of Count von Westphalen during the Battle near La Belle Alliance.

5 August 1815
In camp near Clichy

To Your Excellency,
I feel obligated to comment most obediently on the justification attributed to Major Count von Westphalen regarding the retreat of the two Peine and Hildesheim Battalions on 18 June, the day of battle at Waterloo, as well as on my conduct that day, as also in regard to my own opinion.

Major von Rheden was wounded right at the beginning by one of the first balls which struck the Hildesheim Battalion, and the command of the battalion was passed on to me. A short time later, Colonel von Vincke was ordered to move with two battalions to the highway, and Major Count von Westphalen received an order to have the other two Peine and Hildesheim Battalions form square behind the battery of Major Heise [Cleeves], each battalion by itself but not too far apart to be able to support each other as needed. The two battalions were standing here from four till half past six o'clock. Now an order was received for us to form squares to the right of the highway. We did not stay there for very long when Major Count von Westphalen formed his battalion on the highway and ordered me to form the Hildesheim Battalion in front of the Peine Battalion. The Count now told me: 'We are retiring, your battalion will stay in front.' It was then that I made representations to Major Count von Westphalen against our going back. When I realised that he became touchy on this matter, I told him that I would follow his orders, but that he should keep in mind that he would be accountable for anything untoward, and that I would decline any responsibility in this matter.

I am firmly convinced that Count Westphalen had received the order to retire because I observed an English officer ride up to the count shortly before we formed up on the highway. I was too far away to hear what he said. To me, it remained inexplicable why we were sent to the rear, since the time was already close to eight o'clock, there was no longer any danger, and the outcome of the battle was already as good as assured.

In addition, I feel obligated to inform your Excellency of the good conduct of officers, NCOs and soldiers, about their calmness and un-flagging spirits in following orders, both on the day of battle and during the time that I had the honour to command the battalion. May God grant you an early recovery of your health so that we may soon enjoy the pleasure to see you back soon in our midst. I remain respectfully

Your Excellency's most obedient servant, G. von Ludewig, Major

6th Division of Major General Lambert
4th Hanoverian Brigade of Colonel Best

No. 38 From *Belle-Alliance*

Pflugk-Harttung's letter no. 7 Report of the 4th Hanoverian Infantry Brigade on its participation in the action at Quatre Bras.

Letter no. 22 Report of the 4th Hanoverian Infantry Brigade on its participation in the Battle of La Belle Alliance a preliminary report by Colonel C. Best.[270]

Bavay, France, 22 June 1815

To Lieutenant General von Alten, Excellency, etc, at Brussels

I will not fail to most obediently submit to your Excellency a due report about the actions on the 16th, 17th, and 18th of this month, in which the brigade under my command participated. Since I may be allowed to expect that the generals, under whom I served on those days, will in their reports favourably mention the conduct of my brigade, it is my hope that it will please your Excellency to submit this, my report, to His Royal Highness, The Duke of Cambridge.

On the 16th, the brigade was ordered to support a part of the

5th Division (to which I had been attached because the 6th [Division] had not yet arrived). I therefore had the brigade deploy behind the Scottish [Brigade], of which a part had been engaged. Several men were here lost to artillery fire. The Verden Battalion and the sharpshooters of the Osterode and Munden Battalions were ordered to engage the enemy. Major von der Decken was leading his battalion and had it maintain a vigorous fire throughout the evening. He himself as well his officers and men displayed the greatest bravery and sang-froid, and I therefore feel obligated to commend him to your particular consideration. The sharpshooters also did their duty and quite early lost their leader, Lieutenant Jenisch[271] of the Osterode Battalion, who was severely wounded and died the next day. The Verden Battalion, fighting in open order, lost Lieutenant Wegener who was killed;[272] Lieutenant von der Horst, Ensigns Plate[273] and Kotzebue and several men were taken prisoner because they had mistaken French tirailleurs for Brunswickers. I placed the Luneburg [Landwehr] Battalion along the highway with its right adjacent to the cannon of the horse battery of the KGL[274] behind a ditch that earlier had been occupied by a Scottish regiment. The enemy cavalry made a desperate charge, apparently to take the cannon. The Luneburg Battalion remained very calm, not receiving them until they were quite close. The fire was so well directed that very few of the enemy cavalry turned around, and several had fallen only five or six paces in front of the battalion. General Barnes[275] witnessed this and, no doubt, will make a most favourable report about it.

The Osterode and Munden Battalions were not engaged, but nevertheless lost several men from balls and case shot while still remaining calm and in the best order, as should be expected from such young and inexperienced soldiers. On the same day, Captain Brauns, KGL, serving as major,[276] particularly distinguished himself by skirmishing with part of the battalion, but lost his horse which was shot. The 5th Division, to which my brigade was attached, was commanded by General Sir Thomas Picton.

Towards noon on the 17th we received the order to retreat, and this was conducted in fairly good order. Towards evening, the division was ordered to set up bivouac to the left of the highway. It kept raining continuously throughout the afternoon and the night.

On the 18th, at ten o'clock in the morning, we were instructed to move up to the plateau where we took up position. The enemy deployed his order of battle, and it appeared as if the enemy cavalry was preparing to attack. I came to an agreement with Colonel Vincke, whose brigade [5th Hanoverian Militia Brigade] was on my left, to form a solid square, composed of the two brigades, which was then arranged. The attack began at eleven o'clock, and after the English cavalry had charged that of the enemy I returned my brigade to its original position. The Verden Battalion was posted in front to cover the guns under the command of Major Heise [Rettberg]. That battalion and the sharpshooters engaged the enemy in skirmish fire. The Luneburg Battalion was ordered to form square, the Osterode Battalion stood in close column, and the Munden Battalion in line, slightly to the rear in support. After General Sir Thomas Picton had been killed, command of the division was taken over by General Sir James Kempt. I ordered the Luneburg and Osterode Battalions to advance and engage the enemy; Ensign Schanz[277] of the Osterode Battalion was then killed. The report, already despatched, about the losses of the brigade during these three days will provide more specific details.

After the end of the battle and after the brigade had been assigned a space for its bivouac, Major General Sir John [James] Kempt came to the front of the brigade and expressed to me his satisfaction about the conduct of the brigade on this day in highly flattering terms, adding that he would also take the opportunity to make a most favourable report [about the brigade] to the commander in chief, the Duke of Wellington. He mentioned at the same time that our men had been firing their cartridges at too great a distance, and, considering their inexperience, this would have to be attributed to their eagerness to do their duty.

Although, on the whole, I can be satisfied with the conduct of officers and men during the battle, I regret to have to note that several individuals took advantage of the opportunity to stay in the rear, in particular several assistant surgeons and junior surgeons who failed to provide any help. Senior Surgeon Schulze reported to me during the night from the 18th to the 19th that at his dressing station he had no help at all from these surgeons, and asked me to send him some from other units of the brigade. But even this was impossible because only one junior surgeon from the Luneburg Battalion was present. These useless people returned later to their battalions and offered all kinds of excuses. The musicians were supposed to transport the wounded and to help Senior Surgeon Schulze in dressing the wounded, who had been doing his duty with the greatest dedication. Those men were nowhere to be found and returned to the brigade as late as the third or fourth day after the battle.

Captains Siegner and Ostwald of the Verden Battalion, claiming sickness on the 16th, went to the rear and, allegedly, even as far as Antwerp. Captain von Rauschenplat of the Osterode Battalion also went back due to indisposition. Ensign Schwabe of the Osterode Battalion stayed with the baggage on his commander's order even though the brigade had already given that assignment to Lieutenant

Best. Lieutenant Kuhlmann, of the Munden Battalion, who is of a weak disposition, also went back, feeling unwell. Captain Jormin and Lieutenant Schneider of the Luneburg Battalion also went to the rear due to sickness, although the latter did return. The Quartermaster Sergeant of the Luneburg Battalion was the only one who stayed with his unit; all others had retreated with the baggage. Several NCOs and privates took advantage of an opportunity to retire with the baggage and went to Brussels and as far as Antwerp, and now return day by day. The disgraceful manner in which particularly the assistant and junior surgeons had failed to do their duty and left the senior surgeon unaided would justify appropriate punishment.[278]

C. Best, colonel and brigadier

Luneburg Field Battalion

No. 39 Reminiscences of Captain Carl Jacobi, Luneburg Field Battalion, 1st Hanoverian Brigade

From Erinnerungen aus dem Kriegsjahre 1815 und aus den occupationsjahren 1816, 1817, 1818. Ein Gedenkblatt für seine lieben Angehörigen von Carl Jacobi *[Reminiscences of the War of 1815 and of the Occupation of 1816, 1817, 1818. A Memorial for his beloved family from Carl Jacobi]*, Hanover, 1865.

Carl Jacobi's account of his experiences during the Waterloo campaign 1815.[279]

The brigade of Lieutenant Colonel von Klencke, to whom I was attached as Oberadjutant (at that time the designation of a brigade adjutant) since the autumn of 1814, was one of the first units to move to the French border. It had been stationed at Antwerp for seven months, and arrived at Mons on 7 April. Major General von Dornberg was in charge here, under whose command we had often been in 1813, and who remembered me very well. The brigade was heavily engaged in difficult observation and picket duties. In addition, it had to assist in the restoration of the Mons fortifications, and had to train men in servicing the fortress artillery which was commanded by an English artillery captain. I was myself very much involved in official assignments and I enjoyed doing this demanding work since I often had the pleasure of receiving Lieutenant Colonel von Klencke's expression of his satisfaction.

In the meantime the Duke of Wellington had arrived in the Netherlands and taken up the command of the English and allied troops. On 19 April, the duke inspected our brigade near Mons; everybody was filled with joy and confidence upon beholding the highly respected leader, and his appearance inspired and confirmed our trust in his generalship which foretold victory.

Regrettably, we Hanoverians soon lost much of our willingness to serve and of our feelings of pride in our independent status, although hopefully not our courage. By the terms of a General Order from the duke of 26 April, the Hanoverian brigades were assigned to various English divisions. Until now, the so called Subsidiary Corps (22 infantry battalions, 2, and later 3 hussar regiments, and 2 artillery batteries) had existed as a separate corps under the command of Lieutenant General von Alten. This status was eliminated with the stroke of a pen; we no longer would appear on the battlefield as Hanoverians; we were now individual components of English divisions. Lieutenant General von Alten was still a kind of commander in chief of the Hanoverian troops; but this was only in relation to internal matters (organisation, recruiting, advancement, equipment, higher judiciary, etc.). With regard to the order of battle, discipline, and provisions, the troops were completely subordinated to their English divisional commanders.

There were substantial military considerations that justified this step; the Hanoverian troop complement had only recently been reorganised; only the field battalions formed in 1813 had proven themselves in battle; and the numerous Landwehr (15 battalions) had not had any experience. This would, of course, explain the Duke's point of view of the desirability to provide these new units with an example and a firm support by their close attachment to the old and battle tested English regiments. General von Alten assured me later on several occasions that he could not have assumed the responsibility to object to this decision once it was made. To us at least it was a severe blow to our morale. The English generals were totally unfamiliar with the traditions of the Hanoverians; they were therefore unable to appreciate their good dispositions and to connect to the German soldiers' nature. In their eyes, everything was imperfect, even open to criticism that did not conform to English concerns and institutions. There was no camaraderie among the allied troops, not even among the officers. The ignorance of the other's language, on both sides, the major difference in pay[280] and the resulting great difference in life styles prevented any closer companionship. Our compatriots in the King's German Legion did not even associate with us; the fifteen-year-old ensign with the red sash proudly looked down upon the older Hanoverian officer. In the course of the campaign, these disparities often became unbearably more pronounced, and it redounds to the troops' honour that they did not waver in their dedication and loyalty.

As a result of the General Order of 26 April, the Light Division of Major General Count von Kielmansegge, until then made up of 2 brigades of 3 battalions, each, was transformed into a single brigade. It considered itself fortunate now to become part of the 3rd Division commanded by General von Alten, and thereby to remain under the direct command of this popular and highly respected leader, whereas the existing brigade staffs were disagreeably affected by the order.

Lieutenant Colonel von Klencke ceased to be a brigadier, and as early as 28 April took over the command of the Luneburg Battalion. I was assigned to the battalion's depot,[281] no longer held a position with the field corps, and had to be prepared to be ordered to return to the homeland at a moment's notice. However, one of the battalion's companies was without a commander since Captain von Dachenhausen had just then been promoted to major. But Captain von Rhoden had then been appointed to its command, being the most senior captain at the depot. Lieutenant Colonel von Klencke had full understanding of my urgent desire to participate in the impending war. He suggested that I go to Brussels in person and see Lieutenant General von Alten and submit to him my request to be allowed to at least serve temporarily as commander of Major von Dachenhausen's previous company. The general received me in his customary kind manner, had me explain my situation, and promised to give my request due consideration, but in any case would take care that I be given an assignment with the troops in the field. To my great delight, I was appointed interim commander of the company in question on 19 May.

The battalions of what was von Klencke's Brigade had already been ordered to leave Mons on 30 April and now had moved into the cantonments of what was presently Kielmannsegge's Brigade.[282] On 30 May, our battalion returned to Casteau[283] and environs in the Mons area. This place has left me with the memory of an unforgettable occurrence. The wife of von Klencke, who with their children had stayed at Antwerp, had arrived to visit her husband for a time. I was present on the day she was to leave on her return trip. She was very much concerned in view of the expected start of hostilities; she suddenly turned to me, embraced me heartily, and made me promise never to leave the lieutenant colonel in moments of danger. As it turned out later, I had occasion to keep my promise.

On 12 June we were moved closer to Soignies, and the troops, although cantoned as if in the deepest peace, were each day assembled in larger detachments for their exercises. That was also the case on the morning of 15 June. We were late in returning to our quarters when after a short rest, the officers just having sat down for their meal, the alarm was suddenly sounded to stand to arms. Nobody knew the reason; not a soul thought of war breaking out. The battalion was ordered to march to Soignies immediately; we halted for several hours in front of the town, and the brigade formed up. Late in the evening we were quartered in barns and in large houses of the town. The prevailing, almost war like confusion lent some credence to the rumour that the Prussians had been attacked by the French. Care had neither been taken to provide places for the men to cook their meals nor had any firewood been supplied in time. The English commissary regulations did not allow us to request even the smallest piece of wood from the inhabitants, and it so happened that the greater part of the brigade was only able to start cooking after midnight. This was all the harder on the men since, due to the sudden unexpected march, they had had to forego their midday meal.

The description of the following memorable days is based on notes about my experiences that I wrote down soon after the actual events.

16 June
Suddenly at two o'clock in the morning we were awakened by the signal to break camp quickly. The division formed up on the highway to Braine le Comte; the baggage was separated from the division and went to Brussels. The rumour about the attack upon the Prussians on the day before gained more credibility. After our arrival at Braine le Comte we turned towards Nivelles. Early in the day, the weather became hot and humid; marching was made more cumbersome by the poor country road. It was probably at nine o'clock that we arrived at Nivelles and marched through the town with bands playing. When we halted by chance in front of a bakery I bought some white bread without having an idea how precious it would later be for me.

From Nivelles, the division turned on to the Namur highway, and after half an hour's march it formed up in a field to the side of the roadway. The heat began to become oppressive; the men were allowed to cook as soon as the commissariat would deliver some firewood. After an unsuccessful search for a commissary for several hours, permission was given to obtain wood from nearby villages. During this waiting period everybody enjoyed resting to the fullest extent possible, until a few Prussian stragglers arrived and the first cannon shot could be heard. I am unable to describe the effect of this unexpected sound on all of us, whether officers or men; it aroused feelings of surprise and of impatient resolution. We listened closely to be sure that we had heard correctly, and as now a second and third shot followed, and many more, the spirit of the honourable warriors of yore revived in us. The cannonade seemed to occur at too great a distance to let us assume that we would be part of direct action; but the present certainty that the fighting had commenced filled us with confidence in a favourable outcome.

With few intermissions, the cannonade was sometimes heavier, sometimes weaker; intermixed with it was small arms fire, a sign of the nearness of the fighting. The order to break camp was given at three o'clock; the soup, which was only about to be cooked, had to be thrown out. The division marched left in front, our battalion at the head. After marching for about half an hour, the arms were loaded, and we then continued the march in silence, full of anticipation. In front of the village of Houtain [le Val] we encountered fleeing inhabitants; all houses were deserted and locked. On the far side of the village, the highway led through widely spread fields of corn. After we had continued for some 1,000 paces we observed a body of cavalry in the distance, which hurriedly closed in upon us. The division formed line on both sides of the highway. The artillery readied itself to fire at the cavalry, which careered towards us with loud shouts, when it was suddenly discovered that they were Belgian hussars. With repeated shouts: '*Vive le Roi!*' they had turned their backs on the enemy and now, without stopping, continued their ride on the highway through the lines of the division.[284]

After this incident we marched on in column towards Quatre Bras. When we arrived at the intersection of the highways from Charleroi to Brussels and from Nivelles to Namur, the battlefield all of a sudden opened up before our eyes. The wounded, lying by the wayside, cried for help, and the dead, laid out on the field to the right of the highway, reminded us to fight as honourably as they had done. It was here that the noble Duke of Brunswick, among his brave troops and supported by the Scottish Highlanders and Best's Hanoverian Brigade, had stood up for hours to the enemy assault and, boldly giving his men a shining example, had met a hero's death on the blood soaked battlefield.

We marched in column of platoons along the entire length of the battle-field on the highway, on to the village of Sart [Dames] Avelines.[285] It was occupied by the French, who thus interrupted our shortest line of communication with the Prussians. Enemy tirailleurs on our right flank fired at us, as did the French artillery. We continued our march on the highway past the enemy without stopping and without having fired a shot. Generals von Alten and Count Kielmansegge, together with Lieutenant Colonel von Klencke, rode in front. The enemy cannon aimed in their direction, apparently in order to bring the column to a halt. The balls came whistling, one by one, and, often, a soldier would see the ground he was going to step upon thrown up by a mighty piece of iron.

Leading the foremost (fourth) platoon of my (No. 2) company, Lieutenant Volger was shot in his right arm; I hurried ahead to take his place. At the same time, some of the men of the leading companies attempted to take cover by stepping down into the ditches of the highway; several men of my own company followed their example. Observing how this slowed our march, the lieutenant colonel directed the men back onto the highway. I had held Lieutenant Volger under his arm and asked him to go to the rear, even though he wanted to do his part to restore order regardless of his wound. At that moment he was shot in one of his legs and had to be led back.[286] I then stepped to the middle of the roadway and brought the men quickly back into proper rank and file by shouting these well chosen words: 'Whoever does not want to desert his captain will step up here'.

We arrived at Sart [Dames] Avelines a short time later; the French fell back to the right on the dispersed houses of Pireaumont. Our battalion was sent forward to skirmish. The area was covered with meadows and cornfields which were crossed by dense hedges that had only a few openings. This greatly interfered with the troop cohesion, but our men's courage rose with every step forward. Upon our rapid advance, the French immediately left the first house that might have served them as a parapet, and we took over the remaining farmsteads without delay.

As we were occupying a ridge, we could observe from here how on our left flank Brunswick Jäger and a battalion of the English 95th Regiment attacked a wood before our front that was held by the French. The lower ground between us and the wood located on an elevation was covered with fields of tall corn. We rallied our battalion's men as much as possible who had been widely scattered, and Major von Dachenhausen then led us as the attack was continued. We were severely exposed to the enemy fire from the wood, but we forced it and drove the French back, tree by tree. In the middle of the wood we met the Brunswickers and the English; we closely cooperated with each other in our common aim, and in no time at all were we in possession of the wood. As we left it to pursue the enemy over open terrain, we observed a close column of several battalions upon which the enemy skirmishers were retiring. We were far from our brigade and not in a position for further undertakings; we therefore fell back to the edge of the wood and held on to it.

These moments of rest were most welcome; we had been on our legs since two o'clock in the morning, had kept marching in the oppressive heat of summer, and were under the strains of fighting for more than an hour. Officers and men had had nothing to eat all day except for a bit of bread, and hardly anybody was lucky enough to have something else to eat. On my part, I still had a small hoard of what I had bought at Nivelles, and in my field bottle I had some cognac. I sat down on the roots of an oak tree, next to a completely exhausted Brunswick officer, and shared with him whatever I had. Most happy about the day's work so far accomplished, we refreshed ourselves, and sealed our brotherhood in arms with a hearty handshake.[287] This is how sublime encounters happen in a warrior's life.

We were not allowed much of a rest; the French renewed their attack and were successful at first. In our earlier rapid advance, no care had been taken to have the skirmishers backed up by a formed body of troops in support. While passing through the many hedges and the fields with the corn at a man's height, and from the fighting in the wood, there was a mixing of the troops so that officers would lead detachments composed of men from different companies. In the end, the English, the Brunswickers and the Hanoverians became completely intermingled. At the same time, many men had remained in the area to the rear, partly from exhaustion, partly from their unwillingness to expose themselves. As a result, the foremost line had become very weak. The officers, on their part, were too much in need of rest upon the break in the action to force themselves to rally the men on the wide expanse of the field of action and restore order.

When the French advanced with a superior force we attempted in vain to hold the edge of the wood. One by one did the men fall back when they found themselves deserted by their neighbours. Those more to the rear had lost their senses and started firing. This compounded the confusion, and the entire skirmish line retreated. The French advanced ever more vigorously. The courageous example of our officers and their shouts had no effect; there was no spot to serve as a rallying point where the retreating men could be brought to a halt. All our hold on the wood had been lost. As we came to the cornfield from where our action had commenced, I suggested to a staff officer of the Brunswickers to ride back and try to halt those who had gone farthest on their retreat. This he achieved; as soon as some had formed up in a closed formation, the remainder found this a point where to halt and join up. Eventually, a large part of the skirmishers were rallied and formed up in a sunken road between two hedgerows. At this moment the lieutenant colonel who until then had been on our right wing came to us and, with tears in eyes, told us that just now his horse had been shot dead under him. The animal had with great good luck carried him out of all the battles of former years.

From the wood the French kept threatening the left wing of Wellington's position; probably for this reason an order arrived to renew the attack. This was executed with the support of a detachment from the Grubenhagen Battalion; the advance was slower due to the general exhaustion, and the losses were therefore greater than earlier. The men were encouraged by the presence of the lieutenant colonel, and we penetrated the wood, without regard to the enemy fire which to some extent was directed at us out of the trees. In the meantime the sun had run its course; far fewer shots were fired, and with the onset of darkness we had regained possession of the wood. We were exhausted to the point that nobody uttered a word; not a drop of water could be had that might have stilled our raging thirst; I had let myself drop to the ground from sheer weakness and hoped to fall asleep. But I then received an order to form a picket with the men nearby and to post sentries. My mental resources won out over my physical ones, and with the help of a few energetic comrades I succeed[ed] in rallying some 50 men from ours and the Grubenhagen Battalion and to set up a line of advance posts. We thus faced a not very restful night when to our great delight two companies of the Verden Battalion arrived in order to relieve us.

I led my detachment back to Sart [Dames] Avelines; next to one of the first houses was a well that was crowded by so many thirsty men that hardly anybody had a chance to get some water. Fortunately, a Brunswicker allowed me a few draughts out of his canteen, and that was a most precious refreshment. Our battalion had set up camp on a small meadow at the far end of the village, and here I rejoined it. After a while the companies formed up to receive fresh ammunition, and it was then determined that we had had a loss of 7 killed and 52 wounded. Apart from Lieutenant Volger three more officers had been wounded; Captain Korfes was missing, and nothing became known of his fate; he was probably mortally wounded in the high corn where he was last seen.[288]

Since no foodstuffs had been delivered, the men had availed themselves of meat from the cattle in the village; their superiors elected not to notice; necessity knows no law. Camp fires were lit, and while meals were cooking in the field kettles, the men were exchanging notes about their experiences. Morale was high; General Alten had said that this was a glory filled evening for our battalion, and everybody was cheering when a soldier reported that he had offered his beer filled canteen to the general, who thankfully drank from it. I lay down among my men near a fire; my orderly was with the horses and nowhere to be found; I was given a woollen blanket, and I used a knapsack for my pillow. After I had looked up to the bright starry sky with thanks for my lucky survival despite the many perils, I sent a silent message to all those who were far away and dear to me. I then fell asleep, as gently as one could hope for in the knowledge of having done one's duty on a most trying day and of having partaken in a victorious battle.

17 June

The departing sun had sent her last rays upon those who had honourably fallen and those who had suffered painful wounds; hardly had she again begun to offer to the earth her rose coloured light of dawn when the battle resumed that was to decide the fate of the fatherland. At daybreak the shooting by the advance posts had begun again, and as it became more violent it also ended my sleep. The invigorating god of dreams had us all refreshed. Those battalions that yesterday had not been as heavily engaged as ours now went to battle. My younger brother George, at the time an Ensign in the Duke of York (Osnabrück) Battalion,[289] was also one of the first to greet me while they were marching by. My handshake expressed to him my wish to see him again [later] and in good health, and his [handshake] betokened his pleasure to have found me hale and hearty.

It was easy to see that the action on the 16th would not have had an outcome of decisive consequences since only a part of Wellington's army had been engaged. A rumour was making the rounds that yesterday Napoleon had attacked the Prussians with his main force and that the outcome of that action would determine our own dispositions. Although last night's sleep had filled us with renewed energy, we were out of any foodstuffs. All the bread we had received shortly before marching off on the 15th had been consumed, and provisions had not been delivered by the commissaries. The men thus could not be prevented from appropriating whatever edibles they could find in the village. On my part, I partook of refreshments I had had on my horses that my orderly had returned to me, and I soon forgot all the past discomforts.

It might have been around eleven o'clock in the morning that General Alten's division was ordered to break camp; it was said that the Prussian army was in retreat, and in our case there were also indications of an early retrograde movement. Care had been taken that the lightly wounded were promptly taken to the rear; the severely wounded had to be left behind due to lack of the required wagons. Even some officers were not spared this bitter fate. That the required transportation could not be obtained in this densely settled area was inexplicable and irresponsible. Absence of the commissariat was blamed, which would have to contract for the wagons.

The division marched on rural roads to the area of the town of Genappe that we passed at a quarter of an hour's distance from its right. We marched up in closed columns on a slight elevation, apparently to bivouac for a while. The weather was pleasant, the skies were clear; no enemy was to be seen; and everybody was in good spirits in spite of being on a retreat. I hurried over to Genappe to obtain foodstuffs and wine. Almost all the houses had been locked, the windows firmly shuttered, and the place seemed totally deserted. The right wing of our troops that had fought in yesterday's action retired through the town. I eventually managed to buy some bread, ham, and wine at a high price, after various unsuccessful attempts.

Shortly after my return to the bivouac, camp was broken up all of a sudden and our march was continued. At the same time, dark clouds formed in the sky and discharged such sheets of rain that already on marching off we became soaking wet and were forced to wade through deep mud.

We moved on rural paths parallel to the highway from Genappe to Brussels; marching was slow on the almost bottomless tracks; only with a great effort could one extract one's feet from the mud, and many a shoe remained stuck in it. Added to that were several narrow defiles which increased the congestion. After we had moved for about half an hour we observed the pursuing French on the highway; they were stopped by our cavalry which had taken up position on several ridges in chequerboard fashion, but was forced to slowly fall back. At this moment, all of us were too much concerned with overcoming the obstacles in our march to pay much attention to the peril from the enemy who were rapidly advancing on our flank. The men kept in as good order as the poor condition of the terrain would permit.

We finally moved on to the highway and saw how the several lines of English cavalry posted on its sides retired one by one as soon as the last of our columns had passed. The numerous cavalry, the horse batteries advancing at great speed, and the personal presence of the Duke of Wellington let us surmise that the enemy was pressing ahead at a perilous pace.[290] On the highway we had firm ground under our feet, the rains had ceased, and the men's low spirits were rising, all the more so as the lieutenant colonel rode along the length of the battalion and, calmly and compassionately, asked the men if this marching was not yet becoming too burdensome. Behind us we heard continuous artillery fire and saw our cavalry skirmish with the enemy. Our march was continued without delay in the direction of Brussels until we abruptly turned left off the highway between La Haye Sainte and Mont St Jean, and formed in close column on a ridge, with our front towards the enemy.

We arrived here at about half past seven o'clock; the deployment of many troop formations to our sides and rear indicated that this was the staging area of Wellington's army, and that the retreat was over at least for today. From our position on the ridge we had a view of the entire surrounding region. Most of the English cavalry slowly retired to our rear; only small detachments kept up skirmishing against the advancing enemy who had approached to within 1,000 paces. A French infantry column appeared near a farmstead opposite from us that was located on the highway (La Belle Alliance). We still stood with arms at the ready and awaited the enemy, but the French came to a halt. I observed through the good field glass that I carried with me that the enemy was moving up a battery; we were soon saluted by its balls. The shots were not very effective due to the great distance, but Wellington had three batteries unlimber which soon silenced the enemy fire, as if on this evening to signal to the French: 'Hither you have come but not a single step more!' The cannonade was later resumed more vigorously, but our 9-pounders proved to be superior to the French guns.

Hidden by the clouds, the sun was going down behind the horizon, and as darkness set in, the last shot was fired. Artillery and cavalry moved farther to the rear, the latter maintaining a weak picket line in front of our position. The infantry remained partly in close columns, partly deployed in line in front of these. The rifles were stacked, and the troops were allowed to rest. But what kind of rest was it that we now faced? It brought deprivations of all kinds to the exhausted men. The heavy rain had turned the ground of the fields that served us as camping sites to sludge, into which the grain stalks had been trampled. The rains returned as night set in. There was no thought at all of lighting a camp fire because there was no wood. Foodstuffs had never been delivered since the 15th. Several weeks ago, the troops had received a store of navy biscuits in bags as a provision in case of an emergency. It was to be issued only on orders from above, but was sent back from Soignies with the baggage on the morning of the 16th, and was thus missing when it was needed. Our raging thirst could not be stilled; those sent off to obtain water returned with empty canteens. There were no water streams nearby, and the wells of the surrounding villages had been emptied to the last drop by the troops who had arrived earlier, and by watering the horses.

Lost in dull stolidity, the exhausted men threw themselves down on the watery ground, wrapped in their woollen blankets.[291] The incessant rains streaming down on them had made them insensitive to the dampness of their place of rest. As to myself, I was to experience the most terrible night of my life. When we broke camp near Genappe I had handed over to my orderly not only the dearly obtained foodstuffs but also my coat, and had instructed him to always stay close to the rear of the battalion with the two horses. I was unable to think of my orderly and the horses until there was peace and quiet. I then looked forward to their arrival with such hopeful confidence that I had already cheered several comrades by assuring them that I would share with them my store of provisions and some woollen blankets carried by the horses. The darkening night and the repeated unsuccessful searches for my orderly eventually persuaded me that my hopes had been in vain.[292] They had been the pillars of my endurance, and with their collapse vanished my inner strength.

Here I was dressed only in the short uniform (dolman) and was so thoroughly soaking wet that the falling sheets of rain penetrated directly to my skin. A small fire that some men had kindled with wet straw and a few stray pieces of wood offered so little warmth to the many surrounding it that just standing still stiffened the limbs more than the flame could enliven them. I sought relief by moving about, which, however, I could not do without my feet giving me some pains. At the sudden departure on the 15th, and during the later uninterrupted activities, I had not thought of exchanging the tight fitting boots that I then happened to be wearing for more comfortable ones. By the afternoon of the 17th I had already noticed that on my feet, swollen from my exertions and from dampness, some sore spots had developed; I paid no attention to the pain in the hope of using another pair of boots located in the portmanteau on my horse; but it was not to happen. Tired from walking about I tried to get some rest and a lessening of the pain by standing still, and returned to the fire. Here I met Major von Dachenhausen; upon seeing me entirely without any cover he offered me his orderly's woollen blanket; I accepted it like a gift from heaven. Wrapped in the blanket I hoped to be able to sleep, and flung myself to the wet ground between the soldiers who were lying close together. At this moment, the only one in my whole life in which I had had this feeling, I was reduced to a complete indifference to being alive or not; my limbs collapsed from exhaustion and chill; my soul no longer seemed to dwell in my body. My total exhaustion eventually overcame everything and, notwithstanding my stiffness, I fell asleep.

18 June

That pleasant span of time was much too short during which sleep carried me unconsciously towards the new fateful day. The floods of water from the incessant rains were no longer absorbed by the soil; little pools were forming in the depressions in the ground; when I woke up, I was lying in water. Only with a great effort was I able to rise; sleep had invigorated me somewhat and now I again attempted to warm up by moving about, and I succeeded. Full consciousness and the use of my senses came back, although they did not pass on any pleasant observations to my inner self. From that stationary mass that covered the muddy ground, no sound of rising hopes or manly courage would emanate. Those few who stood around the wretched fire looked like monuments made of rock, numbly staring down, unreceptive to the outside word. Ordinarily even at times of greatest exhaustion and in the most adverse circumstances there would be at least one individual in the crowd who had kept his good humour. But on this miserable night even the most stout hearted were despairing, and no cheerful word was heard from the merriest among the men.

Opposite to us on the enemy side, the number of camp fires increased; it was obvious that masses of troops were gathering there. Since Wellington's army was also closely deployed, it was reasonable to expect that on this blessed and peaceful part of the earth a violent and bloody battle would be fought. A soldier's heart would have been filled with heightened expectations of performing decisive feats if the misfortunes of the moment would not have lowered everybody's spirits.

The darkness of the dreadful night faded gradually but did not yield to a rose coloured Sunday morning; whatever light the grey clouds permitted to pass through revealed to those warriors nothing but their own misery. They rose, one by one, from their wet bedding; but there was no cheerful moving about of well refreshed comrades in arms, instead only the sight of tired pale faces and the sound of stifled groans. The rains had ended, and a few rays of the sun radiated warmth. The exhausted men would have forgotten all their misery if only they could have received some foodstuffs. They hopefully looked forward to the rising day, those brave men who had given ample proof of being worthy of their fatherland, who had endured past exertions and deprivations without grumbling, who willingly and with confidence in their leaders were facing their destiny, they now uttered in vain their modest wish: 'If only we had some bread!'. The officers were in despair over the impossibility of meeting these demands.

With regard to provisions, each brigade depended on the commissary assigned to it, and there may have been instances of individual detachments being relatively well provided by a particularly active agent. Most of the troops, among them the Hanoverians, received nothing. There was no excuse for this failure of the English commissariat; even the Iron Duke and his staff had evidently not paid the required attention to the provisioning of the army. The prosperous city of Brussels was not too far away from the battlefield, where ample stores of navy biscuits and rum had been collected. The decision to deploy the army at Mont St Jean had been made by noon on the 17th, at the latest, and during the evening and the night much could have been brought up. We were, moreover, located in the midst of the densely populated and rich Brabant region; but no contracts had been concluded with the inhabitants, and the available resources could not be used. The soldiers' mettle was to decide the fate of Europe, but nothing was done to raise the morale of the fatigued men. There was hope, little though it was, to end the famine. Early in the morning, General Count Kielmansegge had sent off a mounted officer to bring up the navy biscuits carried in the baggage, if possible. The general had spent the entire night without cover in the midst of his brigade and had thus given an admirable example of enduring hardships. The officer in question happened to be my brother George, the only one of the subalterns with a horse. He had no success, however, because the Brussels highway was completely blocked by disabled carts and wagons.

As we beheld our own army and the enemy one that could be recognised opposite from us, the conviction took hold more and more that a bloody battle was about to be fought. While many millions of Christians peacefully wended their way to the sacred houses of God for their Sunday worship, death and destruction were to be sown on these fields of trampled grains. The first of our officer's duties was to see to it that the cartridges, wetted by the rain, were removed from the loaded rifles and that, above all, the arms were put back into a serviceable condition.

Our battalion's sutler, an enterprising Jew who had stayed with us since 1813, showed up all of a sudden with his wagon full of foodstuffs. The officers of the brigade immediately surrounded him and followed their instinct of self preservation although they regretted not being able to care for their men while taking care of themselves. Charging exorbitant prices, the sutler had nevertheless completely sold out his stores in no time at all.[293]

Towards nine o'clock the skies had cleared up completely; the warming sun shone down on us, and a little dried spot soon enticed me to go to sleep. I lay down next to many comrades, and slumber soon gave us the sweet rest that our exhausted bodies were so much in need of.[294] We may have slept for more than an hour regardless of the turmoil around us when we were suddenly awakened by shouts of 'Get up! Get up!' We stood to arms, and a short time later the French artillery started firing at us. The English batteries responded, and while the iron greetings flew back and forth I took care of a monetary transaction. A short time ago, I had sold a horse to the then Captain von Schlutter, Aide [de camp] to General von Alten, for his brother who served with the [King's German] Legion. Now at the beginning of the battle, Captain von Schlutter came to me and brought the selling price of 30 Napoleon d'ors.[295] The money proved to be most welcome to me and some friends in the coming weeks; the brother died of a severe wound he had received on this day.[296]

Our battalion stood in close column at the left wing of the brigade; we had an excellent view of the area in front of us from the plateau on which we were posted. A marvellous sublime feeling gripped all of us;

we had courageously fought many a battle, but never before had we been part of as great a body of troops as this one; never before had we taken part in a battle which was to decide the fate of countries near and far. As the cannonade became ever more violent, as we beheld the enemy's attack columns descending into the plain, as the foremost French battalions began to deploy, all of this caused the mind to triumph over the frailty of the body; all the misery of the night and morning were forgotten.

We were idle spectators for hours of the fighting that surged before us, particularly of the violent contest around Hougoumont. But when after two o'clock a vigorous attack was launched against the farm of La Haye Sainte which was located immediately in front of us, our lieutenant colonel led us down from our position to confront the enemy. Full of determination and in good order we advanced and threw ourselves upon the enemy who fell back. Part of the battalion, including also my company, was sent into the orchard of La Haye Sainte; the remaining part spread out in the open against the French tirailleurs. In the beginning we successfully defended the orchard; but then the enemy moved up with formed columns against whom the enclosure of sparse hedges offered no protection. We were forced to yield, without any time left to again rally the men. Outside, we fell in with the other scattered parts of the battalion, in the midst of the French cavalry which at this moment carried out its first bold attack against the position. The battalion was completely dispersed. Some of the fleeing men found refuge behind the squares of the brigade, myself included, although French cuirassiers had trotted past myself, 10 to 12 paces away. Nobody among us really knew how he had escaped the horses' hooves or the horsemen's swords. There were moments when the senses of hearing and sight had in fact shut down, and not just figuratively so. Only faintly do I remember that I had told some men fleeing next to me to fire on individual horsemen among the pursuers.

This was the sudden and sad outcome of our action that had been commenced so courageously and auspiciously![297] Would it not have been possible to observe in good time the approach of the enemy cavalry? Or to form with calmness and circumspection, if not a regular square, at least a compact mass? These are idle questions, and the fundamentals are missing for finding an answer. Our losses were considerable,[298] but most depressing was, the evidence that at this moment the Luneburg Battalion had ceased to exist; not even the smallest gathering of its troops could be found anywhere.

I noticed our lieutenant colonel behind the squares of our brigade; his horse had been shot dead and he himself had been wounded by a shot in his right thigh; the bone had fortunately not been injured. He asked me to obtain a horse for him if possible; the Duke of Cumberland Hussar Regiment stood behind us; among its officers were friends of mine and I succeeded in obtaining a spare horse. I brought it to the lieutenant colonel and helped him mount the horse. I thus fulfilled the promise I had made to his wife several weeks ago. The lieutenant colonel rode off to Brussels after exhorting the officers that were present to rally the scattered men of the battalion as best as possible.

But how were we to accomplish this? A number of men who happened to be nearby attached themselves to the officers; they told us that more men had fled to the houses behind the rear of Mont St Jean. We went there, and after some time Captain Rall, Lieutenants Borries, Creydt, Ritter, and Adjutant von Peltz gathered here together with about 50 men. We had the men form rank and file, and I and the senior captain, Rall considered what to do next. In my opinion we had to march back to the brigade. But Captain Rall could not make up his mind; he was completely exhausted and let me be in charge and stayed with us. I divided the small group into five sections, made them wheel into column and had them march off to the position.[299] The road in that direction was covered by incoming projectiles from the French artillery that passed over the plateau in front of us; we were hit by solid shot and howitzer shells and lost several killed and a number of wounded men on our advance. We nevertheless marched on without delay to a spot directly behind our brigade. Adjutant von Pentz had been riding ahead in order to report to General Count von Kielmansegge our coming; he now returned to us and brought the general's order to march to Brussels with the remaining core of the battalion, and to gather as many of the battalion's men as possible.[300]

We now had to pass once more through the area exposed to enemy artillery fire, but without having further losses we came to the forest of Soignes, which is traversed by the Brussels highway. However, it was blocked everywhere by wagons and carts driven into one another that even pedestrians were hardly able to pass through. We were almost always forced to work our way through ditches on the side of the roadway or through thick underbrush, and we were only very slowly getting ahead, but our men held together very well all the time. We arrived near Brussels only at the onset of darkness. Here I met unexpectedly Lieutenant Meyer (later an Oberamtmann[301]) of our battalion who served as brigade auditor at the time. He was riding a horse and had with him his mounted orderly whose horse he now offered me for my use. He invited me to join him on his ride to his quarters in the city. I thought that my presence with the small remainder of the battalion was no longer required. Since my exhaustion had reached a point at which I felt I was almost no longer able to move forward, I accepted, and was most thankful for his invitation. Here I found myself suddenly transferred from the turmoil of the battle and the trampled fields to a quiet, handsomely appointed room. I had to have my boots cut off of my swollen and sore feet. After I had cleaned my self as well as possible and had refreshed myself with meat and drink, I gently fell asleep in a comfortable bed. Such are the ups and downs in a warrior's life; last night hungry and stiff from being cold and wet in muck and mud; this night sated and warmed on a dry and comfortable bed!

When I woke up on the morning of the 19th, Lieutenant Meyer greeted me with the good news that the battle had been won and that in the evening of the18th the French army had completely disintegrated. Our joy, or I should say our jubilation, over this news was all the greater since on the preceding evening the most unfavourable rumours about the adverse situation of the allies had made the rounds in Brussels.

More detailed information about the great decisive victory were, of course, not yet available, but there was no doubt that Wellington's army was on the advance. Lieutenant Meyer had decided to join me in looking for our brigade; I used the morning hours to get some more rest, and I wrote a brief letter home to tell my family that I had survived all the perils of the last three days thanks to God's merciful providence. I procured shoes and gaiters, and in the afternoon we rode over the battlefield which was still covered with the grisly remains of the fighting, and on to Nivelles. On the 20th, I again joined the battalion, which had marched off from Brussels on the morning of the 19th and was now on the road to Binche. About 200 men had gathered again, part of them in a poor condition, without knapsacks and with the most diverse firearms they had picked up on the battlefield. After we had halted in front of Bavay during the night of the 21st, we moved on the 22nd to the Forêt [Domaniale] De Mormal, where we were allowed a day of rest. A number of stragglers also arrived here at the battalion, and so did my orderly with the horses and the personal effects, thus putting me in better circumstances for the bivouacs in the future.

From this camp in the wood I sent a letter to my father; this letter as well as the one of the 19th were among the papers left behind at my father's death, and both of them I will here include since they reflect my state of mind at that time:

Brussels, 19 June 1815

Without delay, dear father, will I write you that George and I have fortunately survived the bloody days of the 16th, 17th, and 18th.

Napoleon has been totally defeated, the victory has cost us much; almost all generals and staff officers of our division have been wounded, killed, or taken prisoner. Of our battalion, only 5 officers, apart from myself, and about 100 men are still fit for service. More to you as soon as we get some rest; we are all terribly exhausted, for three days have we been fighting, and not a single piece of bread. Caroline will, I expect, write to Plau that I am all right, and that Captain von Bobarth is among the fallen. Yours, Carl.

Bivouac between Bavay and Landrecy, 22 June 1815

To expressly put your mind at ease regarding our fate, dearest father, I repeat what I wrote you on the 19th that George and I are healthy and in good shape; if the actions on the 16th and the 17th, and the bloodbath on the 18th had not been as costly for us as they were, those days would have been the most precious of my life. The division of General Alten has suffered terrible losses. On the 18th, it defended the centre against the repeated charges of the cuirassiers with extraordinary bravery, until finally General von Bülow and the Prussians arrived in the evening and assured our victory. The Duke of Wellington and all the English generals are greatly praising the Hanoverians' sangfroid with which they beat off the most vigorous attacks. In my company, one officer has been killed and two were severely wounded. The lieutenant colonel was very close on my side when he was shot in his lower body, which, however, was said not to be very serious. I cannot thank God enough that I have remained in good health. A shell exploded in my section and splashed me all over with dirt. As I held the wounded Lieutenant Volger with my arm, he received another shot at that moment.

Napoleon has lost all of his artillery; each day we follow in the footsteps of his army, and we do not believe that it can rally on this side of Laon. Our division still marches with the rest of the army but can no longer accomplish very much; of my company, which had a strength of 138 men on 16 June, I now have only 41 that are fit for service. George is sitting by my side and asked to give his best wishes to all; I write this in a hurry as I badly need some sleep.

Dearest father, Germany has been liberated once again; the jubilation of the army is beyond words. To mother and sisters, hearty greetings from Carl.

Around this time General Count Kielmansegge had made an urgent request for me to serve as his brigade major after Captain Hanbury[302] had been severely wounded. Under different circumstances I would have gladly accepted this honourable offer and thereby have readily entered an influential field of duties. But our battalion was without its two staff officers; it had only two captains left, Rall and myself, and therefore I could not bring myself to leave the battalion.

The advance towards Paris, beginning on the 24th, occurred in relatively short marches per day; they were cumbersome nevertheless, as they were not conducted very circumspectly, resulting in frequent stops of the immensely long columns; heat and dust made us miserable. Bivouacs were set up for the nights; wood and water often were only to be had from far away; bedding straw was not issued. Provisions were taken care of but consisted only of meat, tough navy biscuits, and rum; the latter had to be provided with the biscuits all the time if possible, according to the English regulations. The officers were usually able to avail themselves of better food stuffs, although at exorbitant prices; our Jewish sutler was untiring.

On 1 July we arrived in the vicinity of Paris and set up bivouac near Aulnay [sous-Bois], where we remained for four days. Those were pleasant sunny days; curious Parisians and dolled up ladies went sightseeing through the camps as if we lived in deepest peace. On Sunday, the 2nd July, we had divine service in the camp. Our army chaplain, Block, talked about the events of two weeks ago and with such gripping solemnity thanked the Almighty for everything he had done for us that all those present were deeply touched by his words. For the fallen and wounded we offered artless prayers to the Lord. I cannot remember a single divine service that had made such a deep impression on me.

During our marches our Lieutenant Borries became sick; our physician suspected a nervous fever and recommended rest and careful nursing. The sick man had a sister in Paris who had been married to a Colonel Chabrier and was now a widow. We procured civilian clothes for our friend, and a Paris cabriolet took him to his sister. On 6 July we moved below Montmartre closer to the city. It was said that Prussian troops had already moved in. Lieutenant Ritter and I were anxious to learn about Borries's condition, who had provided us his address. We had been given leave and rode to the nearest barrier. It was occupied by the National Guard, and we explained our purpose to the commander of the post. He said that no allied troops had yet entered Paris but we could proceed if we wanted to take the chance. Although the matter seemed to be a bit risky, we did not want to appear to be afraid and expressed our desire to take advantage of the permission. On the pretext of showing us the way, two mounted gendarmes escorted us. We thus went right to the middle of the world famous and world shaking capital of France. We were stared at a great deal and rode past many a group who viewed us with their faces full of bitterness, but without going as far as offending us. We found to our regret that our dear comrade had a high fever, and we left him with feelings of grave concern. On our return we happened into streets that were filled with crowds of inhabitants, and learned that Prince Blücher was to make his entrance. We rode to the neighbourhood where he was expected, and were delighted to behold the venerable hero at the head of a hussar regiment. It was the first time that we saw the victorious leader; his appearance made an unforgettable impression on us.

On 7 July, the largest part of Wellington's Army moved into the Bois de Boulogne, and did not march through Paris. After arms had been stacked and the knapsacks laid down under the trees we had no idea that we were to spend almost four months here, until the end of October. It was a tedious period, filled with many unpleasant experiences. The officers had to face many deprivations, but suffered no want. The lofty sentiments from a victory gained, and the many intellectual stimuli and pleasures of a material nature offered by Paris, helped overcome many disagreeable situations. Life was different for the non commissioned officers and soldiers who, after all the sacrifices they had made, suffered privations all the time.

The English troops, with whom we were intermingled, and the King's German Legion, who were on an equal footing with them, were all provided with tents; the Hanoverians had received one tent only for the officers of each company, and several for the battalion staffs. In the beginning, our non-coms and men had no cover besides the trees that existed and they were not to be damaged under any circumstances. Permission was later given for constructing huts with tree branches;[303] but the leaves soon dried up, and the huts offered little protection from the weather. Added to that was the intolerable dust that was often swirled up from the broad sandy carriage ways. Bedding straw was not supplied at first, and later only haphazardly. In the first weeks, no bread was issued, only navy biscuits. The meat was often inedible, and after complaints in that regard, the commissary's answer was that the Hanoverians were given their provisions for free and therefore had no reason to make a fuss.[304] There was no delivery of vegetables, according to British regulations; the English soldiers could buy those with their substantially higher pay, whereas our men were seldom in a position to do that.[305] Water for cooking and drinking water had to be drawn from the Seine below Paris, after all the city's filth had been emptied into the river.

The Hanoverians had nobody at their head who would have been able to stand up for their interests; if General Alten had not been severely wounded, much would probably have been better. Our well justified displeasure became even more acute when in Paris we had to stand guard jointly with the outstandingly well provisioned Prussians. Two times I have been myself on guard duty at the Palais Royal where the Prussians, who served together with us, were brought the best hot food, whereas our men received nothing but dry bread and left over cold meat. When on guard duty in the enemy's capital, we even had to buy our drinking water from water carriers (*In majorem ducis gloriam*[306]). Was it then not natural for our men to ask why such differences existed between the Prussians and ourselves? Was it not understandable that they remembered the costly foodstuffs that their parents and relations had to provide to the French for many years? Was it not understandable that they blamed their English commanders for lack of concern for their well-being? Those commanders were unable to appreciate the Germans' dedication, and lived in another world. To the great credit of our men redounds their willingness to serve, their loyal performance of their duties, and the equanimity with which they endured all the exertions of the many parades and large manoeuvres. The calm acceptance of their depressing circumstances reflected as honourably on them as the feats of arms they had performed.[307]

As officers, all of us having horses, we were able to obtain many delectables in Paris at moderate cost. We had our meal before leaving for the city and then found a repast at low cost in one of the more modest restaurants, after we had become more familiar with the place. Visits to the art collections were free of charge, and if one sat down on the boulevards or in the public gardens a cup of coffee or glass of lemonade would do. Ticket prices for the little theatres were moderate. But if one wished to go to the famous restaurants or the big theatres, one had to dip deep into one's pocket. There was that amazing contrast between this glitter and abundance, and the humble bedding of straw on which one laid down upon returning.

As to my own person, I found in Paris a brother in law[308] who became my guide and mentor; I was therefore oftener in town than the other officers and learned how to live there handsomely and yet at moderate expense. My brother in law was also helpful in several of my purchases and saved me from being overcharged. In this way I bought a beautiful wrap for my fiancée at a bargain that I sent her at Plau; I also purchased several golden rings with a small picture of Wellington that were much sought after at the time, and gave them to dear relatives at home. And then there was the unexpected pleasant surprise of encountering George, the eldest of my cousins of the Thaer family, who was in Paris as an officer with the Prussian uhlans and with whom I renewed the friendship of our youth.

Our much loved comrade Borries had succumbed to the nervous

fever, to our great regret. On 18 July we conducted his corpse from the house of the sister, who mourned him deeply, to the camp with a military honour guard. There he was lowered into the tomb, next to others, who had here also found their last place of rest. As a friend for many years of the deceased, I had asked for the command of the honour guard. We had left Hanover together on 4 April 1813 to take part in the War of Liberation. Who in those hours could have had a foreboding that I would conduct that companion through Paris to the mourning sound of the horns, down the Champs Elysees, to his burial place?

During the last days of July, Major von Dachenhausen returned from captivity and was welcomed by us with great cheers as our commander for the time being. Our battalion was soon transferred to the brigade of Major General Lyon[309] in Lieutenant General Colville's division who wanted to have a light battalion in his division. Although our officers regretted to have to leave Kielmannsegge's Brigade, in which we had seen service for a long time together with the field battalions, we were pleased with this transfer on behalf of our men. This division had a very active officer from the staff of the Quartermaster General who carefully supervised the delivery of foodstuffs which were of excellent quality as a result. The officers were even supplied forage for their horses, whereas earlier we had to have the foraging done off the fields so that our orderlies were often told to go to fields that could hardly supply what was needed.

As it became more likely that we would stay in the camp for a longer period, we officers had a spacious room erected at joint expense that was provided with tables and benches. Walls and roof consisted only of straw, however, which later would not always protect us from the stormy October weather. The structure gave us excellent service nevertheless. Here we did our toilet in the morning, then breakfast together, ate our lunch in comfort, and spent the evenings together in good fellowship. It was an entirely different style of life from what had been ours while separated in confining tents. There was no dearth of part irritating, part amusing episodes. One day we wished to have rice cooked with milk; but when the cook had the dish over the fire it was forming into an incredibly thick mass; instead of milk we had bought starch dissolved in water! We had also bought wine at reasonable prices from a merchant several times who had come to the camp. He visited again one time and asked us to purchase a larger quantity since he would not be able to return in the near future. We tasted a bottle and bought a good supply, but when that wine was served at lunch we discovered that the 'Karnallche'[310] (as the crook was named by Captain Rall) had sold us dyed water; that merchant disappeared never to return.

On 10 August we had the great pleasure of having Lieutenant

Colonel von Klencke come back to the battalion even though his wound had not completely healed; he was welcomed with cheers from all of us. His familiarity with the English language and English manners soon allowed him to become friends with General Colville and his staff, a circumstance that was of particular benefit to the battalion.[311] The lieutenant colonel was ordinarily in command of the brigade when it moved out to parades or manoeuvres because General Lyon lived and stayed in Paris most of the time.

An incident is worth mentioning which illustrates the mentality prevailing at the Hanoverian Kriegs-Canzlei [War Department] of that time. The battalion received as replacements 120 men who had been drawn from different Landwehr battalions that had remained behind. The men arrived in red uniforms with white accoutrements and without any field equipment;[312] these men could not serve with us in that condition, and it had to be corrected in a hurry. The lieutenant colonel had the uniforms dyed to a dark colour in Paris, had the leather accoutrements blackened, and had procured the soldiers' furnishings needed for life at the camp. The bills were sent to the Kriegs-Canzlei in Hanover for the reimbursement of these expenses. This was denied, however, because the expenditure had not been requested nor had it been approved in advance. But this was impossible to accomplish within at least four weeks, given the prevailing slow post service and office procedures. Only after a very unpleasant correspondence, eventually including a hint that an account of the matter might be published in newspapers, was the reimbursement approved as an exception.

Weeks went by, most of the time in a very monotonous fashion. The well-being of the troops was severely threatened by an epidemic of dysentery which spread rapidly and caused many deaths. The impression I had of the situation at the time can be inferred from the following letter I had sent to my father.

Camp at the Bois de Boulogne, 18 September 1815

Dearest father!
Even though our still continuing unpleasant situation offers little subject matter for a happy discourse with our loved ones, I at least will not fail to tell you that George and Fritz as well as myself are in good health. We are particularly grateful in this respect because many officers and men cannot say that of themselves. That the Duke of Wellington would go as far in his preconceived opinion of not at all allowing his army to be billeted in proper quarters, thereby exposing it to epidemic diseases, nobody would have believed [such] of this great man. On one hand the humanitarian Count Munster had assured that every month a certain

sum be paid the Hanoverian troops to at least allow the battalions to purchase, together with part of their own pay, a sufficient portion of vegetables for their men; on the other hand the condition of our troops becomes insufferably poorer every day. During the day, we suffer from the oppressive heat and the incessant clouds of dust, the nights are quite chilly and damp. The soldiers have not yet been supplied a single bundle of bedding straw; the dirty Seine is their only source of drinking water. Instead of receiving their portion of brandy to which they are entitled, they are delivered a kind of wine that back home would have been sold as vinegar. As a result the dysentery epidemic is spreading wider by every day. Formalities to provide proper quarters to a sick officer are such that the officer could have died ten times over before being granted his request. All our complaints about these matters must be submitted to our English commanders, who live the good life day and night in Paris. If they take time at all to listen to our grievances, they will forget them the next moment they spend time again in the arms of a French woman or in a wine tavern. If these conditions would be openly discussed in our German fatherland, not only would the Hanoverian troops be praised for the bravery on the day of battle, but they would also be much respected for enduring without grumbling the mistreatment by the commanding general of the lower ranks, out of loyalty to their King and their love of the fatherland, circumstances that certainly are without equal in military history. Here we exist, after a short but exhausting campaign, after a Battle of three days, after the men's entire equipment has been ruined from the weather and poor roads, and that without having faced an enemy, and now exposed for ten weeks to the weather and the lack of proper drinking water. With the enemy capital next to us, we suffer a want of everything for which we would have to pay three times the price compared to what the local population pays. Whenever Sir so and so or Lord so and so come by for an inspection, the men have to appear dressed up as if their entire pay was to be spent on sprucing up.

I have not been to Paris for more than eight days and have not seen Bastide since then; he cannot make up his mind about travelling to Celle.

Every day our hopes are raised that we will be marching home; God grant that they are fulfilled soon. It is said that on the 25th of this month peace will be proclaimed, and that then a large part of the army will leave France.

In asking for heartfelt remembrances to mother, sisters and our other relatives, I and my two brothers commend ourselves to your enduring love.

Your obedient Carl

On 18 October, a big parade had taken place on the Champ de Mars in commemoration of the anniversary of the Battle of Leipzig, in which all German troops cantoned in and around Paris had participated. The Duke of Wellington was receiving the honours on behalf of the Monarchs. The troops had been formed up in close columns, and as the Duke and his splendid suite passed along their front he was saluted with loud hurrahs by the individual detachments. On coming to the left wing where the Hanoverians were standing, there was no shouting; only the military bands were playing the prescribed tunes. On noticing this, the Duke was much displeased, and he inquired more thoroughly as to the Hanoverians' disposition. It was apparently described him in terms approximating the truth, and the Duke even considered it appropriate to do something on our behalf. The City of Paris was then required to pay a war tax from which the Hanoverian officers were paid the difference between their pay rate and the higher English one for the time spent at the camp. Something was thus achieved by remaining silent that could not have been obtained by complaints. Regrettably, nothing was done for the non-coms and men, and since the money was disbursed to the officers before the beginning of our march home, it was spent for the most part in France.

The weather became worse by the day and caused the closing of the camp on 30 October; the troops were billeted in cantonment quarters. Our battalion was stationed at Saulx les Chartreux, some 5 *lieues* south of Paris; the staff (with the exception of the lieutenant colonel who as temporary brigade commander had his quarters at another locality) and the officers of two companies, including my own, were billeted at a large castle owned by General Dessolles, the French Minister of War at the time. On our arrival we were very politely received by the head butler and then seated at a well appointed table. Even later on, we were served most attentively without having to ask for anything, and we had no compunctions in accepting all the attention since General Dessolles had lived for quite some time in Hanover at the city's expense.[313] We may have enjoyed this hospitality for ten to twelve days when a business agent of the general arrived from Paris who notified us that we had not been entitled to any food service; it had been provided in error as we had been believed to be Prussians. We therefore would no longer receive that service and would have to pay a compensation for what we had been served. Although we had not requested any service and had only accepted whatever was voluntarily offered to us, we nevertheless asked for a bill. This was, however, so exorbitantly high that we suspected fraud on the part of the business agent. We declared that we would pay on condition that the collector of the money produce a properly executed special authorisation from the general. We then set up our own household, had a non-com's wife cook the meals, and had a merry old time in our companionable circle. On marching off, we deposited the substantial sum of money with the mayor of the locality, himself a well off landed proprietor, with the request to make the payment based on our conditions. When later on we had been at Condé for some time, the mayor sent us the money because General Dessolles would not accept it. Our helpful intermediary informed us at the same time that he had been deposed from his position of mayor; we very much regretted that we had caused him this unpleasantness, but were glad to have the money returned to us.

After peace had been concluded, the major part of the allies started off on their return march from France. A certain area at the eastern and northern border with various fortresses was to remain occupied by a mixed contingent of 150,000 men for 5 years under the supreme command of the Duke of Wellington. Hanover was to provide a contingent of 5,000 men, which was formed of six field battalions, one hussar regiment, and one battery; our battalion was part of it. On 11 December we marched off from our cantonment to the northern border; the weather was nothing but storms and rains, the march itself very cumbersome because of certain problems. Due to the large troop formations moving at the same time, units had to be detached far away from their assigned intermediate staging localities. Only deep soft roads led to the remote villages, and, as a rule, all wagons and carts had to be left behind on the major highways. The battalion arrived at Peronne on 17 December, where it remained for several weeks. Here I was given the position of local commandant, and as such was faced with many burdensome obligations due to the columns that frequently passed through and often deprived me of a night's rest. On the other hand, I had very good lodging and was to have my meals paid for by the city; but for my lunches I joined the officer corps.

After some time had elapsed, Lieutenant Colonel von Klencke was unexpectedly appointed fortress commandant at Condé, which was to be occupied by Hanoverian troops. The commandant's staff included the position of Platzmajor [Town Major] to which the lieutenant colonel had me appointed and which I gratefully accepted, without having an idea how this would decide my later career. We departed to Condé, accompanied by an artillery officer (Lieutenant Muller, now a lieutenant general) and an officer with the function of engineer (Lieutenant Westphal, later a state economics advisor), where we arrived shortly after Christmas, if I am not mistaken. The fortress was occupied only by the National Guard and was to be handed over to the lieutenant colonel by a commission of French officers, to include all armaments and many supply stores. It was a peculiar feeling to watch the gate being closed behind us after we had been admitted, and to find ourselves all alone among the population that had a reputation of an extremely hostile attitude towards the Bourbons.[314] The French commissaries that we met were old warriors who did not hide their downcast mood, but behaved towards us in an honourable and comrade like manner. The business of the transfer as such was very arduous; exact inventories had to be made, and all stores had to be inspected at their respective locations, and protocols had to be made out, which were to be the basis for the future return of the fortress.

2nd Netherlands Division of Lieutenant General Perponcher 2nd Brigade Major General Prince Bernard of Saxe Weimar

No. 40 From *Belle-Alliance*

Pflugk-Harttung's Matters Regarding Colonel Prince Bernhard of Saxe-Weimar.[315]
  Letter no. 84 Report of Colonel Prince Bernhard of Saxe-Weimar to General Perponcher about the action at Frasnes.[316]

Quatre Bras, 15 June 1815, nine o'clock in the evening
I have the honour to report to Your Excellency that enemy cavalry and infantry have attacked my advance post at Frasnes at about half past six o'clock in the evening. The 2nd Battalion Nassau and Byleveld's Battery were then forced to yield half the way back to Quatre Bras. The brigade was assembled immediately at Quatre Bras. I then advanced the 3rd Battalion Nassau in column on the highway to Frasnes, posted the 1st Battalion in the Bossu forest to defend the latter and to support the 2nd Battalion. The remainder I concentrated at Quatre Bras and on the highway to Marbais. Operating with great bravery, the artillery prevented the enemy from gaining ground on our side of Frasnes. Enemy pickets are posted at the foremost houses of Frasnes. Enemy cavalry detachments have advanced in the direction of Sart-Dame-Avelines and threaten my left flank. Hardly any Prussian troops have retired towards my position; I do not know anything about possible contacts with other bodies of troops, and whether I am not at risk of being cut off from Brussels. I am unable to indicate the strength of the enemy, since my view is much impaired by woods, elevations of the ground, and high stands of corn. No enemy artillery was observed. All necessary measures have been taken to protect us throughout the night.

By the way, I need to confess to Your Excellency that I am too weak to hold out here for long. The 2nd Battalion of Orange Nassau still has French muskets and is down to 10 cartridges per man. The Volunteer Jägers have carbines of four different calibres, and every man is likewise down to 10 cartridges. I will defend the post entrusted to me as long as possible. I expect to be attacked at daybreak. The troops are in the best of spirits. The words 'Wilhelm' and 'Wiesbaden' I have issued as watchword and war cry.

Colonel Bernhard of Saxe-Weimar.

The artillery has no infantry cartridges.

No. 41 From *Belle-Alliance*
Pflugk-Harttung's letter no. 78 Report of the losses of the 1st and 2nd Light Regiments Nassau[317] at Quatre Bras and La Belle Alliance.

26 February 1825

Strength of the Ducal 1st Regiment on 18 June 1815 before the Battle of Waterloo[318]

	Officers		Rank and File	
Staff	Officers	13	Rank and File	46
1st Battalion	"	18	"	933
2nd Battalion	"	18	"	925
Landwehr Battalion	"	17	"	930
Total	Officers	66	Rank and File	2,834

Because the 1st Regiment did not participate in the action at Quatre Bras, its strength is as shown for the 18th.

Losses of the 1st Regiment on 18 June 1815:

Killed

1st Battalion	Officers	0	Rank and File	60
	Includes the Colour Bearer.			
2nd Battalion	"	3	"	34
Landwehr Battalion	"	1	"	11
Total	Officers	4	Rank and File	105[319]

Wounded

Staff	Officers	3	Rank and File	0
1st Battalion	"	11	"	163
2nd Battalion	"	4	"	142
Landwehr Battalion	"	2	"	83
Total	Officers	20	Rank and File	388

Missing

1st Battalion	Rank and File	163
2nd Battalion	"	132
Landwehr Battalion	"	92
Total	Rank and File	387

Most of these have rejoined the regiment. According to the Absentee List of November 1815 the following are deducted and can be assumed to have been killed:

Staff	Rank and File	1
1st Battalion	"	47
2nd Battalion	"	51
Landwehr Battalion	"	27
Total	Rank and File	126

To be added to the number of killed are those who died in the Brussels Hospital during July and August, to wit:

1st Battalion	Officers	—	Rank and File	6
2nd Battalion	"	—	"	11
Landwehr Battalion	"	1	"	1
Total	Officers	1	Rank and File	18

The total losses of the 1st Regiment on 18 June are then as follows:

Killed

Staff	Officers	—	Rank and File	2
1st Battalion	"	—	"	112
2nd Battalion	"	4	"	96
Landwehr Battalion	"	1	"	39
Total	Officers	5	Rank and File	249

Wounded

Staff	Officers	3	Rank and File	—
1st Battalion	"	11	"	157
2nd Battalion	"	3	"	132
Landwehr Battalion	"	2	"	82
Total	Officers	19	Rank and File	371

It follows that for every man killed there were less than 1½ men wounded.

Strength of the Ducal 2nd Regiment on 16 June 1815 before the Action at Quatre Bras.

Staff	Officers	12	Rank and File	33
1st Battalion	"	23	"	847
2nd Battalion	"	24	"	842
3rd Battalion	"	24	"	853
Total	Officers	83	Rank and File	2,575

Losses of the 2nd Regiment on 16 June at Quatre Bras.

Killed

1st Battalion	Officers	—	Rank and File	3
2nd Battalion	"	—	"	10
3rd Battalion	"	—	"	1
Total	Officers	—	Rank and File	14

Wounded

1st Battalion	Officers	—	Rank and File	40
2nd Battalion	"	1	"	19
3rd Battalion	"	2	"	32
Total	Officers	3	Rank and File	91

Strength of the Regiment on 18 June 1815 before the Battle of Waterloo.

Staff	Officers	13	Rank and File	11
1st Battalion	"	22	"	800
2nd Battalion	"	21	"	796
3rd Battalion	"	22	"	793
Total	Officers	78	Rank and File	2,400

Losses of the 2nd Regiment on 18 June 1815 in the Battle of Waterloo.

Killed

Staff	Officers	—	Rank and File	2
1st Battalion	"	1	"	14
2nd Battalion	"	1	"	8
3rd Battalion	"	—	"	11
Total	Officers	2	Rank and File	35

Wounded

1st Battalion	Officers	6	Rank and File	46
2nd Battalion	"	7	"	45
3rd Battalion	"	7	"	62
Total	Officers	20	Rank and File	153

Missing

1st Battalion	Rank and File	40
2nd Battalion	"	19
3rd Battalion	"	66
Total	Rank and File	125

According to the report of the regiment of August 1815, the following of the missing men must be considered to have been killed:

1st Battalion	Rank and File	13
2nd Battalion	"	5
3rd Battalion	"	16
Total	Rank and File	34

To be added are 2 officers who died of their wounds in Brussels. The losses of the 2nd Regiment on 18 June 1815 in the Battle of Waterloo are then as follows:

Killed

Staff	Officers	—	Rank and File	2
1st Battalion	"	2	"	27
2nd Battalion	"	1	"	13
3rd Battalion	"	1	"	27
Total	Officers	4	Rank and File	69

Wounded

1st Battalion	Officers	6	Rank and File	46
2nd Battalion	"	7	"	45
3rd Battalion	"	7	"	62
Total	Officers	20	Rank and File	153

From this it follows that for every man killed there were more than 2 men wounded.

Communicated to Lieutenant Colonel von Nauendorf.

2nd Nassau Regiment

No. 42 From *Belle-Alliance*

Pflugk-Harttung's letter no. 18 Report of the 2nd Regiment Nassau on its participation in the action at Frasnes and Quatre Bras.

Letter no. 74 Report of the 2nd Regiment Nassau on its participation in the Battle of La Belle Alliance.

The Duchy of Nassau 2nd Light Infantry Regiment, which had been in the Royal Netherlands service since 1814, marched off in the last days of March 1815 from its Maastricht garrison and moved into cantonments in the province of South Brabant. The regiment consisted of three battalions, each of six companies. Each company had 4 officers and 150 NCOs, musicians, and soldiers. With the exception of a small depot group and a few hospitalised men left behind in Maastricht, the regiment was, on 15 June 1815, in full strength under arms. At the time, it had been assigned cantonments at the following localities:

> Regimental Staff and 1st Battalion: Houtain le Val.
> 2nd Battalion: Frasnes and Villers Perwin (Rallying Place).
> 3rd Battalion: Baisy, Sart Dames Avelines and Quatre Bras (Rallying Place).

Also cantoned with the 2nd Battalion at the village of Frasnes was the Netherlands Horse Battery under the command of Captain Byleveldt.

The regiment formed, together with the Orange Regiment, the 2nd Brigade of the 2nd Netherlands Division, the former commanded by the Prince of Saxe-Weimar, colonel of the Orange Regiment, and the latter by the Netherlands Lieutenant General von Perponcher. At the beginning of hostilities, command of the regiment went to the undersigned [Major Sattler[320]], until then senior major and commander of the 1st Battalion, because a short time previous, the commander of the 2nd Regiment, Colonel von Goedecke, had a leg smashed during drills by the horse of his adjutant, and because the lieutenant colonel had remained at the depot.[321] commanders of the battalions were:

> 1st Battalion: Captain Büsgen,
> 2nd Battalion: Major von Normann,[322]
> 3rd Battalion: Major Hegmann;[323] he was mortally wounded by a cannon ball immediately at the beginning of the battle on 18 June and command of the battalion went to Captain Frensdorf.[324]

As soon as the regiment had moved into the above-mentioned cantonments, it was assigned, by Divisional Order, the hamlet of Quatre Bras as its rallying place in case of an alarm, where also an alarm beacon was set up. An order, issued several days before the outbreak of hostilities, instructed the regiment 'To remain under arms during day-time and to set up observation posts on elevations near its cantonments'.

Early on 15 June, heavy artillery fire could be heard in the direction of Charleroi; since no news at all had arrived of an enemy on the move, it was assumed that this came from the Prussian artillery which often performed this kind of practise firing. Because that cannonading could be heard much more distinctly in the afternoon, Major von Normann had his 2nd Battalion, cantoned at Frasnes, and the battery of horse artillery took up position several hundred paces in rear of that village on the highway to Quatre Bras, so that the artillery had a free field of fire. In addition, he left an observation post of 1 sergeant and 12 men on the far side of the village on the Charleroi highway. At the same time, he sent a mounted artillerist rushing to the regimental command post with the information on the latest events. I, at once, had the adjutant major, Captain von Mulmann,[325] take this information to the divisional headquarters at Nivelles, and went with the 1st Battalion to the rallying place at Quatre Bras.

At this time, about five o'clock in the afternoon, the 2nd Battalion's picket in front of Frasnes was attacked and dispersed by French lancers (in red uniform), after it had fired a volley at them. Soon thereafter, this cavalry swarmed around the 2nd Battalion on all sides, which, however, slowly retired in good order along the highway to a farm half way between Quatre Bras and Frasnes. Together with the artillery, it there took up a favourable position that the enemy did not dare attack any more.

During the march of the 1st Battalion to the rallying place, I detached two companies to proceed along the side facing Houtain le Val of the wood that was located between the Nivelles and Frasnes highways [Bois de Bossu]. They were to occupy its extreme tip towards the latter village and to seek contact with the 2nd Battalion. The remainder of the 1st Battalion arrived at the rallying place at six o'clock, where the 3rd Battalion had already assembled. The Orange Regiment moved up a short time later, so that the 2nd Brigade was now present in full force. The 2nd Brigade then bivouacked undisturbed at this position until the next morning, since the enemy, whose strength was unknown, made no further forward movements and limited himself to occupying the village of Frasnes.

At daybreak on 16 June, Lieutenant General Perponcher arrived with the remainder of the 2nd Division. As soon as daylight permitted, Major von Normann advanced with the 2nd Battalion on a reconnoitring mission towards Frasnes but faced only an enemy cavalry picket which turned back. The battalion then moved unhindered to the heights of Frasnes and halted there, after having retaken almost all of the terrain it had abandoned the day before. A short time later, after the Duke of Wellington and the Prince of Orange had arrived, at their orders, the battalion had, two companies engage with the enemy. It then became evident that, during the night, the enemy had received reinforcements of infantry and several cannon that prevented further advances. Towards eleven o'clock, the 2nd Battalion received orders to march back to Quatre Bras, and was then replaced by the 3rd Battalion in the line of advance posts.

There had not been any serious action during the morning of 16 June; the three battalions of the regiment had taken turns in skirmishing with the enemy until one o'clock in the afternoon. By that time, several corps of the British and Netherlands army had arrived. From then on, the attacks by both sides became much more vigorous, because the enemy now deployed the masses of troops that he had kept hidden. The 2nd Regiment had been continuously in the line of fire until darkness set in; it participated primarily in the defence of the wood between the Frasnes and Nivelles highways, during which it repulsed repeatedly the most forceful attacks of the enemy cuirassiers and infantry. Other allied troops involved in the defence of this wood included the Orange [Nassau] Regiment, a Brunswick detachment, and a Scottish battalion.[326] During the night from the 16th to the 17th, the regiment bivouacked at the edge of this wood.

On 17 June at ten o'clock in the morning, I received orders from the commander of the 2nd [Netherlands] Division, Lieutenant General von Perponcher, to have the regiment follow the rearward movement of the division. I arrived in the evening in the line of Mont St Jean, where the allied army had already taken up position. This regiment stood on the left flank of the army and had only the Orange [Nassau] Regiment to its left. In the night from the 17th to the 18th, bivouac was set up at this position.

On 18 June at nine o'clock in the morning, an orderly officer of the Duke of Wellington brought me an order to detach the 1st Battalion of the regiment to the Hougoumont farm on the extreme right flank of the army. Commanded by Captain Büsgen, this battalion marched off immediately to its destination. He defended this farmstead throughout the course of the battle, notwithstanding all the buildings having been reduced to ashes by enemy artillery fire, nor the repeated most violent attacks by the enemy infantry on this post. At eleven o'clock in the morning, I had the 2nd and 3rd Battalions move forward several hundred paces from the position held during the night, thereby facing

La Haye and Papelotte farms. As soon as I saw a strong enemy infantry column turn in our direction, I had these farms occupied by strong skirmisher detachments with strong reserves from both battalions. All enemy attacks made on these farms during the course of the day were steadfastly repulsed.[327] That part of the two battalions which had remained in the line was continuously exposed to the fire of the enemy artillery. A column of English light cavalry stood on the extreme left flank of the 2nd Regiment; as far as I can remember, it was mostly made up by the Hanoverian Legion.[328] The aforementioned position was not changed throughout the entire battle until, towards evening, the Prussians arrived from Wavre and a general advance of the allied army was ordered. Upon nightfall, I had the 2nd and 3rd Battalion set up bivouac at the highway from Brussels to Charleroi, and on 19 June I had the 1st Battalion rejoin the regiment on the march to France.

Sattler, Colonel

1st Battalion, 2nd Nassau Regiment

The following accounts, by Major Büsgen and Private Leonhard are of particular interest, as they highlight a common misconception regarding the defence of Hougoumont. Many British sources claim the laurels for the defence of the chateau complex solely for the British Guards, a calumny that needs to be squashed.

It is very clear from their evidence that Major Büsgen's 800-man battalion had displaced the Guards detachment from the chateau and orchard early on the 18th. This had happened on orders from the Prince of Orange and without Wellington's knowledge and consent, who had positioned four Guards light companies at the chateau on the previous evening.

During the first French attack in brigade strength, Büsgen's 400-man detachment inside the chateau enclosure was the only force to keep this outpost in allied hands. It continued in its defence, jointly with the Foot Guards who soon after moved back into the compound. Those Nassau troops thus should have been allowed a share of the laurels earned by the gallant defenders of Chateau Hougoumont.

The other half of Büsgen's battalion fought in the wood and orchard alongside the other troops there, their fortunes see-sawing throughout the day, but they did not flee on mass as has been generally stated.

Wellington himself was the cause of much of the unfair treatment of these Nassau troops by British historians. From his comment to Count Pozzo di Borgo the Russian attaché on his staff, while watching the Nassau troops in the orchard being pushed back, '*Voila des coquins avec qui il faut gagner une bataille'* [It is with these scoundrels that a battle must be won]; to his later claims that when he had rallied them some shots were fired at him; each further destroyed the reputation of the Nassau troops who had helped the defence of Hougoumont that day.

These two reports should set the record straight and serve to restore the good name of the Nassau battalion detached to Hougoumont.[329]

No. 43 From *Belle-Alliance*

Pflugk-Harttung's letter no. 75 Report of the 1st Battalion of the 2nd Regiment Nassau on its participation in the Battle of La Belle Alliance. Captain Moritz Büsgen's 1st Battalion, 2nd Duchy of Nassau Infantry Regiment reported by Major M. Büsgen.

Description of the Participation of the 1st Battalion of the 2nd Ducal Regiment on 18 June in the Battle of Waterloo during its detachment from the regiment.

On the morning of 18 June, the Ducal 2nd Regiment Nassau was positioned on the left wing of the allied army when its 1st Battalion under my command (800 men) was ordered to immediately break camp and march to, and occupy, the Hougoumont farm located before the right wing of the centre. Shortly thereafter, at about half past nine o'clock, it was led by one of the Duke of Wellington's ADC's past the front of the army to this position. The farm was in the shape of an elongated closed rectangle of which three sides were enclosed by buildings, its left side, however, partly by a garden wall and buildings. The interior of this rectangle was divided into two parts by the residential building and an archway with a gate. The upper part consisted of the large residential building and the farm buildings, the lower part of the stables and barns. Each section had a large gate, the upper facing towards the enemy position, the lower towards the opposite side. To the left and adjoining the farm was the vegetable garden,[330] on its front and left sides enclosed by a wall 5 to 6 feet high, and on its rear by a hedge. This wall bordered on its front onto a wooded area (with tall trees) and, a few paces before that, was masked by a not very dense hedge. To the left of the vegetable garden was an orchard, however without access to the former. On its front it was enclosed by a hedge which was in line with that of the garden wall, but it was open on its rear. The buildings and the vegetable garden were concealed from the enemy by the wood in front.[331]

On my arrival with the battalion, the farm and garden were unoccupied;[332] a company of Brunswick Jäger[333] stood on the furthest edge of the wood. A battalion of English Guards of the Coldstream Regiment under the command of Colonel Macdonell was partly deployed behind the farm, partly in a hollow way behind the said gardens, parallel with the lower part of the former [the farm].[334]

From the existing defence preparations (barricading of the upper gate, loopholes cut in same, and part of them in the garden wall) it was obvious that this post had already been occupied [by other troops]; there was also an ample supply of infantry ammunition in one of the rooms of the dwelling house, as was discovered later.

I immediately undertook the dispositions I deemed necessary for the defence: the grenadier company I stationed in the buildings[335] and two companies in the adjoining vegetable garden; I placed one company behind the hedge of the orchard, the voltigeurs [light company] moved into line with the previously mentioned Brunswick Jäger, and one company served these as a reserve being placed at some distance to their rear.

This deployment was barely completed when at eleven o'clock in the morning the enemy (Jerome Bonaparte's division) began his attack on the wood with a heavy cannonade with shell and case shot. Swarms of tirailleurs then pressed forward, supported by formed troop bodies, and, after tenacious resistance of the three companies[336] posted there, pushed these back towards the farm and the gardens. Closely pursued by the enemy, the retiring troops fell back, partly to the right around the buildings, partly to the left [through the opening] between the garden wall and the hedge of the orchard into the orchard. Kept back by the murderous fire directed at close quarters at the enemy, from buildings, garden wall, and the orchard hedge, he was put to flight at great loss by the combined attack of the already mentioned English Guards battalions,[337] who had moved into the orchard, and who pursued him into the wood. It proved impossible, however, to drive him out of the wood completely during the remainder of the battle, as he was always reinforced by fresh troops. The English battalion afterwards returned to its earlier position. The Brunswick Jäger company, after bravely helping repel the enemy and suffering heavily, rejoined its corps on the main position. Towards one o'clock, the enemy renewed his attack and advanced in a great rush against the buildings and gardens, and attempted to escalade the garden wall and to gain a footing behind the orchard hedge, but was chased off by the skirmish fire from the garden wall and repulsed at all points. During this attack, the enemy set fire to large stacks of hay and straw close to the farm in an attempt to make it spread to the buildings, but without success. Between two and three o'clock, the enemy then moved up a battery to the right side of the farm and started a heavy cannonade with his guns and howitzers on the buildings. It did not take long, and they were all in flames.[338]

The enemy now for the third time made a rash attack, which was mainly directed at the buildings. Aided by the smoke and flames, his grenadiers forced their way into the upper courtyard through a small side door; they were, however, driven out again by the fire from the building windows and the advance through the lower gate and courtyard of a detachment of the already mentioned English battalion. Some intruders were taken prisoner, but seven of our grenadiers were also captured by the enemy during this action.[339] This attack, which ended about half past three o'clock, was the enemy's last serious attempt on the Hougoumont position; the skirmish fire, however, lasted with hardly an interruption until the end of the battle.

Neither upon my being detached, nor during this entire period, was a commander named to me under whose orders I was to operate. No allied troops were drawn up near Hougoumont to either its right or left. If I mention in this account only the battalion of the Coldstream Regiment of the English Guards, then it is because I had seen no other troops sent in support of the battalion under my command; I do not know if and what other troops were later detached to reinforce this position. Due to the continuing fighting, and the view restricted by trees, hedges and walls, I was unable to observe what was happening at a distance.

The battalion occupied this position throughout the night, and, upon receipt of orders, joined the regiment on the Nivelles road on the morning of 19 June.

Büsgen, Major

No. 44 A Nassau Soldier's Remembrances of the Waterloo Campaign

Fragments from the unpublished memoirs of Private Johann Peter Leonhard[340] as cited in Peter Wacker and Guntram Muller-Schellenberg's, Das herzoglich-nassauische Militar 1813–1866 *(Taunusstein, 1983).*

On arrival [at Hougoumont] we noticed that this big farm was surrounded by a wall; the doors were open, one could see the freshly broken loopholes in the walls. Ha, I thought to myself, here you'll settle in but leave nevermore, good night, world! The farm was now occupied at the greatest speed by us Nassauers, the right wing of the 1st Battalion, 2nd Nassau Regiment, on the inside [the grenadier and two line companies], the left wing on the outside [the light and two line companies].

We had hardly taken up position at the loopholes when masses of French came out of the wood, apparently all set to capture the farm, but they were too late! A shower of balls that we loosed off on the French was so terrible that the grass in front was soon covered with French corpses. Their retiring and advancing thus went on alternately, and we were attacked four times in our farm, but each time the French were again repelled.

The fifth attack that the French launched against the Hougoumont farm was beyond description. The hornbeam trees of the garden alley, underneath which we stood, were razed by the immense cannonade, as if mown down, and so were the beautiful tall trees along the outside of the farm. Walls were collapsing from both the heavy bombardment or from the severe thunderstorm that raged above us, the likes of which I have never experienced before; one could not distinguish one from the other.[341] The skies seemed to have been changed into an ocean of fire; all of the farm's buildings were aflame. The soil underneath my feet began to shake and tremble, and large fissures opened up before my very eyes.

After the Battle of Waterloo, the Nassauers were again drawn up ahead of the entire army, and were forced to be the vanguard, or avant-garde, through all of France to Paris. For the most part we had to march with loaded muskets and fixed bayonets. During these rapid advances, the Nassauers were never treated to delectables nor wine, but rather to the opposite, hunger, thirst, want, and all kinds of hardship. We were never quartered in towns or villages but had to camp at night under the open skies! It is thus understandable that oftentimes on this march to Paris we were in dire needs because the food supplies could not follow our fast marches in pursuit of the French. We eventually arrived at Paris and moved into this capital city on 1 July 1815, where we camped in the Boulogne Wood until 30 October.

2nd Battalion, 2nd Nassau Regiment

No. 45 From *Belle-Alliance*
Pflugk-Harttung's letter no. 76 Information on the participation of the 2nd Battalion of the 2nd Regiment Nassau in the Battle at La Belle Alliance.

Excerpt from a letter[342] from Captain von Reichenau[343] to Lieutenant Koch[344] at Wiesbaden.

Our two regiments were still separated on this day (18 June) because the commander of the division, General Perponcher, did not want to lose the 2nd Regiment. But now, both were united under General von Kruse.[345] Since Colonel von Goedecke had broken his leg in the beginning of June, Major Sattler commanded the [2nd] Regiment and the colonel of the

Orange Regiment, Prince Bernhard of Weimar, the brigade. This good man would have done better if he had stayed at home.[346]

The 2nd and 3rd Battalions of our regiment were stationed on the left wing of the English army in order to occupy a small village, La Haye Sainte by name (if I am not mistaken).[347] Towards evening, our entire [2nd] Battalion was posted there as skirmishers when, unfortunately, the Prussians, who operated against the French right flank, mistook us for Frenchmen and loosed an unbearable fire on us. I stole myself to get to them through a sunken path to alert them to their error. [Together] we moved quickly against the French and were about to overrun two French guns just 50 paces away when I was hit by a ball near my left knee. Rettberg, whose company had shrunk to about 30 men and who himself had a big bruise on one of his legs, had me bandaged and carried back to Waterloo on crossed muskets. During the night I slept there fairly well among the wounded and dying.

On the next day I hobbled along the road and, fortunately, met Captain Ahlefeld[348] who had me carried on a stretcher to Brussels, together with Major von Weyhers.[349] Major Hegmann has died here after two amputations of his leg. Of our (2nd) battalion, Lieutenant von Trott[350] was killed and eight have been wounded, but besides that, we have no news at all about the regiment.

The people of Brussels distinguish themselves by their care for the wounded that cannot be praised enough, particularly since the number of wounded who were brought here rose to 30,000 in the first days after the battle. Poor Holleben[351] suffers from fits of fever for four weeks now, which make us fear that he will end up losing his mind.

3rd Battalion, 2nd Nassau Regiment

No. 46 From *Belle-Alliance*

Pflugk-Harttung's letter no. 77 Report of the 3rd Battalion of the 2nd Regiment Nassau on its participation in the Battle of La Belle Alliance.[352]

Biebrich, 28 December 1835

Report about the 3rd Battalion of the 2nd Regiment Nassau during the battle near Waterloo on 18 June 1815.[353]

The 2nd Regiment, with the Orange Nassau Regiment, formed a brigade under the command of Prince Bernhard of Saxe Weimar. On the evening of 17 June, the brigade took position of the extreme left wing of the battle line at the farms of Papelotte, La Haye, and the village of Smohain.

The 3rd Battalion, under the command of Major Hegmann had to its right the 2nd Battalion of the 2nd Regiment [Nassau] and somewhat removed to its left the 1st Battalion of the Orange Nassau Regiment.

Between eleven and twelve o'clock, the enemy columns and their gun batteries deployed opposite [our position]. One of the first cannon balls wounded Major Hegmann, and Captain Frensdorf took command.

Between twelve and one o'clock, a line of enemy skirmishers advanced towards Papelotte. The Prince of Saxe Weimar sent me with my company, the 3rd Flanqueurs, against them. Shortly thereafter, a detachment of the Orange Nassau Regiment occupied the village of Smohain and La Haye, and I linked up with them.

Papelotte, a square complex built of stone and surrounded by sunken roads and hedges, is most suitable for a determined defence. I was able to drive the enemy skirmishers back to the outermost hedge at the border of the meadowy valley which separated our line from the enemy's, and there take possession of several small houses.

Between three and four o'clock, a stronger enemy skirmish line advanced again, followed in support by a considerable infantry column. I was forced to leave my position and fall back on Papelotte, which I had fortified as much as possible in the short time available.

At my request for reinforcements, Captain Frensdorf placed No. 10, No. 11 and No. 12 Companies under my command, with the Flanqueur Company of 2nd Battalion of our regiment following suit. The enemy column, being held up by the fire from Papelotte and from the small houses, whose occupiers had bravely held out, was now driven back in a quick bayonet charge and pursued to the just mentioned outermost hedge. Here it was that an enemy battery now received us with case shot from a distance of less than 500 paces. Even though we had significant losses, the 3rd Flanqueurs lost two officers in this position, and the rank and file was reduced to half of the men by the end of the battle, the enemy no longer attempted a serious attack and only kept up a vigorous musketry fire from a hedge on the far side of the meadowy valley at the foot of his position. That attack had been attempted by a part of Durutte's division, the exact strength of the detachment I do not know, but it was certainly superior in number to my own.

At about six o'clock the enemy suddenly appeared on my left flank. I no longer had any contact with the 1st Battalion of the Orange Nassau's. The enemy had taken possession of Smohain and La Haye, and a skirmish line advanced towards Papelotte. Although [the French] attacked vigorously, they were not supported by infantry columns; due to my favourable position, no particular effort on my part was needed to hold the enemy off.

After seven o'clock, the enemy suddenly retreated from my side, without even being forced. This event was inexplicable to me, and so was a vigorous gun and musket firing that seemed to originate from the direction of Smohain and Plançenoit. Shortly thereafter, my own line, which I had moved forward to La Haye, was driven back to the road that separates La Haye from Papelotte by numerous skirmishers, followed by infantry columns. Skirmishers even attacked me from the hedges in my rear. When I repulsed these, I became aware that we were faced by Prussians. They in their turn recognised their error, which had lasted less than 10 minutes but had caused several dead and wounded on both sides.

I then left Papelotte which I had held without interruption. Remaining there any longer was rendered extremely difficult if not impossible by a rapidly spreading fire which had suddenly erupted in the right wing of the building. I then joined the Prussians on their advance towards Plançenoit and reported this to Captain Frensdorf. Since my three hornists had been killed or wounded, I was unable at the time to gather on the rugged terrain more than only a small part of my men. The orders I had left for the remainder were not followed. I was informed later that the Prince of Saxe-Weimar had directed them back to the two companies of the 3rd Battalion which had held their position throughout the battle.

Jointly with the Prussian skirmishers, I believe they belonged to the 18th Regiment,[354] we did battle with the enemy who fought tenaciously, however, [they] began to yield ground more readily between eight and nine o'clock. At this time and not far from Plançenoit, Captain von Reichenau[355] was wounded at my side.

Soon thereafter, I left the Prussian troops who followed the fleeing enemy, and retired to the farm of Mont St Jean where I spent the night and, on the next day, rejoined the 3rd Battalion.

Rettberg, Major & ADC to his Highness the Duke

1st Battalion, 28th Orange Nassau Regiment

No. 47 The experiences of Sergeant Johann Heinrich Doring,[356] Orange Nassau Regiment during the Waterloo Campaign.
From Historische Beilage *[History Supplement]* Dill Zeitung *(Herborn 1988), vol. 56 no. 11.*

Prelude to the battle of Quatre Bras[357]
After entering Belgium, we took quarters in the little town of Genappe. Myself and some NCOs and soldiers were billeted at a tavern on the Brussels Road, right at the beginning of town, which was owned by a widow. It was same place where, later, the fleeing Napoleon had to leave behind his coach, jewels, money, hat, sabre, etc. and would have

been taken prisoner by the pursuing Prussians, had it not been for the speed of his cavalry horse.

Since we had to be prepared for an early attack by the French, we conducted exercises all day. Quite often at night, general quarters were called, and we had to march off for hours with full equipment, in order to keep our soldiers in constant readiness. Upon the news that Napoleon had in fact invaded Belgium, our battalion, the 2nd Regiment Nassau[358] (quartered next to ours and where my uncle Hegmann was a major), several Dutch Militia battalions, and a horse battery of the Netherlands artillery, all had to move by forced marches towards the Quatre Bras farms, in order to halt the advance of the French Marshal Ney's forces.

We ourselves marched off from Genappe on this Thursday, 15 June, at 3 p.m. on the Brussels chaussee towards Quatre Bras. On our way we met several cartloads of wounded Prussians, who had been fighting Ney's forces on this side of Charleroi. Our men who, until then, had been singing and were otherwise in good spirits, calmed down on beholding these wounded soldiers, and more so, as our sutler women shouted at them 'You will yet forget about singing!', and as orders were given to load the muskets with live cartridges. Inexplicably, on arrival at the height of Quatre Bras we were not bothered very much by the enemy, in spite of his twenty fold superiority on this day,[359] and we bivouacked not far from him. We did not have to worry very much about provisions because our Genappe hosts had been quite generous in that regard. The rest of this 15 June passed by with only some skirmishing on both sides. In spite of his superiority, the enemy was held in check until well into the next morning by the previously mentioned Netherlands battery (whose men later received the King William Order), and by our battalion and several Dutch battalions.

The Battle of Quatre Bras

It seems that only on the morning of 16 June, Marshal Ney realised that he faced very weak forces, and he then attacked us with all his might. A battalion of Dutch [infantry] was driven back right away, because they had been posted on the main chaussee in the centre of our line, their falling back put us and the other corps in great danger. These Dutchmen had suffered severely from the enemy's fierce cannonading and musketry and had become totally disheartened. They left their position, some throwing away their muskets. In order to meet the danger and to push the French back from that position, our colonel, Prince Bernhard of Saxe Weimar ordered our battalion to attack the enemy, as our battalion had stood next to the Dutch. By the way, the colonel was one of the tallest persons I have ever seen. A very brave and courageous soldier, he rode at the time a big black Arabian stallion, which was a gift from the Tsar Alexander of Russia. He at first called for volunteers, but then the entire battalion stepped forward and, with all drummers in front, marched off with levelled bayonets and without loosing off a single shot, [went] straight at the all important position left by the Dutch and now occupied by the enemy. The French were thrown back, and in no time was the centre of our line again in our hands.

It was in this affair that Sergeant Geise from Dillenburg had the hilt of his sabre ripped off by a cannon ball; he was knocked unconscious and fell to the ground, perhaps from the air pressure, but had suffered no further harm, except for the terrible shock. On our advance in the wood that had been abandoned by the enemy, I came upon a Brunswick Jäger leaning against a pine tree who had a musket ball stuck firmly under the skin of his belly. He was as pale as death, complained about terrible pains, and begged for a surgeon. Our battalion surgeon J. G. Neuendorff,[360] who by chance had followed me, was able to cut out the ball, as I found out later from him, and thus probably saved the man's life. Many years later, the surgeon received a valuable gift from this man, along with a note, expressing his warmest thanks.

The French now moved against us with an ever greater force. But our side was also reinforced by English, Hanoverian, and Netherlands troops, who earlier had been widely dispersed behind us and now entered our line with all arms. At this point, the fighting became fiercer and bloodier. With the addition of more regiments, Marshal Ney attempted to force a breakthrough. He did not succeed because all our troops, particularly the Scotsmen and the Brunswickers, fought like lions in spite of the terrible cannonade. The latter were all the more incensed when they saw that their duke, leading their regiment, had been fatally wounded by a French dragoon and had to be taken off the battlefield. A regiment of French cuirassiers who were about to break through our lines were counter attacked with levelled bayonets by a regiment of Scottish Highlanders, who knocked the riders about so that most of them had to kiss mother earth. As the day ended and the firing from both sides let up, we had lost no ground and, in fact, had maintained the position we had held all day, in spite of all of Marshal Ney's efforts.

Retreat to Waterloo
We now believed that the battle would be continued the next day in this area. But shortly after midnight[361] the news arrived at our camp that Blücher had been beaten by Napoleon at Ligny, five hours' march from us. In order to avoid becoming surrounded, our whole army would have

to break camp immediately and march back through Genappe to Waterloo. We had to leave in a hurry and on an empty stomach, but not without having taken in the sad sight of a lot of our dead and wounded having been plundered and stripped to their bare shirts by the French. Among the wounded was an officer named Engel from the Nassau Siegen area, who had been shot through his neck. It had swollen terribly and was horrible to look at. He was still living, and in this condition was carried by some soldiers of his company to a merchant's house in Genappe where he had been billeted earlier, and had been engaged to the man's only daughter. That officer died a short time later.

On our part, we now retreated this 17th of June under a steady downpour to Waterloo, pursued all the time by the French vanguard and their cannon fire. All along the main chaussee from Quatre Bras to Waterloo, the side of the roadway was filled with overturned ammunition carts, demolished guns or guns jammed into each other; and on the road were ambulances carrying the wounded and an endless wagon train with the camp followers of the Scottish troops (as was their custom at the time). Cavalry and the infantry could not advance on the chaussee and had to march on the adjoining fields and pastures, slogging their way through some terrible mud. At one point, we had to cross a creek, over which there was only a very narrow footbridge. Only one file could use the bridge [at a time]; the other had to wade through hip deep water to reach the other side. Some soldiers refused to pass through the water and caused some disorder and a loss of time. General Kruse[362] immediately ordered a troop of English dragoons of the so called 'Grey Horse Guards',[363] which regiment without exception rode dapple-grey horses to strike the recalcitrants, who then made their way through the water. Under these circumstances and feeling that everything was lost, we eventually reached the Waterloo farm under continuing downpours, and with the fire of the pursuing French following us.

A terrible night at Waterloo
Instead of marching on through the Soignes forest on the road to Brussels, we were ordered to halt at the Waterloo farm.[364] The entire army was then put in battle order on both sides of Waterloo, involving an unending marching back and forth. During this manoeuvring I lost one of my shoes which remained stuck in the heavy mud and which in the general rush I could replace only after a good while with another one from my backpack. Even if found later, that lost shoe is unlikely to grace somebody else's foot.

Both armies now set up camp, about a cannon shot apart from one another. Within a short time the pitch black horizon was lit by thousands of camp fires. Due to the continuing rain, the muskets had to be stuck downward into the soil by their bayonets to prevent the cartridges inside from getting wet and to be ready for [the] next day's dance. Dead tired from the day's exertions, everybody threw himself down into the mud, the backpack serving as a headrest, and no thought was given to food and drink, even if available. Our desire for some rest was not to be granted for about midnight some Englishman's musket went off from carelessness. That caused some shouting all along the line that the French had managed to break through at our right wing and were upon us in full force. Within a short time, that news proved to be unfounded. But only someone who has been through all this, on a pitch dark night with constant rain and even a thunderstorm, can have an idea of what that did to our spirits. My comrade Sergeant Achenbach, who was with me and the first of us to wake up to that unfounded news, broke out into a series of the most violent curses. Never had he been through a night like this, he said, not in the Spanish campaign, nor in any of the others that he had been in, and he was sorry that a ball had not made an end to his life during the past days. Lying down, we both had burrowed so deep into the mud that [it was] only with difficulty we could get up again.

That Achenbach was a man of superhuman strength. He had run away from home and had joined the French Lanciers de Berg. But during his first days with this regiment he had become involved in an argument with the regimental fencing master. In the ensuing duel he almost chopped off the man's left hand, whereupon he was put in chains for some time and was sent to Spain as an additional punishment. The rest of the night we spent in relative quiet, and without being molested by the enemy. Still, all this adversity and the past hardships had taken their toll on our spirits. But this must have equally been the case with the enemy, with the same kind of sky overhead, the same roads and bottomless fields to pass over. There was this vast difference, however, that he was advancing and we were on the retreat, which deeply affects the soldiers' morale.

As the day had hardly dawned, it was still raining cats and dogs; we had to get our muskets ready for their next use as best as possible, in particular clearing the locks with rags and other means. In the course of the lining up for the battle, there seemed to be no end to the corps' continuous marching back and forth. Still, our stomachs insisted on their right, and as our hunger was getting worse, the farms, mills, etc. located between the lines were plundered, both by our troops and the French, for cattle, pigs, geese, ducks, chicken, potatoes and other edibles. Some of the buildings were burned down.[365] To lose no time, all of this, half boiled or half grilled, was devoured with the greatest haste and appetite; no wonder after several days of fasting and the past hardships. I even noticed one time that some soldiers had brought along a pretty fat pig. Rather than first slaughtering it, they cut out with their sabres entire pieces from its hind parts, held them over a fire and devoured them half grilled with the greatest appetite, hard to believe but true. During all this plundering, our soldiers and the enemy's were the best of friends, and nobody gave a thought to the prospect that in a few hours they would meet in a fight for life and death.

The Big Battle

After the weather had improved somewhat, at about eleven o'clock in the morning, Napoleon signalled the beginning of the battle by a single cannon shot. A description of the course of the battle throughout the day would be too lengthy and even unnecessary, because its history has become well known. In regard to what took place during the battle on 18 June, I will confine myself to what I remember and whatever a single person can recall from the turmoil of fighting, and in particular to what I myself have seen and experienced. The battle now began to rage with the thunder of 300 to 400 guns. This as well as the firing of thousands of muskets caused a steady thunderous and earth shaking rumble. The powder smoke unfortunately blew towards us and was so dense at times that the enemy opposing us could only be recognised by the fire flashes from their guns and muskets. Added to that was the moaning of the dying and wounded. No pity nor consideration could be shown them. Because of the terrible noise, the officers' orders could no longer be understood, and the necessary commands were largely communicated by the tambours, buglers and half moon hornists.

Our battalion was posted for several hours on the left wing of the plateau, at the chateau and farm of Frischermont, which was surrounded by a 3 to 4 foot high wall. We were able to defend this fairly important position for quite some time against the attacks of a regiment of voltigeurs. They attempted several times to force the wall, albeit without success, until they were reinforced by the arrival of a corps of some 4,000 men. We then had to retire from this position in a hurry, and we continued our defence further back at a hamlet [Smohain].[366] It so happened on this retreat that our Major Dressel[367] was heard to cry, full of anguish 'Are you grenadiers going to leave me behind?', as his orderly had already left with his horses. Somebody then helped him in time by bringing him a riderless horse.

For us, this was the day's most critical and dangerous moment, as the French moved against us with ever more powerful columns. We were separated from the enemy by a distance of not more than half the range of a musket shot. Due to the huge clouds of powder smoke, blown into our faces by the wind, we could recognise the enemy much of the time only by the flashes of their musketry fire. The turmoil became more general by the minute, and there could be no thought of some form of order. Without interruption, we loaded and fired into the enemy's ranks; no use in aiming at a particular target. As the enemy was forcefully pushing forward, getting more reinforcements all the time, we could hardly have withstood his thrusts much longer. Wellington, moreover, had pulled many regiments towards his faltering centre.

The Prussians arrive – Victory!

It was at this critical moment that the vanguard of Bülow's Corps descended behind our backs. Believing that these were French troops, we turned around and fired at them for a short time, until some Prussian officers waived at us with white cloths. As great as our relief was, there now followed the hottest affair of the entire day. Of the tumult and confusion of battle, the hurrahs and cheering, the rumbling thunder of cannon and musket fire, nobody can have an idea but he, who has taken part in this terrible spectacle. There was no place for human sentiments. The wounded and dying were run over or marched over without consideration, regardless of whether friend or enemy, it just did not matter. Everybody was only concerned with his own self. Of this furore, I remember one incident in particular. A Prussian Landwehr NCO was running by me, shouting 'We will yet make them smoke some Prussian tobacco!' A short while later he fell down, whether killed or wounded I could not make out.

The battle now had ended in a victory that was primarily owed to the Prussians, because our army could hardly have held on any longer. The Prussians under General Gneisenau took on the pursuit of the French troops. At night we camped on the battlefield at the centre of the line among dead and wounded who, in places, were lying above each other in piles as high as 3 to 4 feet. There was no thought of food or drink, there was none in the first place; everybody dropped down where he was, backpack and all, the musket in his arms. Still, this night's rest lasted only until about two o'clock in the morning. My brother[368] then wrote a brief note, a drum serving as a table, to our people at home that the two of us had come away from the battle unharmed. He had an orderly take it to Brussels to be put in the mail. Shortly thereafter, on the 19 June, our army broke camp. I will mention here that, as we passed the last buildings of Waterloo, a place in front of a barn was full of amputated legs and arms, some still with parts of uniforms, and the surgeons, with rolled up sleeves like butchers, still busy at work. The scene looked like a slaughterhouse.

Off to Paris

We took the other chaussee, that leading past Namur to Soissons etc. It was getting hot quite early on our march. Due to the past heavy rains, the surface of the road had turned very rough and uneven. I noticed on this day that many men fell down and died from sheer exhaustion. There was not much resting in between, and nobody was allowed to be left behind, since the Brabanters were not to be trusted, much less so than the French. What made things worse was the fact that the cavalry, artillery, caissons, ambulances, etc. used the centre of the road, and that the infantry had to march on the sides of the road. On the evening of the second day we camped in some orchards next to the chaussee, a few hours' march away from Peronne fortress. The kettles filled with chicken, ducks, etc. were already cooking over the camp fires, and everybody was looking forward to a hearty meal, when general quarters were called. Several battalions had to break camp and were ordered to attack the French in that fortress at once and take it by storm if necessary. Unfortunately, ours was one of those battalions. The half cooked contents of the kettles had to be thrown out. Our equipment was put back in order, and we marched off with empty stomachs. After we had marched for an hour, and the fortress was already in sight, an English staff officer came galloping towards us and brought the news that the French had capitulated. Then followed the order to return to our camp site. But in the meantime, others had already settled there and taken advantage of the food stuffs discarded by us. We had no choice but to forage and start cooking again, which did not take much time. Still, we had to break camp again at around two o'clock. As long as we passed through the Brabant province, where the English army was the only one on the road, we had enough of everything. But as of that point where both armies started using the same road on their march towards Paris, the Prussians having advanced before ours, no life seemed to be left in the villages. Only a few people could be seen, and more rarely yet, a living animal. Staircases, windows, etc. were lying in the streets. From now on, we were limited to our daily rations, which were 2 lb of bread, ½ lb of meat, ½ lb of rice, and ½ pint of rum; not too bad, after all. Quite often, water for drinking and cooking had to be obtained from fairly distant places, because nearby wells had been made unusable with gunpowder. The rest of our march towards Paris was without major incidents; we arrived there in the beginning of July. As we neared the city, the road was often barred with the trunks of what had been beautiful alleys of linden trees bordering the road. Those obstacles caused many delays and disruptions on our march.

End of the Campaign – the Victory Parade

On arrival in Paris our troops set up camp in the Bois de Boulogne. Beautiful fruit and other trees growing on those wide spaced grounds were chopped down in a hurry for building thousands of huts, a work of several hours. Each of these housed eight to ten men. After staying some time at this camp, the army was partly dispersed to localities outside Paris. Our grenadier company and the flanqueur [light] company, as well as the entire staff, were assigned quarters in Senlis, about five hours' march from Paris. One day, several weeks after the arrival of the allied forces, a festive entry of the entire army into the city was to take place. Never again in my life have I seen this or a similar spectacle, and it will never fade from my memory. Beginning several days before the event, uniforms and equipment were put in the finest condition. On the day of the parade we had to march off to Paris at three o'clock in the morning. All our troops began to gather there, at least 80,000 men, cavalry, infantry, and all our guns and the captured ones. On this occasion I happened to see Old Blücher up close. When riding by us with his staff, he noticed General Perponcher before our front. Recognising him as an old friend and fighting comrade, he rode up to him, warmly pressed his hand and said 'How are you, old man? ['*Nun, Alter, wie geht's?*'] I believe this is going to be a boring and hot day.' I could hear all this quite well since both had halted in front of our company, a few paces away from me. After a brief conversation, Blücher returned to his staff.

If I am not mistaken, it took until noon before all regiments had been lined up and the train was in place. The parade through the city now started off, all troops, cavalry, artillery, infantry, in their full dress uniforms. Each regiment marched with its band, its drummers, buglers, and hornists in closed ranks, in brigades and divisions, all this accompanied by an unimaginable deafening noise. The army proceeded through many streets and then, at the Tuilleries, marched past the Allied monarchs, who were gathered on a grandstand decorated with guns, flags, drums, and other military emblems. All roofs and trees were crowded tight with people, particularly in this area, so that one could no longer see the roof tiles nor the leaves on the trees.

After an hour of marching we arrived again at the city barriers, where the various corps separated and went on to their cantonments. On this day with its oppressive heat, we suffered some extreme trials, on our legs almost without interruption from early morning until late evening, with a full backpack, musket, and side arms, without a moment of rest, nothing to eat all day, and only occasionally a sip of rum. All the more did we enjoy the hearty meal on return to Senlis after five hours' march. [In concluding] I should mention that, in 1806, my Senlis host had been billeted in my home town [Herborn], while he served with the 14th Dragoons in the French army, which was undoubtedly true, as he was well informed of the town and some of its people.

2nd Battalion, 28th Orange Nassau Regiment

No. 48 Notes on the Battle of Waterloo by Captain Friedrich Ernst Eberhard,[369] formerly with the Orange Nassau Regiment

Den Uhrturm *[Nassau Family History News]*, Wiesbaden, no. 27, July 1940, pp. 551–3.

In 1815 I was a first lieutenant in the 2nd Battalion, Orange Nassau Regiment. In the evening of 15 June the said battalion already faced the enemy at Quatre Bras. When on 16 June fighting started with the arrival of daylight, the battalion was unable to take part in the skirmishing with the rest of the brigade due to the low supply of ammunition for its French muskets. Its services on that day seem nevertheless to have been substantial. When the action warmed up, around noon, the battalion moved from the height on the left of Quatre Bras down to the Namur road where it joined two Hanoverian battalions.[370] Together with these it covered the Brussels road as a protection for our artillery which had taken up position on that road. It was either the enemy's attempt to take out the guns because of their destructive fire, or his intent to open the Brussels road, that made him try several times to overrun the guns. But the attacks of his considerable cavalry detachments were repulsed each time by our well directed gunfire and musketry. The limited view from my location and my little knowledge of military matters will not allow me to judge as to the probable consequences, had the enemy's foiled attempts succeeded.

Around noon on the 17th the battalion retreated from Quatre Bras to Waterloo, along with the remainder of the army. As the battle line was formed in the evening, it was assigned its position at the extreme left wing. During the night from the 17th to the 18th, one of its companies occupied a village (Smohain) located in front of the battalion. Defending this village and maintaining contact with the localities to its left and right was the battalion's objective.

Our lack of ammunition was barely alleviated by cartridges being obtained from the Duchy of Nassau Regiments.[371] But before these supplies arrived, the battalion was already facing the enemy, and his tirailleurs were engaged with our skirmishers. At first, holding the village seemed not to be overly difficult. But when in the afternoon the French right wing started to press hard on our left wing, in support of his operations in the corner space,[372] our lone company was no longer able to withstand the enemy assaults. It had to be reinforced, first with the grenadier company, and then with No. 1 and eventually with part of No. 2 Company. It was during this phase of fighting that Lieutenant Muller[373] was wounded, then myself, and finally Captain Hartmann. Both these two died from their wounds,[374] whereas I, still alive, have not yet fully recovered. The battalion nevertheless held on to the village, and although contact [to adjoining units] was sometimes interrupted, it was promptly restored again.

Letter from First Lieutenant Eberhard to his wife after the battle

Brussels, 21 June 1815

To Mrs Eberhard in Dillenburg,
Don't be upset if I report to you that I have been wounded. My wound is not a dangerous one. In the battle on the 18th, I had the misfortune to be hit by a musket ball in the lower part of my right arm; one of the bones has been damaged, while the other has remained unharmed. I was standing with crossed arms in the ranks, and this circumstance saved my life, otherwise the ball would have penetrated the right side of my body. It must have been between one and three o'clock, during the fiercest part of the action, that I was wounded. After having been carried behind the front line and having received an emergency dressing, I had to put an extremely burdensome march of five hours behind me through some terrible confusion in order to get here. I did not go to a hospital but took lodging in an inn where I am well taken care of although I am still confined to bed. As soon as my condition is improved, I will seek permission to return home to you to fully recover under your good care. I will write you more about this. Until then all the best, my love, from your truly loving Eberhard.

PS I have dictated this letter to Sergeant Dartell who has accompanied me here from the battlefield and is now my personal attendant. Among the wounded of our battalion, beside myself, are Captain Hartmann and Lieutenant Muller, the former also in his arm, and the latter in his foot, neither of their wounds being dangerous. Fritz (von Reichenau) has been hit in one of his legs, and Major Hegmann had a leg shot off.

Nassau Reserve of Major General Kruse

1st Nassau Regiment

No. 49 From *Belle-Alliance*

Pflugk-Harttung's letter no. 71 Report of the 1st Light Regiment Nassau on the events from 15 June to 18 June.

Strength
Brigade staff : Major General von Kruse; Captain Morenhoffen[375] serving as Chief of the General Staff; Adjutants Captain von Bose,[376] 2nd Lieutenant Count Walderdorff;[377] Freiherr von Breidbach Burresheim[378] serving as Major à la suite; 3 mounted orderlies.

1st Infantry Regiment
Staff: Regimental Commander Colonel von Steuben,[379] Lieutenant Colonel von Hagen.[380] Commanders: 1st Battalion, Major von Weyhers, 2nd Battalion, Major von Nauendorf, 3rd Battalion, Major von Preen.[381]

15 June
At readiness for the expected departure. At eleven o'clock in the evening, the regiment is ordered to be ready to march off.

16 June
Order of 1:30 a.m. The regiment was to be present at seven o'clock in full strength at the rendezvous at the Leuven gate and wait for further orders. Because of the distance of several of the quarters, only the 1st and 2nd Battalions were able to appear at the rendezvous at the time ordered, and part of these only with great effort. Without waiting for the 3rd Battalion, at nine o'clock the march was commenced around the city and on the road to Charleroi. Short halt in the forest of Soignes, a longer one at the village of Mont St Jean to rest up the young men who had been marching since the night and were exhausted from the heat. The road was filled with the troops of Lieutenant General Picton, the Brunswick cavalry, the headquarters personnel and baggage, etc.

While we rested at Mont St Jean, a cannonade could be heard coming from Ligny, and soon thereafter also from Quatre Bras. General Kruse and his adjutants ride ahead in a hurry. The regiment continues its march by sections, right in front, [encountering] returning baggage, a large and increasing number of wounded of the 2nd Regiment Nassau, of Brunswickers, and of the Scottish regiments. Due to a misunderstanding, Colonel von Steuben has the regiment make a halt at a place by the side of the road, after several hours marching, only to have it immediately move to another one further ahead. After remaining there for a quarter of an hour, an order was received from General von Kruse to continue the march in all haste.

Towards eight o'clock the regiment arrives at the first houses of Quatre Bras shortly before the end of the action, and here meets the 3rd Battalion of the 2nd Ducal [Nassau] Regiment that had been taken out of the firing line due to its losses. The regiment forms up to the right of the highway in closed column by divisions and heads drawn forward, in support of the 2nd Regiment in front of it. The skirmishers of the 1st Battalion, 2nd Regiment, backed up by its battalion, were still heavily engaged in the wood in front, under the eyes of General von Kruse. The enemy guns fire at the position. The 3rd Battalion arrives as dusk sets in. The 1st [Nassau] Regiment had no losses. The troops set up their bivouac at this position.

17 June

The regiment took up position forward and to the right from that at night, close behind the wood, the battalions unformed and spread out. At ten o'clock, forming up for the retreat on the Genappe road, in double closed up [solid] section column. At this village, the Dyle is crossed by wading. The retreat was executed with perfect calm and in good order. Behind the outpost of La Haye Sainte, a left turn is made onto the road. This is followed to the centre of the plateau, and with heads turning right and at a distance of 100 paces off the road, the regiment marches up in line, thereby facing the road. Heavy showers; then stacking of arms and dispatching men to pick up foodstuffs and go for water. An alarm is sounded. The regiment moves forward into the position. After the exchange of a few shots, everybody returns and bivouacs. The rains last throughout the entire night until the following forenoon.

18 June

Strength of the regiment under the colours: 66 officers, 2,834 NCOs and privates, a total of 2,900.

At nine or ten o'clock movements are observed on the enemy side on the opposite ridges. Quiet then returns. The skies are brightening, although remaining cloudy and overcast. Towards twelve o'clock, the regiment stands to arms. The battalions are marched off, the 1st battalion in closed column to the right, the 2nd and 3rd to the left. After a roll call, all battalions turn about, move down the gentle slope on this side of the plateau and take up position about 200 paces to the rear in the 2nd line.

A short time later the 1st Battalion was drawn forward into the 1st line, at about 300 to 400 paces to the right forward of the 2nd Battalion. The cavalry of the army was deployed in several lines at about the same distance to the rear, in the plain before and to the side of the Mont St Jean farm and village.

At twelve o'clock the first cannon shot was fired. The enemy commenced his movement against the right flank, which was opposed by 40 guns and several battalions. This action lasted without great exertions for about one hour. By that time, the French artillery had been emplaced and began a most violent cannonade from well served heavy guns. Most of this vigorous fire was directed at the plateau. Placed on this were four to five Hanoverian battalions, two English battalions and the Ducal 1st Regiment, of which, as already mentioned, the 1st Battalion was in the 1st line, and the 2nd and 3rd in the 2nd line. After remaining in their first position for one to one and a half hours, during which only the 2nd Battalion had one man killed, the two last mentioned battalions were drawn 60 to 100 paces nearer to, and close behind, the slope, while maintaining enough distance between each other to be able to deploy. The 1st Battalion now began to suffer heavy losses, as also the 2nd Battalion, with 30 men killed and 50 to 60 wounded within a short time. The 3rd Battalion suffered less, either by accident or perhaps from being better protected.

At about four o'clock the flanqueur company of the 2nd Battalion was detached to the La Haye Sainte farm as reinforcement for the battalion of the German Legion. On its advance, it lost its commander, Captain von Weitershausen,[382] who was killed. Together with other troops, later on it drove the enemy out of the said outpost, but had one corporal and seven privates taken prisoner. The remainder returned again to their battalion.

After the enemy artillery had caused great harm to the various battalions, and in particular to the 1st Battalion of the 1st Ducal Regiment, and after our artillery was for the most part demolished or out of ammunition, very strong masses of French heavy cavalry now moved up. The time may have been five o'clock. Covered by their guns, they attacked uninterruptedly our infantry for over an hour, which, without artillery and only weakly supported by cavalry, was made to depend on its courage. The enemy's cuirassiers broke through the 1st and 2nd lines and eventually halted only 100 paces from the first English infantry line, bravely defying their fire. Due to the havoc caused in the 1st Battalion of the 1st Regiment by the canister fire at short distance from a French battery, and taking advantage of the smoke, these cuirassiers, who were halted nearby, were able to at once charge into the battalion. They wiped out about 1½ companies and took two officers, one of them badly wounded, and 20 wounded men prisoner.[383]

Much weakened by this noteworthy action, it [the enemy cavalry] retreated, partly of itself, partly upon being driven back by the English and Netherlands cavalry, and infantry moved up in its place. Napoleon's Guard took possession of the plateau, with our infantry withdrawing only 100 paces. A violent fire fight broke out.

Between about six and seven o'clock, on orders from General von Kruse, the 2nd Battalion of the 1st Regiment moved into the first line. Together with the remnants of the 1st Battalion, it was led by the Crown Prince of the Netherlands and the said general in a bayonet charge. The Prince of Orange was badly wounded in this attack.[384] Most of the enemy mass wavered upon being attacked, in spite of its earlier effective and murderous fire, but failure to press it further kept the attack from turning into a success. The much weakened battalions returned in passable order to the site from where the attack had been started.

Several battalions on both sides in the first English line were retiring[385] so that the plateau was now only held on both sides by some weak troop bodies. General von Kruse joined one of these with the 3rd and the remainder of the 2nd Battalion at the left flank of the centre near the highway (where there was a shack built of brick). The 1st Battalion, by now almost completely wiped out, remained in the 2nd line. These troops returned, as best as they could, the fire of the French infantry now spreading out on the plateau. Sounds of firing from the left flank and the rear made it appear as if the extreme left flank of the army had been considerably pushed back.

After a glorious charge by the English cavalry, the battle took a turn for the better. The Duke of Wellington had all the infantry on the right flank move to the centre. The Prussian army now also appeared on the enemy's right flank; the entire line went over to the attack, and victory was won in less than half an hour.

At sunset, the 2nd and 3rd Battalions of the Ducal 1st Regiment advanced onto the highway at La Haye Sainte farm, out of whose yard and gardens the last enemies were making off before them. The road was covered with a large amount of war material and wounded Frenchmen of the Imperial Guard.

After a short halt below the ridge of La Belle Alliance to restore order, the battalions continued their advance, passing by an enemy horse artillery park of about 40 guns with caissons, to the outer buildings of La Belle Alliance where they found Captain Schuler[386] of the 1st Battalion who had suffered many wounds. They [arrived] at Rosomme at the same time as the Royal Prussian troops, and in order to avoid the crowded and impassable village of Maison du Roi they attempted to regain the highway by bypassing it to the right across the fields.

But the battalions turned too far to the right in the darkness and after an hour of a fatiguing march over the soft soil they were led back by General von Kruse to a camp of straw huts that had been occupied by the French Guard on the day before. Located on the far side from Maison du Roi across from the house named La Gros Caillou, they arrived here around midnight, numbering about 500 to 600 combatants (the 2nd Battalion had only 238 men left with its colours).

19 June
The regiment remained at its bivouac . . .

No. 50 From *Belle-Alliance*
Pflugk-Harttung's letter no. 70. Strength of the 1st Light Regiment Nassau at the Time of the Battle of La Belle Alliance.

Duchy of Nassau 1st Regiment, statement by ranks
Strength of the above regiment as of 18 June 1815 before the battle.

Staff	
Colonel	1
Lieutenant-Colonel	1
Majors	3
Adjutant Majors	3
Regimental Surgeon	1
Battalion Surgeons	3
Divisional Surgeon	1
Sergeants	12
Corporals	1
Privates	<u>33</u>
	59
1st Battalion	
Captains	6
1st Lieutenants	6
2nd Lieutenants	6
Sergeants	47
Corporals	67
Musicians	18
Privates	<u>801</u>
	951

2nd Battalion

Captains	6
1st Lieutenants	6
2nd Lieutenants	6
Sergeants	46
Corporals	66
Musicians	18
Privates	795
	943

Landwehr Battalion

Captains	6
1st Lieutenants	5
2nd Lieutenants	6
Sergeants	40
Corporals	63
Musicians	18
Privates	809
	947

Steuben, Colonel

1st Battalion, 1st Nassau Regiment

No. 51 Major General F. A. Weiz's cover letter to his Waterloo report to Duke Adolph of Nassau

Hessisches Hauptstaatsarchiv Wiesbaden, Manuscript File No. 130 II 2915, 9v–11.

Report of Major General Friedrich August Weiz on the 1st Battalion 1st Nassau Regiment at Waterloo[387]

Wiesbaden, 12 June 1863

Most serene Duke,
Most gracious Duke and Lord!
Your Highness's so very gracious letter of the 22nd of last month and the opinion expressed therein, of my account regarding my experiences in Your Highness's 1st Regiment, viz. 1st Battalion, in the Battle of Waterloo, which honoured me in the highest measure, has caused me the greatest pleasure and happiness. The most graciously given permission to wrest this event from oblivion obligates me to the deepest and most humble expression of my gratitude.

Your Highness may find a measure of the depth of my gratitude in that there can be no second human being who takes a greater interest in the past trials and fate of Your Highness's regiments than myself, or rather in the regiments in whose ranks I had the rare fortune to experience the most interesting and happiest times of my life.

Due to this interest, it has been my desire, entertained for a long time, to preserve this history of the ducal troops. To the preservation thereof is attached a special wish, that the present and future commanders may hereby be guided at least to some extent, towards knowledge that cannot be learned from books alone. Every single experience that a superior lacks in our profession may have to be gained in war at very great expense.

Apart from Your Highness's satisfaction and approval, I would consider as the greatest reward for my modest efforts, if some of the few suggestions that I believed I was permitted to make, could be of use to one or the other of the ducal officers.

I would not deprive myself of the opportunity to write in my own hand this copy of my work desired by Your Highness. It may serve as my intercessor, whenever it comes before Your Highness's eyes, to remind Your Highness that I remain in most grateful and deepest respect, as Your Highness's most humble, most obedient

Weiz, Major General

No. 52 Copy of the report of Major General Friedrich August Weiz on his experiences as a captain and company commander in the Duchy of Nassau 1st Battalion 1st Regiment during the Battle of Waterloo

Wiesbaden, 20 May 1863

The following report on the events during the action on 17 and 18 June 1815 relate only to those which involved the 1st Battalion of the Ducal 1st Regiment and happened within its line of sight, and are truthfully described by an eyewitness.

As is well known, the Duke of Wellington's army retreated on 17 June 1815 past Genappe to the Waterloo position, in advance of Mont St Jean, where the battle took place on 18 June. The retreat occurred in three parallel columns, as follows:

1 the artillery and the train column on the main chaussee,
2 the infantry to its left, and
3 the cavalry to its right

A cavalry corps under Lord Uxbridge covered the retreat on this side of Genappe, it was heavily engaged with the pursuing enemy cavalry and suffered significant losses. But owing to the leadership of its commander and the bravery of the English cavalry, the army's retreat could proceed without any more difficulties.

The command work regarding [the progress of] the several columns, as well the positioning of the individual regiments and battalions, etc., etc., was handled in exemplary fashion and certainly redounds to the highest credit to the staff officers in charge. The competency and circumspection displayed by this high level of leadership resulted in three most favourable preconditions for next day's success, which have seldom occurred in history, to wit:

1 a gain in time,
2 the troops not being unnecessarily and thoughtlessly exhausted from marches and counter marches, and finally
3 The required trust in their leadership being raised in all corps, which was needed towards assuring success in the impending battle.

To understand fully and appreciate the value and meaning of this kind of trust, one needs to assess, for example, the make up and condition at the time of the Ducal 1st Regiment. Except for the staff officers and captains, the great majority of subalterns and more than nine tenths of the rank and file had never faced an enemy or fought in a battle. Of the 2,900 men that this regiment consisted of at the day of marching off from Wiesbaden, which was on 20 May, more than 2,000 were raw recruits who had left their homes only four to five weeks earlier.

The training of these men in such a short time had, of course, to be limited to that absolutely necessary. It was indeed a most challenging task due to the small number of experienced officers and NCOs. However, the active cooperation and the good will, which inspired all men, overcame all difficulties in a manner which should never be forgotten in the history of the Nassau regiments. There was no question of parade ground drill, to assure staying in rank and file and the effective use of the weapons were the most important objectives. That this was achieved by all company commanders has been proven in the outcome. It would be difficult to obtain similar results nowadays [May 1863]. Although the present generation is more intelligent than that of 48 years ago, it cannot be denied that military virtues; loyalty, obedience and good will, cannot be found any longer in the same degree as in the troops of yesteryear.[388] To cite an example: throughout the campaign, not a single case of serious misconduct had occurred in No. 5 Company, and only a very few reprimands had to be issued for minor infractions of discipline.

It will not be out of context to mention here that, from the day of marching off from Wiesbaden until arrival in the Brussels vicinity, besides the six to seven hours of marching a day, several hours of exercises were put in. This was possible because the units marched off at dawn each day, that no rendezvous was held and that they proceeded on the shortest route to their next quarters, with each company being given its route from here [Wiesbaden] to Brussels. As already mentioned about the army staff work on 17 June, this had its advantage in three respects:

1 a gain in time,
2 the young men's vigour was not needlessly and thoughtlessly squandered, which had been strained to the utmost since their induction into the regiment, and finally
3 in this manner, the individual commanders were given a better and more extensive opportunity for gathering experience in independent command duties and in training their units. All of this would not have been possible, had there been a daily regiment size rendezvous and a marching in a large composite column.

This arrangement was found to be advantageous and practical to the extent that it was retained on the regiment's march from Paris back to the Fatherland.

The unexpectedly rapid arrival of the French army and the resultant sudden mobilisation of the English army were the likely cause that little, or even no, preparations had been made for the latter's food supply. He was an ill advised commander who had failed, due to inexperience or indifference, to advise the young soldiers to avail themselves of the necessaries from their hosts at their quarters, depending upon the hosts' willingness and resources. Even if a battle is to be fought in a land of plenty, the concentration of hundreds of thousands of troops, if only for a few days, makes it impossible to assure a regular food supply. Under these conditions the introduction of a so called 'iron rations', as used in the Holstein campaign, is strongly to be recommended and should never be overlooked.[389]

As already mentioned before, the various corps and regiments had been placed in their positions by the staff officers and had settled themselves in, as well as possible, with those having something to cook starting a fire under the kettles. [However], between about seven and eight o'clock in the evening, a strong French force, supported by numerous guns, advanced towards our position and began a cannonade.

The Duke of Wellington in person gave the necessary orders to repulse the attack, as, by coincidence, he had been riding over from the army's left flank and happened to be nearby. The nearest regiments, among them the 1st Regiment Nassau, were called to arms and advanced into a position more favourable for the defence. Several batteries were moved forward and responded vigorously to the firing of the French, who then retreated. The enemy obviously intended to verify whether the English army was preparing to accept battle in this position.

Also to be noted is the foresight of placing the old battle tested regiments in between the less seasoned ones; as an example, the 1st Battalion of the 1st Regiment was posted in the first line,[390] with an English regiment to its right, and to its left a battalion of the German Legion, etc. etc. The 2nd and 3rd Battalions of the 1st Regiment stood in second line, about 150 paces behind the 1st [Battalion], and behind those were the artillery reserve and a large corps of heavy cavalry.

All in all, the troops posted on the plateau of Mont St Jean consisted of two English regiments, four Hanoverian battalions, the 1st Regiment Nassau and two battalions of the German Legion, of which Major Baring's rifle-armed Jäger Battalion had occupied the farm La Haye Sainte, which was situated close to the main line and next to the chaussee.

Soon after the enemy's retreat and our corps' return to their state of rest, dusk set in and with it [came] heavy rains which lasted until the morning of 18 June. This, as well as the heavy soil and the corn [standing] up to a man's height, made it a most uncomfortable night for the troops. There was no rest for the men, badly though they were in need of it.

Upon daybreak, and after the rains had eased off, the first order of business was that of cleaning the muskets, at that time still fitted with flintlocks and making them usable as best as possible, after these had been in the rain throughout the night and had become totally unserviceable. Drying the wet clothes and putting equipment, uniforms, and ammunition back in shape were other duties this morning.

In this way, what appeared to be impossible was achieved through the officers' efforts, and another purpose was served, that of leaving the young men no moment for reflection by keeping them busy all the time, which otherwise might have badly affected their fighting morale. The morning hours thus passed quite rapidly; at about eleven o'clock the call to arms was given, as the beginning of the battle came closer and could be expected at any moment now. The companies and battalions moved into position, the muskets were loaded, and it was at 12 noon that the first cannon shot announced the beginning of the terribly serious game.

Some comments need here to be made regarding the formation of the battalions of the 1st Ducal Regiment and certain related items. The 2nd and 3rd Battalions, in the second line, were formed in attack columns.

The 1st Battalion stood in the first line and, inexplicably, was formed in columns of divisions, with the right wing *in front* that is, every two companies at that time formed a division, or two pelotons; of 160 men per company.[391] The pelotons were too strong and unwieldy. This formation of the 1st Battalion was retained throughout most of the day; its serious disadvantage was that, due to the depth of the column, it suffered heavy losses from the incessant artillery fire, and that, during the cavalry attacks, only the two companies in front were able to fire [at the enemy riders]. Many of the soldiers passed the day or were killed without having fired even once. There can be no worse situation for young soldiers or honourable officers.

The 1st Battalion was commanded by Major von Weyhers, a well educated man and an in the highest degree energetic and brave officer; he, however, lacked the talent and competency to train and lead a battalion of young men, such as this one. To this day, this officer must be blamed for never for a single moment having commanded and exercised the battalion entrusted to him, from the day it was mobilised until the day of battle. The men had never heard their commander's voice. If the battalion preserved its honourable name on the day of battle, it was not his, but rather the battalion officers' merit, and theirs only. Least understandable was that the higher authorities let the matter slide, as it did; it was not clear if and what considerations were here at play. Everybody was of the opinion, and justifiably so, that under these circumstances no special considerations can and should be allowed.

The battalions in the first line to the immediate right and left of the 1st Battalion, each at a strength of about 600 to 700 men, were kept moving all the time by their commanders through ployments and deployments. Under the exposure to well directed artillery fire, these were conducted with great competency. These commanders should be commended for always knowing the right moment when to put their force in best defensive order. They had their battalions deployed [in line] if exposed to heavy artillery fire; they ordered them to form hollow squares whenever threatened by cavalry attacks. This procedure had the advantage that the men paid less attention to any danger, busy as they always were, and that their losses were much less in comparison to those of the 1st Battalion. In its case, not even a single attempt was made to follow a similar procedure, even though there was no reason not to do so. All that was thus left to the battalion was to face the death dealing gun fire for hours on end.

The battle started at 12 noon, as mentioned earlier, hundreds of guns on both sides kept up a devastating cannonade for several hours. To keep the infantry which defended the plateau from remaining a ready target, it was retired to the rearward slope. Still, the battalion's ranks were struck by many cannon balls.

On our side, the artillery had been placed at the crest of the plateau with as many guns as the terrain would permit. It happened several times during the counter battery fire that fresh batteries had to replace the demolished ones. In an early instance, three guns of a recently arrived battery were smashed before having fired a single shot, one of this battery's caissons blew up at the very moment that it was passing near the front of the 1st Battalion. With the caisson all ablaze, its horses panicked and drove it straight towards the large artillery park, from where they had come. A major disaster was averted when some dragoons rode up in a hurry and, while racing along, stabbed and brought down the horses.

Between two and three o'clock, the firing by the enemy artillery slackened off; it had caused terrible losses among our battalions, even though nobody had yet come face to face with the enemy.

As of this moment, the enemy's assault could be expected to take on a different form, and for that reason the battalion had to move forward again to the crest of the plateau. The artillery, on the other hand, was retired; only two guns that had no horses left remained right in front of the 1st Battalion. Of the gun crew, only a few, four or five men, had been left unharmed. They remained with their guns and serviced them until the attacking force came so close that they just had time to seek protection in the battalion's ranks. As soon as the assailants had been repulsed, these gunners rushed back to their cannons and performed their incredible feats. These soldiers, Hanoverians,[392] as intrepid and brave as they were deserved the highest recognition. It has remained unknown whether they indeed received it.

The advance of the infantry towards the plateau was directed by the generals in charge in the area, Lord Hill and his Highness the Crown Prince of the Netherlands in person. They hurried between the several corps and kept up the soldiers' spirits with encouraging words. For the Nassauers, the best example was given by their own commander, the brave and highly respected General von Kruse, who with his sensible and circumspect leadership inspired confidence and courage.

At the time when the firing of the artillery had ceased and the infantry had advanced to the plateau, everybody was filled with an all encompassing, vitalising, uplifting, and even solemn, feeling. Morale was at an all time high, [particularly] in view of the generals hurrying back and forth with their retinue. There was a feeling that victory was near, and yet, the most arduous fighting was still to occur, only in a different form than heretofore.

In the face of a skilled and energetic adversary, and with five to six hours left until dark, such was to be expected, and became reality as our eyes perceived the wide ranks and deep columns of the [approaching] enemy.

We did not have to wait long before the enemy appeared. Our eyes had hardly adjusted to the new situation, when cuirassiers moved to the attack from the lower ground in our front. At first, only their helmets could be seen, an instant later their cuirasses, and, finally, did the men and their horses come into full view. With every moment, the threatening storm was moving closer to our front the battalions were ordered, and warned not to open fire too early at the attacking cavalry. Our young soldiers were still unfamiliar with using their weapons effectively. To prevent them from starting to fire unless ordered, the officers of our first line units moved before the front of their companies.

The cuirassiers approached in three echelons on a two squadron front spaced not too far apart. It was probably a fortunate circumstance for the 1st Battalion that the enemy's most advanced echelon first attacked the English regiment to our right.[393] By exemplary behaviour, it fired its first volley when the riders were at a distance of 60 to 80 paces. The effect was spectacular, many riders and horses fell, and the remainder of the squadrons scattered like chaff. But as soon as the muskets were reloaded, the next echelon attacked. It was received in the same successful manner as the first assaulting wave.

These examples happening in our immediate vicinity were of the highest significance for our young soldiers. The third echelon of cuirassiers now attacked the 1st Battalion and the German Legion battalion to our left [actually the Hanoverian Feldbattalion Bremen] at the same time, and was most forcefully repulsed. Although the cuirassiers now continued and repeated their attacks most energetically, it became obvious that their confidence waned to the same degree as it was gaining in the ranks of the infantry, and that all their assaults were to fail. In their support there now appeared a strong regiment of heavy cavalry, carabiniers, having yellow helmets and cuirasses. Part of the remainder of the cuirassiers joined this regiment and another part remained as *soutien* [reserves]. All our battalions on the plateau were now attacked at the same time, but none wavered. They all stood like rocks. But then several squadrons, animated by their officers, stormed through the space between two battalions towards those in the second line. These battalions were in a precarious situation, they could not fire their muskets because of our own troops before them, and they thus had to face the attack with only their raised bayonets.

In no time was that danger averted as the nearest English dragoons rushed towards the French riders. There ensued a heated clash of arms.

The horsemen on both sides displayed feats of unexcelled bravery in this cavalry duel between our two lines, as was confirmed by all who were able and near enough to witness [the encounter].

Finding themselves without support, the French, at least those who still could, all of a sudden stormed back in a wild flight through the space between the 1st Battalion and that of the German Legion, Englishmen and French pell-mell intermixed. In their running battle, they rushed through the battalion intervals like a storm cloud. Their impact was so heavy and so close to the men on our flank that they could protect themselves against being overrun only by stabbing with their bayonets at the passing host.

As long as the cavalry attacks were continued and repeated on the plateau, the enemy artillery had held its fire, as mentioned earlier. But their guns resumed their cannonade after the horsemen had failed in their assaults and were retreating to the lower ground in front of our line, and just as fast, our own artillery went into feverish action. During this time, two exploding shells fell in short succession into the tightly packed column of the 1st Battalion and did great execution.

After this artillery duel had lasted for about half an hour, the battle went again into a new phase [by that time, the Anglo-Allied artillery in the 1st Nassau's sector had been disabled or was out of ammunition]. In the next attack against the defenders on the plateau, several horse artillery batteries moved up, accompanied by strong cavalry formations. Soon, one could quite clearly see that sets of two guns were spaced at a considerable distance from one another, the reason being, as it turned out, to enable each of them to fire case shot at every one of our battalions with greatest effect. Their cavalry moved up behind their artillery and also to the side of the guns.

Two guns unlimbered in front of the 1st Battalion at a distance of 200 to 300 paces and started at once to cover us with case shot (at about this time, a light rain set in; the enemy artillery therefore used portfires instead of matches to ignite the next charge. Whenever this happened, the circular movement of the portfires to the fireholes could be clearly seen, even at a distance, and each time that this occurred, a certain uneasiness or painful sensation could be noticed in our soldiers' eyes. The cavalry stationed at the side of the guns gradually moved closer, yet stayed at enough of a distance from these to avoid obstructing their line of fire. The 1st Battalion's situation became ever more perilous with each moment, and extremely so, on its front the two murderous guns, and finally on its right side, 100 paces away at the most the cuirassiers who waited for signs of disarray in our ranks to charge at the battalion; that disarray threatened to happen any minute now under the increased cannonade of case shot.

The first rounds from the two guns went too high and caused no losses to the battalion; all the more terrible were the following ones. From now on, so many men were levelled by each shot that it took superhuman efforts by the officers to have the dead removed and to close the ranks and to keep them closed. At this time, the three officers of the No. 1 Company, Captain Rohm[394] and Lieutenants G. Niess[395] and Menzler,[396] had been wounded, and its sergeant had been killed, and all it had left were some young inexperienced NCOs. What must be repeated here is that the battalion was formed in right marched off division column and that therefore, the Grenadier and No. 1 Companies were at the head. The fate of the battalion depended more or less on the steadfastness of these two companies; No. 1 Company could therefore not be left without a leader. Major von Weyhers put Captain Weiz in charge of that company, whose own No. 5 Company stood behind No. 1 Company.[397] First Lieutenant Koehler[398] of No. 5 Company was also wounded at the same, and Lieutenant Macco,[399] a well-educated, though very young and inexperienced officer, depended for support and assistance on two older brave sergeants named Dittmann and Munsch, and on Corporal Hemming, whose names should never be forgotten in the annals of the regiment.

Any change in command creates by itself an awkward and difficult situation; but it becomes extremely so when this is to happen in a moment of the greatest danger. To the aforementioned officer there was some comfort, if such it can be named, in being well known to the men of No. 1 Company and having established with them a feeling of mutual trust. He had led the company in its exercises during the eight days of its stationing at Wezembeek near Brussels, due to the indisposition of Captain Rohm, its commander.

That moment of greatest danger just mentioned occurred when Major von Weyhers, the battalion commander, decided to have his men rush at, and disable, the two guns which threatened to annihilate the battalion. Captain Schuler, who was the battalion's most senior officer and well recognised for his bravery in battle, made the most strenuous representations against such a move, and with good reason, because it impaired the other battalions' defensive stance, but primarily because it was liable to fail in view of the closeness of the threatening enemy cavalry. Major von Weyhers could not be dissuaded from his decision and gave the order to attack. After the battalion had advanced some 40 to 50 paces, it received two more rounds of case shot which levelled the major and his horse and many soldiers. The resulting disarray and gaps in the ranks caused an unforeseen halt before order could be restored and the ranks be closed, one of the Duke of Wellington's ADCs hurriedly rode up with the strict order for the battalion to move back to its former position at once.

This retreat to the original position could have been executed if one of our cavalry detachments had faced the enemy cavalry in a way that the latter would have been unable to attack our battalion on the move. However, this was not the case; the seriousness of the situation either had not been observed or evaluated, or there was no cavalry of our own at hand. This was a grave mistake or failure on the part of the general in charge of this sector. Even though Major von Weyhers had made the wrong decision by moving out of the battle line, without an order but still with the best intentions, the absence of any effort to rescue [our detachment] was a much graver mistake.

With the wounded Major von Weyhers out of action, Lieutenant Colonel von Hagen [of the regimental staff] assumed command of the 1st Battalion and at once ordered its retreat to the main line. The rearmost four companies turned around and marched off: however, the two in front held their place. In the general turmoil they either did not hear or understand the order to retreat, or kept firing and were too concerned about the approaching enemy. Not the slightest blame can be laid against the two companies.

Barely had they found themselves separated from the others when they were already surrounded and attacked by the cuirassiers. By this time, the fighting strength of the two [companies] amounted to 130 to 140 men at most. There now started a most severe and bloody battle. Pressed together, this cluster of soldiers defended itself in the bravest manner, as was confirmed by all who observed the action. How long this struggle lasted, can no longer be determined, but at least long enough for any allied cavalry to free the embattled detachment from its attackers. That this did not happen, can be considered another great mistake which is all the harder to understand, since not far off a dragoon regiment of the legion had taken up position. Those riders certainly lacked neither courage nor prowess [in battle]; their inaction was a case of absence of decisive leadership at this moment

Since the cuirassiers received reinforcements all the time, the defeat of our detachment was a foregone conclusion, yet in the hope of relief it fought on to the last. Captains Schuler and Weiz, as well as Lieutenant Wollmerscheid,[400] were the only officers with this detachment that was left to its fate. The grenadier company still had 30 to 40 older intrepid soldiers whose bravery made it at all possible that our resistance lasted as long as it did. Two men, Sergeant Schellenberg, from Wehrheim (Usingen district), and Sergeant Jorg, from Limburg, excelled everybody with their steadfastness and gallantry. Both men, of athletic build, conveyed those military virtues already through their demeanour, which now came to the fore: their well aimed fire and their sharp bayonets had disabled many an enemy. For example, the latter [of the two], Jorg, had bayoneted two cuirassiers from their horses, one after the other, although he was wounded by several sabre cuts and had his right eye stabbed from its socket which then hung down on his face. Both NCOs received the Golden Tapferkeits Order[401] for their valour, at Captain Weiz's request.

However, all this led nowhere, with every passing moment the situation of the detachment became more desperate and hopeless. With the defenders' number dwindling, and in the degree that their fighting strength lessened the enemy's pressure increased and became more forceful. In a final thrust, this little troop was totally overrun and dispersed. Some of the men managed to reach the remainder of the battalion; many, however, were to feel the full wrath of the cuirassiers. Still others became prisoners, Captains Schuler and Weiz among them, the former after having been severely wounded in three places. The latter suddenly found himself pressed between the horses of two cuirassier officers and could not but follow their order to surrender. But Captain Weiz was not a prisoner for very long; after being handed over by these officers to a trooper, he managed to escape from his guard within a short time and to hurry off to the safety of the nearest English battalion.

Captain Weiz was prevented for a while, half to three-quarters of an hour, from returning to his battalion, due to the continuing and always renewed cavalry attacks at the time. Meanwhile, this [battalion], or rather the remainder of four companies, had resumed its former position in the line, but, severely weakened, could no longer serve as an independent unit. It was replaced by a battalion from the [army] reserve. General von Kruse combined the remainder [of the battalion] with the 2nd Battalion, before the four battalions of the Imperial Guard advanced to the attack (see his relation dated Malplaquet, 21 June 1815).[402]

Fresh battalions were moved into the line from the reserve and from the right wing. The Guard, and, in fact, the entire French army, were defeated and, due to the timely arrival of the Prussian army and its further pursuit [of the enemy], annihilated to a point that from this hour until the arrival in Paris no enemy soldier was seen anymore. As dusk set in, victory had been completed. The night was spent on the battle field, after our helpless wounded men were sought out and collected. Most of them could not be transported to Brussels until the following day.

The so called Contingents Brigade (1st Light Regiment Nassau) under the command of General von Kruse consisted of:

The 1st and 2nd Battalions of the 1st Regiment, and a Landwehr [Militia] Battalion, at a total of 2,900 men.
The 1st Battalion was commanded by Major von Weyhers.
The 2nd Battalion was commanded by Major von Nauendorf.
The Landwehr Battalion was commanded by Major von Preen.
The regiment was under the command of Colonel von Steuben, and under him was Lieutenant Colonel von Hagen.
The staff of the commanding general consisted of Captains von Morenhofen and von Bose, Major a la Suite von Breidbach, and Lieutenant Count von Walderdorff. The latter two served as adjutants on a voluntary basis.

No. 53 The losses of the General Staff and of the Ducal 1st Regiment on 18 June 1815

	Killed	*Wounded*
General Staff	0	2 Officers
1st Regiment	5 Officers, 249 Rank	19 Officers, 370 Rank
Total	5 Officers, 249 Rank	21 Officers, 370 Rank
Total killed and wounded	26 Officers,[403]	619 Rank and File

2nd Battalion, 1st Nassau Regiment

No. 54 The Waterloo letter of Second Lieutenant Heinrich von Gagern,[404] in the 2nd Battalion, 1st Duchy of Nassau Light Infantry Regiment

Nassauische Heimatblatter, *vol. 46, no. 1, 1956, pp. 17–26.*

Auteuil, 26 July 1815

Dearest Mother!
You will have received my first letter from Paris, and now I keep my promise and give you a more detailed report, not about the battle itself, but about the events and parts of the battle that I witnessed myself. I assume this is of interest to you, although you may already have read quite a few printed and written descriptions of the battle.

During the night from 15 to 16 June we received an order at around half past eleven o'clock to break camp immediately. We packed up everything right away, and by four o'clock in the morning everybody was on the move. The entire regiment assembled outside Brussels, and we then marched as one unit through Brussels, where we heard all kinds of rumours which, however, I will disregard here and on towards Quatre Bras. We already heard the sound of firing several hours away from there. In between, we rested somewhat, but then our columns moved off again and marched towards the battlefield, without us having had either food or drink. Two hours away from the battlefield, the regiment halted and closed up and awaited further orders. General Kruse was riding ahead, however. At this point, we were faced with an extraordinary commotion: an entire baggage column was on the retreat. The immense English baggage train blocked the road in a way that the troops had to march on the fields next to the road and became even more tired than they had already been. We had hardly spent half an hour on this spot when we moved on again through and by the side of the retreating baggage train. But this kind of spectacle ended soon to make way for an even more unpleasant one. For an hour and a half we marched between two files of wounded soldiers, among them quite a few men of our 2nd Regiment.[405] Some of their lightly wounded unwisely told their comrades and fellow countrymen in our regiment that everything had been lost, their entire regiment dispersed, etc. The look of these wounded men was not encouraging, but, as one can imagine, their words made an even worse impression on our young soldiers. Most of the wounded that we met were Scottish Highlanders and Brunswickers, the latter having lost their sovereign on this day.[406] I was most impressed by the Scotsmen, only seldom could one hear one of them moaning or crying. They were walking quietly, these unfortunate men, like lambs being led to the slaughterhouse. Because on and after the day of battle, field hospitals are even more terrible places than slaughter houses.

Towards dusk, we arrived very tired at the battlefield and took position somewhat to the right of the battlefield and the road, which passes through Quatre Bras on to Brussels. There is a crossing of two roads here, which is the reason for the name Quatre Bras. It was now only that we learned about the actual beginning of the affair and, indeed, of the whole campaign. Since this is part of the introduction, I must mention some of this, even though it may appear superfluous.

On 15 June, the French invaded Brabant, overran our advance posts and pushed forward all the time. Major von Normann, in command of the 2nd Battalion, 2nd Regiment [Nassau], was on the drill ground with his battalion when to his surprise he heard the sound of firing coming ever closer. He immediately notified his corps headquarters whereupon he was told to take it easy since this was caused by the Prussians holding firing exercises. As soon as he became fully convinced that he was faced by French troops, he acted with distinction on that day by not waiting for any orders. He withdrew his battalion to a more favourable position, and from there kept a superior French force in check for many hours, so that the other [allied] troops gained the time to concentrate and move to his support.[407] Earlier that day, a Prussian corps under General Ziethen had already been driven back. They [the Nassauers] then held their position throughout the night. The outcome by the evening of 16 June was that the Prussians on the left wing had, in fact, been totally beaten, and that the English army, or rather part of it, since only its smallest part had been in the battle this day, had lost many wounded and killed, although it had maintained its position. On this day we did not come under fire anymore. Some balls whistled over our heads, but not a single man was wounded. As it became really dark, the firing ceased and we had a quiet night. This was the first night I ever spent in the open air. I lay down at the rear of my battalion, next to a wall of the last house of Quatre Bras, and fell asleep, wrapped in my overcoat and hungry after all the exertions of the day.

The French announced that another day had dawned with a cannon shot that went over our heads. The regiment took up arms. We thus stood quietly for several hours. During this time His Serene Highness, our brave Hereditary Prince, came riding up to us; he was still sleepy eyed.[408] Some time afterwards we marched along the right side of the wood, which covered the left wing of the French which was immediately in front of us.[409] We then rounded the extreme corner of the wood and took up position on the right side of the wood. Before us were several battalions of English in front of the wood, leaning with their left wing against our line, although at some distance. Behind us was the 2nd Regiment, which was not at all dispersed, as had been rumoured the day before.

After we had taken up that position, the companies of Captain Waldschmidt and Captain Weitershausen,[410] to the latter of which I belonged, were told off to skirmish and keep an eye on the enemy. Waldschmidt was in charge, being the oldest officer. His order was to search out the Brunswickers who, to the left of us in the wood, were skirmishing with the enemy, and for us to hold back the French. Waldschmidt now led us to the part of the wood that was opposite to where we had been posted in the evening of 16 June. At this place, the French cavalry piquets were several hundred paces in front of us, almost at firing distance. They remained peaceful, and so did we because we were in a delicate situation, not having found the Brunswickers and, moreover, half a company [was] detached to search for the Brunswickers. We found them at last and then realised to our consternation that they were as weak a force as ours; both sides questioned one another who was to depend on whom, they on us, or we on them. The commander of the Brunswickers, in charge of our body of troops, had now been ordered to follow the allied army, which had retreated several hours earlier. Things were becoming scary: the French were already in possession of Quatre Bras, and we had to pass by them at a distance of a rifle shot. Fortunately, they appeared to be too busy plundering the place to be paying any attention to what was going on around them. In short, we were lucky to be off without having lost a single man on this day. We had even made two prisoners who had lost their way. But just five minutes later, and we all might have been prisoners ourselves.[411] That is the way things were going.

We followed the army as fast as possible on our march. Wellington had left another corps behind which, while retreating, was to keep the French from advancing too fast. But that corps operated on the other side of Quatre Bras and could not support us in our retreat. It was around noon that we left the wood and, without having had any rest or food, joined the full army in the evening at five o'clock. Its major part had arrived about two hours earlier.

So the army had retreated on this day and had taken up position at Waterloo and Mont St Jean, in the first place because the French position at Quatre Bras was very much in their favour, whereas ours was inferior to theirs. We also needed to give the Prussians the opportunity to come to our help if there was to be a battle. They had retreated to a point from where they could not have helped us at Quatre Bras because of the great distance. Napoleon's planning had turned out quite well so far, because he wanted to beat the Prussians first, and then fall upon us. But he had been mistaken in one respect; he believed that, once beaten, the Prussians would not recover very soon, much less be able to attack again right on the second day. But one has to give the Prussians their due, they are tenacious and not easily deterred. Still, they cannot work miracles, because the age of miracles is far gone.

Our feelings of relief to be back with our regiment can only be imagined [by one] who himself had been in danger of being taken prisoner by the French.

This day, 17 June, and the following, the 18th, were the days on which I had to suffer the most hardships. The 17th was the very first day on which I had to walk on foot for a day's march because I had to leave my little black horse with the regiment when we advanced on our skirmishing assignment. So I had to walk for the entire length of the march, and this after I had nothing to eat but dry bread for two days, and, secondly, after I had a fit of nausea that very morning, and, thirdly, having to suffer through the fiercest heat until about three o'clock in the afternoon, which left me all wet [with perspiration]. At three o'clock we had a terrible downpour. Everything that had become wet from the heat was now totally soaked by the rain. At first I had my coat slung over my shoulder; but then it became too heavy for me and I gave it to a soldier to carry, and so I slogged on through the mud. The rain had let up a bit, but continued on and on even after our arrival. While under way, I had quickly cut a piece from a pig that the soldiers had slaughtered, and looked forward to a delicious meal. We had hardly reached our position when the firing came ever closer; the French misbehaved to a point that their balls were flying over our heads. They could easily have hit somebody! Besides, they could at least have waited until my pig's meat had been fully cooked, but no, I had to take it out of the kettle and fry it on a stick over an open fire to get it ready a bit quicker. Still, they did not even allow me that much time, and in the end I had to eat it half raw with a piece of bread. That certainly was not very considerate of the French, polite people that they are otherwise.

By now, our rearguard had reached our forward posts. Wellington had left it behind to delay the enemy's advance. Yet the French continued pushing ahead and it was decided to stop them right then and there. Everybody was ordered to take up arms. The French now moved up some artillery pieces and fired at us, although with little or no loss to us, in fact, none in our regiment. On our side, some English batteries moved into action and silenced the French guns with enfilading fire, and the French corps then retreated. Thus ended 17 June.

The night from the 17th to the 18th was awful. I was able to sleep for only three hours, and, in fact, until there was not a single dry thread left on me. I had my coat dried on the evening before, but it was wet through and through again. For my bedding I had gathered some wheat straw, and then fell asleep. By twelve o'clock I had had enough and started to stand by the fire to dry myself on all sides. My portmanteau had been left with the baggage and I thus could not change clothes.

On the morning of the 18th we had to see to it that the soldiers cleaned their muskets. They would not have been able to fire a single shot because they were all wet and rusty inside and out.

After ten o'clock word arrived that the French were coming. I joined Major von Nauendorff[412] as he went over to the highlanders in the first line. From there we saw them advance on a broad front. Soon thereafter our regiment took up arms, as did the others; Wellington now rode along the entire length of the army and gave orders for the positioning of each regiment. What I could see of our army had all been formed in squares. At around twelve o'clock noon the guns started a vigorous fire, particularly those on our side. After all, ours had to do double duty since in the morning there were 40,000 on our side, and the French had 105,000 men according to the lowest estimate,[413] which seems to be the correct one, and then theirs were the best of their veterans. In the beginning, most of the balls flew over our heads; but after about 1½ hours, things were heating up. The second one killed one of our men standing right in front of me, and I received such a blow on my arm that I was tossed aside for several files. Now I do not know exactly whether the blow against my arm was from the spent ball that had killed that man, or whether it was from a piece of a smashed musket. In short, it hurt quite a bit for several minutes but then I no longer felt a thing.

Not much later, a stupid ball from a canister shot hit the upper yellow fitting of my sword scabbard and ripped the sword-belt apart; I threw it away along with the scabbard because I did not want to carry those with me anymore. That ball certainly was mistaken if it thought I had enough money to pay for a new one; thank God that the Duke will have to pay for it 'that Ibel and my bad luck' [a pun on the name of the Duke's chief of cabinet][414] will allow me that much. But that was not all of it yet. Before long, there comes a shell which has the impertinence to explode at the very corner where I am standing; it kills three soldiers and slashes at my foot which still gives me trouble, tears apart my trousers and moreover shatters my sword that I had stuck into the ground next to me. Now that made me really angry because that thing had hellishly burned me, and at first I could not step down on this foot. But then I saw that everything was still in its right place, the skin as well as the flesh. My poor trousers which I still wear at this moment I wrapped with my handkerchief. I picked up the musket of a dead soldier as a replacement for my sword and returned to my square. In the meantime, it had advanced 40 paces because too many balls had come down at the former place. But we were not spared at the new place, and I must admit in all seriousness that we had a dreadfully high number of killed and wounded during these hours.

Immediately after I had been wounded, the company to which I belonged was detached forward to assist the Brunswickers in their defence of a farm.[415] Major von Nauendorff ordered me to remain behind; he apparently intended to send me back because of my wound, as I found out later. He seemed to believe that my wound was more serious than it was. Before the company arrived at the farm, my company commander was wounded, and when he was about to be carried back he was killed by another bullet. Captain Waldschmidt had also been wounded during the first half hour. On my part, I would hardly have been hurt if I had worn boots. But that was not possible at that time because of my sore feet, and I wore large gaiter shoes.

This immense artillery fire lasted from twelve until after seven o'clock, interrupted only by some cavalry charges, which, however, were repulsed by the brave English cavalry. It was then that our battalion was ordered to make a bayonet attack against a battalion of the French Guard.[416] Things had come to a crisis because the long awaited Prussians still had not arrived yet. Some Allied battalions had already been completely dispersed, and the French attacked with renewed vigour. Our battalion advanced, however, the Landwehr Battalion somewhat back to our left; we were covered by the cavalry. The major drawback was that our artillery was completely out of ammunition and that we were not supported by even a single gun. We attacked two times, and were repelled each time. The brave Crown Prince of Orange rode by the side of our square during the first time and encouraged our soldiers, but was also wounded next to our square.[417] A short time before, I had seen our brave Hereditary Prince riding back, who had also been wounded.[418] We had to pause quite a while between each attack, partly in order to regroup the soldiers, partly to allow them some rest.

In the [final] advance of our square we passed by the farm that our company had earlier defended and had been driven out of by the French in their assault on the farm with the support of cavalry. There must have been some murderous musketry going on, our men shooting [at the French] through the loopholes they had made in the walls earlier, and the French sticking their muskets through the same loopholes and shooting at our men inside. In the end, our people had to yield to the enemy's superior numbers and, in retreating, lost many men as the French cavalry went after them and also made prisoners of some of them. Our men could hardly move because of the soggy soil. One sank into the mud up to one's knees. Had I been with my company, there is no question but that I also would have had it; I still could hardly keep up with the battalion due to my wound. Just think, if half a dozen of those cuirassiers had been after poor old me.

After our first attack had been repulsed by the terrible musket fire that had then started, we had some rest before the second one was to start. I sat down on a drum and, as luck would have it, fell asleep in spite of the raging musketry. Still, I was soon awakened by the preparations for the second attack. Regarding the first attack: I forgot to mention that Major Preen had been wounded and that Major von Nauendorff had lost his Polish horse. As to our battalion, old Captain Dern had been wounded and died shortly afterwards on the battlefield; First Lieutenant Ruckert, now a captain, was also wounded although not severely.[419]

Our second attack was also beaten back. But now, a rumour was suddenly heard that the Prussians had arrived. That filled our people with renewed courage, and we regrouped one more time, since the moment of decision had come. The French were driven back, and everybody ran who still had legs to run, and we ourselves after them over the entire battlefield until we arrived at the road. It was here that one saw signs of the confusion in which they had fled. Here we also met the Prussians. Everything became mixed up. No longer could one see regimental units, here there were some six Nassauers in between a group of Prussians, and yonder were others. I myself rode on a captured cuirassier horse towards a house where I wanted to refresh myself with a drink of water. Since everybody was struggling for some water I was forced to stay there for a while, but on returning to the street I no longer saw any of our troops. I thought that, of course, they must have advanced down the road while I lingered some time [at the house], and so I rode on for more than hour. I made inquiries everywhere, but nobody could give me the information I needed. Getting tired, I eventually rode back, but on the way the Prussians arrested me at least six times, mistaking me for a French officer since on that day I had forgotten to wear my sash. I even had to take the cover off my shako for one of these Katzbach officers so he could see my [Nassau] badge.[420] While the Prussians had earlier filled the road well enough, they now jammed it tight. On top of that, the roadway was blocked by all the guns and caissons that the French had left behind. The best guess by all was 250 guns and an untold number of ammunition carts. The road was jammed to such an extent that, regretfully, I had to leave my tired steed, which could hardly stand on its own legs, and make my way by foot through all kinds of nooks and crannies. Eventually, I heard our [unit's] roll call signal. By God, what a relief to be with them again, because this erring around is a most disagreeable experience. They had marched off to the right, just when I had ridden to the house.

The place at which we had stopped was a former French bivouac near the large village of Maison du Roi. All the huts were still standing, to us a great convenience, since hardly anybody would have been inclined at this evening hour, it was already twelve o'clock, to spend another few hours searching for straw.

So this was the great Battle of Waterloo, which meant a decision in Germany's favour for the second time.[421] All the old officers who had been through many a battle say that they had never experienced as terrible a cannonade as in this battle.

That same evening, the severely wounded Captain Schuler was found in a house in Maison du Roi among wounded French officers; he had been taken prisoner, and was transported to Brussels.

We stayed here at Maison du Roi for two days in order to regroup. I stayed with Major von Nauendorff in one hut. My own company did not rally until the second day, and my orderly arrived quite late that day with my horse. At that place, I bought a French draught horse for a ducat, to use as a pack horse. On the third day we marched off on the direct route to Paris. There we are now in this cowardly capital city in the expectation of things to come.

My intention to write you a letter has now been accomplished. Whatever else might be of interest to you I am going to leave for a letter to Amalie. You better take three days time to read my scrawls, or else you could turn blind. In other respects I flatter myself that you will be pleased with me. All the best!

Your ever loving son Heinrich von Gagern

Brunswick Contingent

No. 55 From *Belle-Alliance*

Pflugk-Harttung's letter no. 9 Report of Colonel Olfermann[422] to the Princely Privy Council at Brunswick on the action at Quatre Bras. First Report. In the night of 16 to 17 June 1815 at the bivouac near Quatre Bras.
Letter no. 67 Report of Colonel Olfermann on the Battle of La Belle Alliance.

Late in the evening of the 15th at eleven o'clock we had received marching orders, we took off on the 16th towards Quatre Bras, [a distance of] some ten to eleven hours from the cantonments of the corps. One of the bloodiest battles happened there, in which our much loved Duke was struck by a musket ball, after, with his inborn intrepidity and courage, he had involved himself most actively in all command decisions. [The ball] had smashed his hand and pierced his abdomen and liver. This tragic incident occurred at about six o'clock in the afternoon. His Highness was personally leading two battalions against a strong enemy column which was threatening our entire right flank, and held it back for a long time despite its immense superiority, but was finally forced to retire to the second line. The only words that the Duke said before his death were to Major von Wachholtz,[423] and were, 'Oh, my dear Wachholtz, where is Olfermann?' Captain Bause went at once in search for him [Olfermann], but sudden death kept the duke's last wishes from being fulfilled. Apart from this irreplaceable loss, we regret the deaths of Majors von Strombeck and Cramm.[424] Major von Rauschenplatt[425] has been severely wounded. All three were by my side, either when they were killed or were wounded. As soon as more detailed information is available on all those killed, wounded or missing of the corps, which now is impossible to provide due to the ongoing operations, I shall report to the Princely Privy Council the particulars immediately and in detail. Most of the losses were suffered by that part of our corps which operated at the right flank of our army, from a heavy cannonade lasting for three hours. We had no artillery to respond because our corps' artillery had not yet arrived due to its remote cantonments. The cavalry suffered in particular at this point. However, it closed with great sang-froid the ranks from time to time that had been taken out by howitzer or canister fire, as also did the infantry battalions near there. The Duke was here, also, almost during the whole time that the heavy cannonade lasted, and by his presence instilled the utmost intrepidity and calm in his soldiers.

Of particular distinction was the conduct of the 2nd Line Battalion, the 2nd Light Battalion, and the Leib-Battalion. The first of these had formed square and completely threw back with great steadiness and sang-froid the repeated charges of enemy cuirassiers, and hindered the enemy's advance, inflicting a considerable loss in killed. The last two battalions contended with the enemy for the possession of a wood, which was lost three times and regained just as many times. The battalions eventually remained masters [of the wood]. All in all, these mostly young troops have conducted themselves in the bravest manner, and even more so as they were led by the duke himself against the enemy and by his presence were filled with unlimited confidence. I cannot praise enough the performance of the officers of the General Staff, Lieutenant Colonel von Heinemann,[426] Majors von Wachholtz, von Grone, and von Marenholz, the captains von Lubeck and Bause, as well as of my adjutants, Captains von Morgenstern and von Zweifel. All of them displayed the strongest initiative and most outstanding bravery, and their support was of particular help to me after the command of the corps was handed to me upon the duke's unfortunate demise. Majors von Grone and von Marenholz were in charge of the duke's corpse.

The Duke of Wellington's army has been victorious, notwithstanding the enemy's superiority. His advance posts are positioned one hour beyond the line that the French had held before the beginning of the battle. We are facing another battle tomorrow. Prisoners claim that Napoleon and Ney under him had been in command of the enemy army.

No. 56 From the same

Bivouac near Braine l'Alleud, 18 June, 9 a.m.
After having passed a night bivouacking in the heaviest rain, we are still

at the same position we took up yesterday, the 17th, after a rearward movement, without anything special to report. I hasten to send this off to ensure its early arrival in Brunswick. Olfermann (Colonel and Brigadier)

No. 57 Second report from the same

Laeken, 19 June 1815

(In greatest haste.)
When I attempted to continue my last letter, the army was suddenly attacked and we were forced to break camp. At first, the Brunswick corps stood in the 3rd line; however, after two hours I received an order to have the corps advance to the 1st line. This movement was promptly executed, and the infantry battalions formed attack columns on the [rearward] slope of a ridge, on which English and Hanoverian artillery had been emplaced and, for two hours, traded fire with the enemy cannon. Until then, only a few balls had struck our battalions, and there were only minor losses. During this cannonade, the enemy had formed up considerable masses of cavalry, which soon launched the most violent charges against the allied artillery, although always without success. A short time later, one of these masses debouched from the corn fields at our side. This cavalry, perhaps consisting of four to five cuirassier regiments, was apparently emboldened by not being fired at and, possibly, did not expect squares ready to fire on the other side of the ridge. They crossed the plateau and were about to charge the battalion squares at full gallop. But this forceful attack was repulsed, and entire ranks of this cavalry were shot down.

Since this moment, the Duke of Wellington stayed for quite some time with the infantry squares of our corps, while these were attacked in renewed cavalry charges. But to those, the same happened as to the earlier one: they were always forced to turn back with heavy losses. A short time later, the Duke of Wellington ordered me to have 3 battalion squares advance and move over the ridge. This movement was calmly commenced by the battalions, although it was on everybody's mind that heavy canister and infantry fire was awaiting us on the other side of the ridge. That expectation unfortunately turned out to be true enough. Hardly had we passed the ridge when entire ranks of the battalions were shot down in quick succession. The enemy soon became aware of the effectiveness of his fire, and began to support the cavalry attacks with his horse artillery. It was impossible to hold out here any longer.

I gave the order to return to our earlier position. Soon thereafter, we were here also most violently attacked, but at no gain to the enemy. The 2nd and 3rd Jäger [Light] Battalions and the 3rd Line Battalion stood like rocks. The Duke of Wellington was still near us, and again sent orders to advance. An attempt was made. But the enemy moved up with a stronger force, particularly in artillery, and the losses in our infantry battalions became ever greater. The three just mentioned battalions nevertheless occupied repeatedly the slope on the far side of the ridge, but were forced to return each time to the former position. This we held despite the continuous enemy attacks, even though the allied artillery had almost totally been demolished. During one of these attacks, several of my fingers were smashed and the right hand shattered; these wounds forced me to go to the rear. I handed the command over to Lieutenant Colonel von Heinemann towards seven o'clock in the evening. Lieutenant Colonel von Butlar[427] had suffered a contusion and had to leave the battlefield. Around nine o'clock the greatest victory was won in conjunction with the Prussian Army Corps. 100 cannon and 15,000 prisoners were captured. The enemy is in full retreat.

The losses suffered by those three battalions is quite considerable. They made an essential contribution to the army through their steadfastness and outstandingly good conduct. The badly wounded commanders of the brave 2nd and 3rd Jäger Battalions, Majors von Brandenstein and Ebeling,[428] and also Captain Hausler and Major von Normann,[429] have excelled in a most brilliant manner. Captain Hausler had led a skirmish line and, with great bravery, had done considerable damage to the enemy. The adjutants of the late Duke, Captain von Lubeck and Bause, as well as my Adjutants, Captains von Zweiffel and Morgenstern, have greatly distinguished themselves. Through their superior activities they contributed outstandingly to the performance of the corps, and repeatedly gave proof of their intrepidity and their competency in the military field.

Signed: Olfermann, per Captain Bause.
The Colonel was unable to write due to his wound.

No. 58 From *Belle-Alliance*

Pflugk-Harttung's letter no. 1 Brunswick Report on the Belgian Campaign. no. 68 Brunswick Report on the Belgian Campaign.

Army Report on the United Corps Under the Command of the Duke of Wellington

The hostilities commenced on the 15th of this month[430] at the Sambre. The Prussian vanguard troops posted along the length of this river retired on their main bodies after very tenacious resistance. The direction of the advance of the French army, commanded by Bonaparte himself, showed his intention to attack between the Allied Army under the Duke of

Wellington and the Prussian Army under Prince Blücher and to separately wear them down. In order to foil this manoeuvre, the Prussian detachments posted behind the Sambre turned to the right, and General von Ziethen, who was particularly pressed by the French, retired to the plain of Fleurus. The Duke of Wellington assembled near Genappe all the troops that were quartered in and around Brussels. These consisted of two brigades of English infantry, one Hanoverian brigade (Best), the Duke of Brunswick's corps, and three regiments of Netherlands troops. The Prince of Orange had the 1st Army Corps take up position near Nivelles.

These preparations had hardly been completed when, on the 16th at three o'clock in the afternoon, Bonaparte attacked most furiously along the entire line with 150,000 men, including much cavalry and artillery. There was a terrible cannonade near Fleurus which lasted until nine o'clock in the evening. At this place, French superiority gained temporary advantages, in spite of the Prussians' outstanding bravery. The Duke of Wellington was similarly attacked by a superior force at his position near Genappe; however, his gallant troops repulsed every assault with the greatest sang-froid, although they suffered significant losses. It was here that the widely respected brave Duke of Brunswick died an enviable death, for Germany's independence and for Europe's peace; pierced by a musket ball, he fell at the moment that with his in-born intrepidity he led his splendid uhlan lancer regiment against an enemy battery. Embittered by the death of their sovereign, the Brunswick troops fought with incredible fury.[431] The other troops also remained true to their character. A brigade of Scots Highlanders distinguished itself in particular. Best's Hanoverian Infantry Brigade conducted itself admirably. Von Vinke's [Hanoverian] Brigade arrived towards evening as [an additional] reinforcement. The action ended at nine o'clock; the battlefield remained in our hands,[432] and the French left in a slow retreat.

While this happened at the left flank, the 1st Army Corps under the Prince of Orange was attacked at Nivelles by Generals d'Erlon and Reille.[433] The enemy was here also thrown back at all points after continuous and tenacious fighting. The outcome of this affair would have been more outstanding if the total absence of cavalry had not prevented a pursuit of the enemy. Because of the large distance, Lord Uxbridge and his cavalry were unable to arrive at the battlefield before late in the evening.

During the night from the 16th to the 17th, the Duke of Wellington had the corps of the Prince of Orange and the cavalry join [his body of troops] so that in the morning of the 17th the army was assembled near

Genappe, except for General Hill's Corps, the garrison troops, and the reserves. The French had withdrawn from the Genappe area; Lord Wellington himself had marched with part of the army for two hours beyond that locality, and it was assumed that the enemy would return to his first position behind the Sambre. This expectation turned out to be unfounded upon the news of the not very favourable outcome of the action near Fleurus. The Duke of Wellington was thereby induced to undertake a retrograde movement towards Waterloo in the afternoon of the 17th and to deploy the army in front of the large Forest of Soignes, in order, possibly, to effect from here a juncture with the Royal Prussian troops.

On 18 June at ten o'clock in the morning, the French army began marching from its bivouacs behind the ridges of Genappe in three columns, led by Bonaparte in person, towards the position of the Duke of Wellington. The Duke deployed his entire line in battalion squares and the cavalry in the 2nd line. Around noontime, Bonaparte directed the first attack against the Duke's right flank at the Hougoumont farm. Soon thereafter, however, he vigorously assaulted the centre near La Haye Sainte and attempted to break through, although in vain. His major attacks were now undertaken with his artillery and closed masses of cavalry, which tried to overrun our squares. Several of our Landwehr battalions have repulsed these attacks of the French cavalry, which were repeated three times. At half past six o'clock in the evening, Bonaparte launched the last furious attack at our line and particularly at our centre, but this one also failed before the unshaken bravery of the troops. This last attack had hardly been thrown back when the Duke of Wellington astutely recognised the decisive moment and ordered the entire army to advance to the attack. This master stroke had the most brilliant result. Exhausted by his own efforts, the enemy was unable to resist this sudden and unexpected manoeuvre and was driven back at all points. At nine o'clock his rout was complete, and darkness prevented his total defeat.

By the evening, this memorable victory had already resulted in the capture of 5,000 to 6,000 prisoners, 130 cannon and a number of eagles. That same evening, the army readied itself to energetically pursue the enemy, jointly with the corps of the royal Prussian General von Bülow. Prince Blücher had also gained a brilliant victory on this day. He had captured several thousand prisoners and 60 cannon. By the time the courier was despatched from Brussels on the 19th,[434] it was already learned that the French army had retreated behind the Sambre in the greatest disorder.

Thus ended the first offensive operation [of 1815] of the French general, which he had probably started with the greatest expectations. His army is completely disorganised and has lost confidence in him and in itself. Since the beginning of hostilities, his losses cannot have been less than 30,000 men.

It can be easily imagined that these splendid gains could not be obtained without losses on our side. However, these were in no comparison to those of the enemy. By the way, particulars about these have not been received yet. The following list includes the names of the killed and wounded officers, to the extent that they were known by the time of the courier's departure. No exact details have been learned about the losses of the English officer corps. Definite information has been obtained only regarding the fate of the following generals and staff officers.

1 Killed: the Quartermaster General Sir William Delancey; Colonel Gordon, aide-de-camp to the Duke of Wellington.
2 Wounded: the Hereditary Prince of Orange, severely; Lieutenant General Count Uxbridge, lost a leg; Lieutenant General Lord Fitzroy Somerset, lost an arm; Lieutenant General Cooke, Major General von Dornberg, lightly; the Adjutant General Major General Barnes, severely.

No. 59 From *Belle-Alliance*
Pflugk-Harttung's letter no. 3 Table of the Field Strength of the Brunswick Troops and List of [Brunswickers who served with] Distinction.[435]

On 17 April and the following days, the Field Corps moved out with:

Combatants	
Staff of the Field Corps	13
Hussar Regiment	727
Uhlan Squadron	246
Line Infantry Brigade (Staff, 1st, 2nd, 3rd Line Battalions)	2,075
Light Infantry Brigade (Staff, Light, 1st, 2nd, 3rd Light Battalions)	2,765
Avantgarde Battalion (2 companies skilled Jägers and 2 light infantry companies)	690
Artillery (1 8-gun horse battery with 188 combatants and 1 8-gun foot battery with 227 combatants)	415
Commando of Police Hussars (Constabulary)	17
	6,948

For the most part, very young men seventeen to twenty years old. During the Westphalian period [Kingdom under Napoleon's Brother Jerome], the older age-groups had to serve under Napoleon's colours in Spain and Russia, and there were few survivors.

Following is a list, forwarded later by Colonel Olfermann, of officers, NCOs and privates who had particularly distinguished themselves during 16 to 18 June 1815, names with some interesting information on how and where they distinguished themselves:[436]

Hussars:	von Hennings, Major,
	von Holy, Cavalry Staff Captain,
	Schelle, Cavalry Captain,
	Eigener, Cavalry Captain,
	Schwenke, Lieutenant,
	von Unger, Lieutenant & Adjutant,
	Flotho, Lieutenant & Adjutant,
	Engelbrecht, Cornet
Uhlans:	Matern, Lieutenant & Adjutant,
	Lüderssen, Cornet
Avantgarde:	Mahner, Captain,
	Leuterding, Lieutenant & Adjutant
1st Light Batttalion:	von Specht, Captain,
	von Meibom, Captain,
	Wagenknecht, Ensign
1st Line Battalion:	von Munchhausen, Captain
	Pressler, Staff Captain,
	Scherf, Lieutenant.
2nd Line Battalion:	Rudolphi, Staff Captain,
	Hartmann, Lieutenant & Adjutant,
	Matern, Lieutenant,
	von Meyern, Ensign
3rd Line Battalion:	von Brugmann, Captain
	Geyer, Lieutenant,
	Kubel, Ensign.

Brunswick Medical Services

No. 60 From *Belle-Alliance*

Pflugk-Harttung's letter no. 95 Letter of Company Surgeon Wilhelm Schutte to his parents about the activities of the Brunswick Troops at Quatre Bras and La Belle Alliance.

Merxem, 2 July 1815

Dearest Parents![437]
It is about time now that you hear from me to learn that I am still alive.
Yes, strange things happened to me until now, but I believe it is best not
to become discouraged, to avoid just giving up. It's the fate of a soldier
on campaign to bivouac for five or six days under rain and then sunshine,
accompanied by the roaring of guns, quite often to have only dry bread
with one's spit, without a drink of decent water, and not even dry
bedding. A lucky man was he who managed to get some brandy and a
piece of bread out of deserted houses ruined by cannon balls, or a
chicken looking for its coop; how often was it not my dearest wish just
to have a cup of coffee or some tobacco for my pipe? I still don't
understand how my miserable weak body was able to endure all of this.
The hunger I had to suffer was so bad that it cracked the skin on my
body; as soon as I had taken a chicken away from a crying woman and
already had it cooking in a pot, some damned shell was likely, with a
'pss, pss, slitt', to hit the ground next to oneself, and one was glad to have
got away with the skin still untouched. But let me start off with the old
story from the beginning.

As you know, we were quartered at Asche, two hours this side of
Brussels, where I still received several letters from you, and the last one,
in which Jette[438] asked me not to poop in my pants when things were
getting rough. Now that certainly did not happen. During the night to
the 16th of this month, the artillery was ordered to be collected at the
Laeken headquarters at two o'clock in the morning. But that was not
possible because our men were quartered as much as two to three hours
away from our village and could not get together as fast as needed. We
marched off at eight o'clock in the morning from Asche to Laeken. The
Duke and the other corps had already left. We therefore passed through
Brussels to Waterloo, where we arrived at two o'clock in the afternoon.
Now we could already hear the roar of the guns, and my heart leapt for
joy to perhaps be able to dispatch some Frenchmen out of this world.
Hardly had we been marching for one hour when one of the Duke's
ADCs met us with an order to join the corps as fast as possible. We now
set off at a fast trot towards the battlefield at Quatre Bras. There now
already passed us some wounded soldiers, one with a rag around his
head and otherwise unrecognisable from the blood, another one with an
arm wrapped in a cloth, and so on. We were sometimes unable to move
through all those baggage carts, the wounded, and the likes, even some
regiments on the retreat, until an advance guard was formed with the
task to push everything off the street. I was so filled with rage about
these misfortunes that the French had brought on us, and anxious for

revenge that I never stayed behind but rode ahead up front. I do not know what gave me this kind of courage. What filled me with particular pleasure was having been able to take a pair of pistols away from a fleeing Dutch Hussar. Now no dog was safe from me; whoever failed to get out of the way was run over, and so things went on. After a couple of hours and before we arrived at the battlefield, I found the Wilhelms' boy[439] lying by the roadside who had completely passed out. The infantry had been marching since midnight without rest and without anything to eat or drink, and on top of that there was this terrific heat. I tried to make him wake up, and went on my way. Soon, I saw one lying there and crying, another one who was on the run and had thrown away his knapsack and everything, only to get away faster, that third one had a comrade on his back and carried him off, then again there was one lying too, but he was dead, and another one was filching him, and so the scenery changed all the while. It was at four o'clock in the afternoon that we arrived at Quatre Bras where we took up position on a little hill. Now such a cannonade went on that I believed the skies were to fall in. Later, I had to laugh at myself for having been leaning my head sideways whenever a shell passed by my ears, the ones one can recognise right away by their whistling. So I remained with the battery until the major[440] asked me to set up shop in one of the neighbouring houses where he could send the wounded. There I met Vorlop,[441] Kruger,[442] Schmidt[443] and Meineken[444] being quite busy since they had already arrived at two o'clock in the afternoon. Now the butchery was really beginning, so that soon one was looking like a knacker's helper. Towards evening I returned again to the battery, which had moved left beyond the road to Maubeuge. While on the way I found one lying dead in his own blood, then there was a [dead] horse, here there was an arm or a leg or a head, and so on. Then a damned mischief happened to me: I am trotting along on a country road, without a care in the world, and all of a sudden here comes a shell and blows up next to me in the bushes and fences so that I was showered with loose branches and stakes and dirt. Now I began to give free rein to my horse so that he broke into transports of joy and rushed off over fences, ditches, dead people and horses, and everything that was in my way, until I was back with the battery. It was drawn up in a field of rye; only a few men had been killed, and that right on the spot; and some seven to twelve horses had been lost. The roaring of guns continued until it was getting so that one could not see anything anymore, which offered me a nice spectacle on that evening. We bivouacked that night in a splendid field of rye. The shooting started up again very early in the morning, until about noon, but nothing special happened. About that time, my batman returned who had remained with the baggage. A horse was his booty. I was overjoyed to have him back. At around ten o'clock [a.m.] we started on a retreat which took almost six hours. Some really bad weather began in the afternoon, with rains lasting almost through the entire night. I almost forgot to mention the most important news: at about four o'clock in the afternoon of the 16th, our Duke was killed by a ball that went through one of his hands and then through his body. His wrath would not allow him to stay behind. He was up front all the time. Now to continue, the French left us in peace on the 17th and until noon of the 18th, by which time a terrible blood bath began again, which lasted until night. Both sides put up a tremendous fight, and the French stood like lions. Their damned tirailleurs hid in trees, hedges, shrubs, and ditches, from where they caused much damage. After we had been under fire for about two hours, the brave Lieutenant Dietrichs[445] was killed by a shell which hit the ground behind him and then exploded with a thrust through his back. I still can see that brave fellow before my eyes. We lost no more officers, but many men and horses. All in all, our corps has been terribly weakened; hardly half of it has been left. But it fought most valiantly because our men were full of a hellish wrath. Wherever they could do in a Frenchman, they would do it. Here is an example that I witnessed myself: at four o'clock in the afternoon some 100 French prisoners were brought in; one of them escaped at a favourable moment. A hussar chased him and with his pistol shot him through his head, others ran towards him and everybody stabbed at him, and even wounded ones took a piece of wood or whatever they could find and clubbed him, until no single piece of him hung to another. Only a couple of companies are left of some battalions. Almost all of our uhlans are gone from attacking squares some seven times, same thing with the hussars. I would never have believed that the Brunswickers could have fought as bravely as they did, considering that theirs was a newly formed corps. An enormous number of men perished on the 18th, both on our side and on the other. Well, it almost seemed as if the skies were to collapse on us. Several villages in the vicinity were shot to smithereens. The battlefield was entirely covered with corpses; one could hardly move through all the dead bodies. There were piles of them, in particular wherever there had been a square. Towards evening the French retreated in a total defeat. Many of them had been taken prisoner, several generals among them and the devil knows what else. Quite a few of their generals were said to have been killed. It was not until Maubeuge that they came to rest. In truth, much the same might almost have happened to us if the Prussians had not come to help us.

Nobody can have an idea of a battle and a battlefield who has not been there. It is a horrible scene, the splendid flowering fields all wasted and covered with piles of corpses. The villages were vacant, desolate, half turned into ashes, and deserted by their inhabitants. In their despair those people wandered aimlessly through woods and forests. But after all this, I thank God that things have turned to the better in the end.

On the following day, our artillery had to return to Brussels for repairs from the terrible beating it had taken. On one of the guns, one thing would be amiss, on another some parts were broken. Since there was nothing to do for me at the battery, I rode to Laeken every day to care for the wounded in our field hospital that we had set up there. Here I ran into Meineken who had lost all of his baggage; I gave him one of my shirts. Also Uhlan Bringmann[446] who had been shot through one of his knees and had to have the leg taken off; and then the one who had served at Oehl . . . , but who was only lightly wounded, and several others. After I thus had helped out for some four days, I was ordered to go to Antwerp, where there was one of our hospitals, since not all of our wounded could remain at Laeken. I found it at Merxem, a quarter of an hour outside Antwerp. Here I then had 1 hospital under my inspection, where the wounded were lying in three pavilions. In my own [hospital] there were Wihelm Keitel,[447] who was soon off to the army having had only a contusion, then the son of linen-weaver Schumann,[448] who lives at Martinis Graben, also only lightly wounded, furthermore Huhne,[449] son of the shoemaker who lives in the Neue Dorf, who died yesterday from gangrene, then several from the Neue Dorf whose names I do not remember just now, all only lightly wounded, also from Hillebrechts-hausen, badly wounded, from Oppershausen and several villages along the Leine [river] and Bentgerode. I have three surgeons serving under myself, and the four of us have to care for 150 wounded. The director, with his five assistants, has about 180 in his, and Schnelle,[450] with one assistant, has some 120 in his, the latter only lightly wounded ones. When the wounds of our patients are about healed, we send them to Schnelle's hospital for final care of the scars. I have already taken off several arms and legs, and every day something is happening. I am terribly busy, and I can assure you I would have written sooner if this had not been the case. On one of them I had to open the skull, but he died four days later. I extracted four pieces of bone from his brain, and on dissection I found another one embedded deeply in his brain which, in effect, had caused his death. The Antwerp people take great care of our wounded; every day they send wine, shirts, bandages, fruits, foodstuffs, in general anything that one could ask for. When the Hospital was first set up here, the poor devils had to lie on bare straw without covers or anything. But now thanks to the beneficence of the Antwerpers, everyone of the wounded has a straw mattress, two bed-sheets and two blankets, one white of wool, and a red one; it really is a pleasure to behold all of this. There is one family in particular, under whose special care we are, the Van Hauers; all the time they send us wine, vegetables, butter, lemons, underwear, bandages, medicines, and more things like that. All we need do is give them a list of our needs, and the next day the things are in our hands. Indeed, we really could not even have started without this great support.

In order to buy something I needed, I rode to Antwerp yesterday. While there, I went to the harbour to see the ships and, just then, French prisoners were put on board ships heading for England. They were packed hellishly tight and looked fearfully bad. Among them were grey haired fellows of the Old Guard, and so on. Some still had the courage to shout, '*Vive Napoleon.*' But to those they teach a thorough lesson. It has been said that Napoleon has left the army and has gone to Paris, where he has been deposed from government, and more of that. I do not know where our army now is, but it must have advanced quite a bit.

I now come to the end, as I see that this letter is long enough, and I also intend to better wait until I get a similar one in return. When you write, address the letter by Military Post to Pockels[451] [Chief of Brunswick Medical Corps], who will know where I happen to be, in the event I should no longer be here. I hope you all are up and well, and if I should make it to Paris, I will get Jette a shawl as promised. Greetings to all the friends, all the best to you, and do not forget your obedient son,

    W. Schutte

A propos: The Prussians caught Napoleon's baggage; I saw his coach yesterday as it was about to be taken to Berlin.

Prussian Army

No. 61 Journal of Lieutenant Von Reuter, 6th Prussian Artillery Battery

'A Prussian Gunner's Adventures in 1815' by Capt. E. S. May, RA, United Services Magazine *vol. IV, new series, no. 755 October 1891, pp. 43–50.*

Ordered on 25 May 1815 to join Ziethen's Corps and quartered in the village of Suarlee.[452] 15 June, heard guns[453] while breakfasting and by two o'clock ordered to Fleurus where he arrived on the evening of the 15th.

'Towards evening we came upon the enemy not far from Fleurus, and I took up a position on the far side of the village and on the left of the road. We remained all night in this position, which, by the way, was a most uncomfortable one. When day broke the next morning the general was horrified to find that my battery was alone, without any escort, right under the noses of the enemy's advanced piquets. During the night the remainder of the troops had all received orders to retire; but I and my guns had been completely overlooked! We would have fared badly indeed had the enemy attempted any enterprise against us under the cover of the darkness.'

He received orders to take up a position near the windmill at Ligny. About midday, while Wellington and Blücher were talking together on an eminence near the battery, General Von Holzendorf came up and ordered number one gun to fire a round.

'We were told, at the time that this was a signal to our army corps that the Prince had made up his mind to accept battle.

'I suppose it was between two and three o'clock in the afternoon when I received an order to take four guns of my battery and accompany the 14th Regiment in its advance towards St Amand, while the howitzers and two remaining guns took up a position opposite Ligny, so as to be able to shell the open ground beyond the village, and the village itself, too, in the event of our not being able to hold it. I halted my guns about six hundred paces from St Amand, and opened fire on the enemy's artillery in position on the high ground opposite, which at once began to reply with a well-sustained fire of shells, and inflicted heavy losses on us. Meanwhile the 14th Regiment, without ever thinking of leaving an escort behind for us, pressed gallantly forward to St Amand, and succeeded in gaining possession of a part of that village. I myself was under the impression that they had been able to occupy the whole of it. The battery had thus been engaged for some hours in its combat with the hostile guns, and were awaiting the order to follow up the movement of the 14th Regiment, when suddenly I became aware of two strong lines of skirmishers which were apparently falling back on us from the village of St Amand. Imagining that the skirmishers in front of us were our own countrymen, I hastened up to the battery and warned my layers not to direct their aim upon them, but to continue to engage the guns opposite. In the meanwhile the skirmishers in question had got within three hundred paces of the battery.

'I had just returned to the right flank of my command, when our surgeon, Zinkernagel, called my attention to the red tufts on the shakos of the sharpshooters. I at once bellowed out the order "With grape on the skirmishers!" At the same moment both their lines turned upon us, gave us a volley, and then flung themselves on the ground. By this volley, and the bursting of a shell or two, every horse, except one wheeler, belonging to the gun on my left flank, was either killed or wounded. I ordered the horses to be taken out of one of my ammunition wagons, which had been emptied, and thus intended to make my gun fit to move again, while I meanwhile kept up a slow fire of grape, that had the effect of keeping the marksmen in my front glued to the ground. But in another moment, all of a sudden, I saw my left flank taken in rear, from the direction of the Ligny brook, by a French staff officer and about fifty horsemen. As these rushed upon us the officer shouted to me in German, "Surrender, gunners, for you are all prisoners!" With these words he charged down with his men on the flank gun on my left, and dealt a vicious cut at my wheel driver, Borchardt (a good artillery name, this), who dodged it, however, by flinging himself over on his dead horse. The blow was delivered with such good will that the sabre cut deep into the saddle, and stuck there fast. Gunner Sieberg, however, availing himself of the chance the momentary delay afforded, snatched up the handspike of one of the 12-pounders, and with the words, "I'll soon show him how to take prisoners!" dealt the officer such a blow on his bearskin that he rolled with a broken skull from the back of his grey charger, which galloped away into the line of skirmishers in our front. The fifty horsemen, unable to control their horses which bounded after their companion, followed his lead in a moment, rode over the prostrate marksmen, and carried the utmost confusion into the enemy's ranks. I seized the opportunity to limber up all my guns except the unfortunate one on my left, and to retire on two of our cavalry regiments, which I saw, drawn up about 600 paces to my rear. It was only when I had thus fallen back that the enemy's skirmishers ventured to approach my remaining gun. I could see from a distance how bravely its detachment defended themselves and it with handspikes and their side-arms, and some of them in the end succeeded in regaining the battery. The moment I got near our cavalry I rode up to them and entreated them to endeavour to recapture my gun again from the enemy, but they refused to comply with my request. I, therefore, returned sorrowfully to my battery, which had retired meanwhile behind the hill with the windmill on it near Ligny. We there replenished our ammunition wagons and limber boxes, and set to rights our guns, and the battery again advanced to come into action on the height. We had, however, hardly reached the crest of the hill when the enemy issued from the village of Ligny in overpowering numbers, and compelled all our troops which were there with us to fall back. The movement was carried out with complete steadiness and regularity. It was now about eight o'clock p.m., and the

growing darkness was increased by the heavy storm clouds which began
to settle down all round us. My battery, in order to avoid capture, had,
of course, to conform to this general movement. I now noticed that
there was an excellent artillery position about 1,500 paces behind the
village of Brye, close to where the Roman road intersects the road to
Quatre Bras. I made for this point with all haste, so that I might there
place my guns and cover with their fire the retreat of my comrades of
the other arms. A hollow road leading to Sombreffe delayed my
progress some minutes. At length I got over this obstacle and attained
my goal; but just as I was going to give the word, "Action rear", Von
Pirch's [II] infantry brigade began to debouch from Brye. The general
saw in an instant what he took for a selfish and cowardly movement of
retreat on my part, dashed his spurs into his horse, and galloped up to
me nearly beside himself with passion, and shouting out, "My God!
Everything is going to the devil!" "Truly, sir," said I, "matters are not
looking very rosy, but the 12-pounder battery, No. 6, has simply come
here to get into a position from whence it thinks it may be able to check
the enemy's advance." "That, then, is very brave conduct on your part,"
answered the general, at once mollified. "Cling to the position at all
hazards, it is of the greatest importance. I will collect a few troops to
form an escort to your guns." While this short, but animated, discussion
had been going on his brigade had come up close to where we were. He
formed it up to cover us, and sent every one who was mounted to collect
all retreating troops in the neighbourhood for the same purpose, while,
as they came up, he called out to them, "Soldiers, there, stand your guns,
are you not Prussians!"

'During the time that a sort of rear-guard was thus formed, the
battery had opened fire on the enemy's cavalry, which was coming up
rather cautiously, and had forced them to fall back again. Later on a 6-
pounder field battery and a half a horse artillery battery came up and
joined us. The fight then became stationary, and as the darkness came
on, fighting gradually ceased on both sides. During the course of the
night this rear-guard, which, meanwhile, had come under the command
of General von Roeder, continued its retreat unmolested by the enemy,
crossed the Dyle on the 17th at Wavre, and there we again found our
baggage. During the retreat I had the good fortune to be able to horse
three guns of Meyer's battery which I found on the road unable to get
along, and drew them off with me. Yet Captain Meyer, annoyed at still
having to leave three of his guns behind, was extremely rude to me
because I could help him no further!'

During his march to Wavre, Prince Blücher rode and chatted
alongside him; when the Prince heard of the lost gun of the day before,

he comforted him with the words, 'There, now! don't let that trouble you. We will very soon take it from them again.'

His account of the night of the 17th describes the bivouac on the soppy grounds under the heavy downpour, which extinguished all efforts towards a fire, but the Prussians were more uneasy, as to the enemy's doings, and could not understand why he did not make his appearance. His battery arrived at the battlefield as night closed in.

The evening was 'as lovely a one as I ever remember, here and there, a burning homestead. The wounded, as we came rushing on, set up a dreadful crying, and holding up their hands entreated us, some in French and some in English, not to crush their already mangled bodies beneath our wheels. It was a terrible sight to see those faces with the mark of death upon them, rising from the ground and the arms outstretched towards us. Reluctant, though I was, I felt compelled to halt, and then enjoined my men to advance with great care and circumspection. And soon I saw that I could in any case have no share in the glory of the day, for the enemy had begun to break and fly on all sides.'

Not at Waterloo

Veteran Battalion, King's German Legion

No. 62 From *Belle-Alliance*
Pflugk-Harttung's letter no. 39 Information on the activities of 60 men of the Veterans Battalion of the German Legion at La Belle Alliance.

This detachment (60 men of the Veterans Battalion), commanded by Lieutenant Tatter[454] of the Veterans Battalion, earned a commendation from General Mackenzie, commander at Antwerp, for its conduct and efforts during the critical moments of the Battle of Waterloo when on 18 June refugees from the battlefield streamed into the city and there caused confusion. [The commendation] was brought to general knowledge of the garrison by way of a public order.

2nd Hussars, King's German Legion

No. 63 From *Belle-Alliance*
Pflugk-Harttung's letter no. 57 Report of the 2nd Hussar Regiment of the German Legion on its activities during the month of June.

Since 31 March, the regiment formed a line along the French border from Courtrai to the North Sea; it occupied Courtrai, Menin, Ypres, Loo [or Lo] and Furnes;⁴⁵⁵ to maintain over all security, the individual pickets consisted of 5 officers and 203 men.

The Duke of Wellington rode along this position and on this occasion, inspected the individual squadrons. The regiment remained here until setting off for Paris, notwithstanding the fact that it formed, since 6 June, a brigade together with the 7th and 15th Hussar Regiments, under the command of General Grant. Only in the last days of June was an order issued to join forthwith the army, which, since the victory at Waterloo, was on its march to Paris. The regiment was assembled at Courtrai as fast as possible; it marched to Tournai on 1 July, and to Mons on the next day.

NOTES

1   Published January 2010.

2   Canada and Australia proving especially fruitful.

3   *The Waterloo Letters*, London, 1891, published by Herbert Siborne, the son of William Siborne, famous for his models of the Battle of Waterloo. To ensure accuracy of his models, William sent a circular to all surviving British officers asking for their memories of the battle, he received over 400 replies, of which Herbert published 180.

4   Von Ompteda, Louis (ed.) in the *King's German Legion: Memoirs of Baron Ompteda, Colonel in the King's German Legion during the Napoleonic Wars*, reprinted by Ken Trotman 1987.

5   Hibbert, Christopher. *The Wheatley Diary: A Journal and Sketchbook Kept during the Peninsular War and the Waterloo Campaign* Longmans, Green and Co., London, 1964.

6   *History of the King's German Legion* 2 vols, London 1832–7.

7   *1815 – The Waterloo Campaign*, 2 vols, Greenhill Books, London, 1998–9.

8   *Letters from the Battle of Waterloo*, Greenhill Books, London, 2004. In this work the 200-odd letters in the Siborne files not printed by Herbert Siborne were finally published.

9   The Osnabrück and Quackenbruck Landwehr Battalions were also known as the Duke of York's 2nd and 3rd Battalions but I use their alternative title to avoid confusion. The Duke of York 1st Battalion was also named Osnabrück but is referred to throughout as the Duke of York's to differentiate.

10   This regiment is omitted in the Waterloo Roll Call.

11   Most of the 4th Division missed the battle, except Mitchell's Brigade which did participate and von Rettberg's battery joined Picton's Division. The report of this battery is letter no. 14 in this volume.

12   Note by Pflugk-Harttung. See Schwertferger, *Geschichte der Koniglich Deutschen Legion 1803–16*, II, pp. 332ff. The report is for the year 1825.

13   There is no village of this name in the area, it probably refers to Bray.

14   Almost certainly Havre.

15   This is an error, as the Gemioncourt Farm was initially within the allied line and occupied by the Dutch 5th Militia Battalion.

16   Both Captain Bijleveld's Horse Battery and Captain Stievenart's Foot Battery were involved in this operation at Quatre Bras. Siborne states that while

retreating Stievenart lost a gun disabled and Bijleveldt abandoned one gun following the explosion of a caisson. See Colonel Zuylen van Nijevelt's 'Report on the Operations of the 2nd Netherlands Division', in vol. IV of *The Waterloo Archive*.

17 This shows how worried Wellington still was for his flank while the army was on the march, as these veteran troops would have been invaluable at Quatre Bras.

18 A *lieue* or French league equated to approximately 2.4 miles.

19 Captain Charles von Rettberg Hanoverian Foot Artillery (Beamish no. 33). His letters have been published in the author's *Letters from the Battle of Waterloo* (nos 90 and 91).

20 Major Brome's Foot artillery battery.

21 Spelt Cleves by Dalton and the Army List but I prefer the spelling used by Beamish which agrees with Pflugk-Harttung.

22 The cavalry had arrived during the night.

23 1 *rute* equals 3.76 m.

24 Battalion 2nd Nassau Regiment; the light companies of the Coldstream and Third Guards of 100 men, each, 1 Feldjäger company and 100 men, each, of the Luneburg and Grubenhagen Battalions of the 1st Hanoverian Brigade.

25 The Papelotte farm was held throughout the battle by troops of the 2nd Regiment Nassau. See Major Rettberg's, 'Report regarding the 3rd Battalion of the 2nd Regiment Nassau during the Battle near Waterloo on 18 June 1815', letter no. 45 in this volume.

26 Pflugk-Harttung's footnote: 'The troops are mentioned in the order in which they stood in the battle from the right to the left wing.'

27 Lieutenant Colonel Hugh Halkett, number 646 in Beamish.

28 The more specific report of the 1st Hanoverian Brigade indicates that 100 men, each, of the Luneburg and Grubenhagen Battalions were detached to Hougoumont. See letter no. 28 in this volume.

29 This probably refers initially to Roger's battery which stationed itself to the left of Cleeves' around 2.30, it was relieved by Sinclair's around 4.30 and eventually by Ross's battery around 6.30.

30 Major von Dachenhausen was recorded as missing after the battle.

31 There is a general theme throughout these reports from the German troops, that instead of sending wagons back for ammunition from the reserve; the whole unit, guns and all, retired. This is possibly the cause of Wellington's ill humour with the artillery at Waterloo.

32 Beamish (Number 1211) states that Frederick Lewis Augustus von Wurmb was a colonel in the Hanoverian service when he was killed at Waterloo commanding the Field Battalion Grubenhagen.

33 Siborne totals 47 officers, and 715 men killed, wounded and missing.

34 Major George Baring (Beamish no. 335). His letters have been published in the author's *Letters from the Battle of Waterloo* (nos 163 to 165).

35 Waters's 'morning state' records that the 1st Light Battalion numbered 478 and the 2nd Light Battalion 432 men present. This figure is significantly higher than Siborne's figures, particularly in relation to the second battalion.

36 The Nassau unit in question was the musket-armed Flanqueur company of the 2nd Battalion, 1st Regiment Nassau, of about 160 men.

37   Colonel Christian von Ompteda (Beamish no. 972).
38   Major General William von Dornberg, commander 3rd British Cavalry Brigade (Beamish no 86), was severely wounded.
39   An interesting excuse for leaving the battle!
40   Lieutenant Colonel Frederick Lewis Meyer (Beamish no. 816) was severely wounded at Waterloo and succumbed to his injuries on 6 July 1815.
41   The term *rott* means 'files', i.e. two men, therefore 60 *rott* would equate to 120 horsemen.
42   Captain Bolton's battery.
43   Pflugk-Harttung's footnote, addition in the Berlin MS: 'so-called shrapnel-shells, which were here used to good effect'.
44   Captain Sandham's battery.
45   It would seem that many artillery units did not leave their guns on the crest with the men retiring to the adjoining squares as ordered, but actually removed their entire units to safety in the reserve until the cavalry attacks ended.
46   Another example of the artillery batteries retiring completely with their guns, rather than simply sending their caissons back to be replenished.
47   Dalton and Adkin mistakenly show Braun attached to Colonel Vincke's brigade of Picton's division.
48   Captain Bernhard von Bothmer, 1st Dragoons KGL (Beamish no. 92).
49   Lieutenant Colonel Charles Frederick de Jonquières, 2nd Dragoons KGL (Beamish no. 127).
50   They had formerly been heavy cavalry and equipped with heavier straight swords.
51   Philip von Sichart (Major in Beamish, no. 89).
52   Captain George Henry von Hattorf (Beamish no. 93)
53   Lieutenant Lewis Henry von Sichart was an officer of the 2nd Line Battalion, but was attached to the staff. Another letter of his has been published in the author's *Letters from the Battle of Waterloo* (no. 15).
54   Major Augustus Reizenstein (Beamish no. 88).
55   Captain Frederick Peters (Beamish no. 803).
56   Lieutenant Frederick Charles Lewis von Levetzow (Beamish no. 810).
57   Lieutenant Otto Kuhlmann (Beamish no. 812).
58   Lieutenant Colonel John von Bülow (Beamish no. 87).
59   Adjutant William Fricke (Beamish no. 121). His letters have been published in the author's *Letters from the Battle of Waterloo* (nos 37 and 38).
60   Lieutenant William Mackenzie (Beamish no. 103).
61   Lieutenant Henry Bosse (Beamish no. 104).
62   Lieutenant Staats Henry Nanne (Beamish no. 107).
63   Cornet Edward Trittau (Beamish no. 115).
64   I can discover no evidence to support this statement.
65   3 km east of Nivelles.
66   Lieutenant Colonel Augustus Friedrichs (Beamish no. 128).
67   Shown as Captain Antony von Streeruwitz (Beamish no. 219).
68   Captain George von Decken (Beamish no. 172).
69   Lieutenant Colonel Augustus von Wissell (Beamish no. 168). Another letter of his has been published in the author's *Letters from the Battle of Waterloo* (no. 66).

70   Pflugk-Harttung footnote: 'Captain G von der Decken was commander of the No. 1 squadron (No. 1 and 7 companies) since 3 April 1815.'

71   On the western outskirts of Genappe.

72   Colonel Frederick Levin August von Arentschildt (Beamish no. 247) had risen through the ranks of the KGL, being present at the battles of Talavera, Fuentes d'Onoro, Salamanca, Vitoria and Toulouse.

73   Actually still recorded as the 3rd Light Dragoon Regiment in the report.

74   Major George Baron Krauchenberg (Beamish no. 249).

75   It seems very strange that this regiment was sent to Brussels and then ordered to return for the battle. Perhaps further evidence of the disorganised staff work all too evident in this campaign.

76   Captain Agatz von Kerssenbruch (Beamish no. 801) was killed at Waterloo.

77   Captain George Janssen (Beamish no. 802).

78   Lieutenant Henry Bruggemann (Beamish no. 808).

79   Cornet William Deichmann (Beamish no. 815).

80   Lieutenant Christian Oehlkers (Beamish no. 267).

81   Lieutenant Hermann True (Beamish no. 266) died on 31 July 1821.

82   Cornet Conrad von Dassel (Beamish no. 276).

83   Cornet Hans von Hardenberg (Beamish no. 279). Beamish who gives his name as Hons von Hodenburg, but the spelling throughout this report is immaculately consistent and I have sided with this version.

84   Captain George Meyer (Beamish no. 258) was severely wounded but survived.

85   Captain Quintus von Goeben (Beamish no. 88). His letters have been published in the author's *Letters from the Battle of Waterloo* (nos 67 and 68).

86   The 13th Light Dragoons actually fought with Grant's Brigade.

87   Beamish states 29 men killed.

88   Captain William von Schnehen (Beamish no. 255).

89   Beamish records Anthony Frederick Hoyer as a lieutenant in the regiment, his no. 271.

90   Beamish states 24 horses which appears to be an error.

91   Colonel Hermann Segeband Gotthelf Friedrich August von Estorff (Beamish no. 5).

92   Almost certainly General Augustus Frederick von der Bussche (Beamish no. 869) who left the KGL on half pay in 1813.

93   1 km north of Saintes.

94   Major (at Waterloo) Henry Jacob Kuhlmann (Beamish no. 28).

95   Cooke commanded the 1st (Guards) Division.

96   Captain Sandham's Foot Artillery.

97   Lieutenant Colonel Stephen Galway Adye.

98   This is confirmed by Best's own report, see letter 37 in this volume.

99   Most plans of the battle (see Adkins's for example) show Kuhlmann and Sandham in the centre of the right wing. However if he was in front of the Guards he must have been stationed nearer the eastern edge of Hougoumont.

100 The only howitzer battery at Waterloo was Bull's: he was moved up from the reserves at approximately twelve o'clock to take position on the rise above Hougoumont to bombard the French troops assaulting Hougoumont wood. The fact that Kuhlmann witnessed this movement further supports my belief

that these regiments were further to the right on the crest than normally accepted. See footnote 95.

101 Another reference to the guns pulling back during the cavalry assaults.

102 Lieutenant General Frederick Count von der Decken (Beamish no. 24).

103 Second Captain Samuel Rudyerd. In his letter (no. 98 in *Waterloo Letters*), Rudyerd does indicate that he was with two guns supporting the 69th Foot until they were dispersed by cuirassiers then rejoined Lloyd. Lloyd's battery was not 'lost', but took a severe pounding and was finally ordered to retire behind Quatre Bras to re-equip. Rudyerd does not mention Rettberg's Battery, however, Rettberg is specific and his report has the ring of truth, it seems that Rudyerd did not like to leave the fighting and joined Rettberg.

104 Picton managed to conceal his wound until it was discovered after his death in the battle.

105 Clear evidence that Bijlandt's men did not simply flee.

106 Second Captain (at Waterloo) William Braun (Beamish no. 38) was severely wounded at Waterloo. He had previously fought with the KGL since 1805 and had served with the Portuguese army from 1810–12.

107 It is now a northern borough of Ghent.

108 Lieutenant Charles Detlef von Schulzen (Beamish no. 787) was killed at the Battle of Waterloo.

109 Lieutenant Colonel Sir George Julius Hartmann (Beamish no. 26).

110 Lambert commanded the 10th Brigade.

111 First Captain Andrew Cleeves (Beamish no. 34).

112 First Lieutenant William von Goeben (Beamish no. 52). Another of his letters has been published in the author's *Letters from the Battle of Waterloo* (no. 87), he was severely wounded at Quatre Bras.

113 First Lieutenant Henry Hartmann (Beamish no. 56) was severely wounded at Quatre Bras.

114 2nd Lieutenant Charles Hermann Ludowieg (Beamish no. 67).

115 Actually Captain von Rettberg's 2nd Hanoverian Foot Battery; Heise was commander of the Hanoverian artillery.

116 An error, he almost certainly means the 28th, which was in Kempt's Brigade.

117 Whinyates's Troop.

118 The restricted visibility owing to smoke in a Napoleonic battle should not be underestimated.

119 Adkin et al. show Sympher advancing at around 3 p.m., but Cleeves indicates that it happened later, at around 5 or 6 p.m.

120 This would seem to indicate that Sandham's battery had also retired from the crest.

121 First Lieutenant Henry Mielmann (Beamish no. 46) had been severely wounded at San Sebastian in 1813.

122 Sinclair's battery had remained in reserve near Mont St Jean until moving forward to a position on the crest to the right of La Haye Sainte (this certainly occurred much earlier than Adkin indicates at 4.30). Having run out of ammunition he retired to replenish and hence Cleeves found him here.

123 He seems to indicate that Sympher took position near his battery, whereas Adkin has him near to Hougoumont.

124 This is a particularly late notification!

125 Captain Augustus von Saffe (Beamish no. 985). He was promoted major on the field, it not being known immediately that he was dead.
126 Captain Charles von Holle (Beamish no. 989).
127 Ensign Hartwich von Luken (Beamish no. 1014).
128 Beamish records the killed rankers as 1 sergeant major, 2 sergeants, 1 drummer and 27 men. The apparent discrepancy may be explained by some men succumbing to their wounds soon after the battle.
129 Major William von Robertson (Beamish no. 376).
130 Captain Gerlach von Schlutter (Beamish no. 383) was very severely wounded and died at Stade on 29 June 1818.
131 Lieutenant Frederick Schnath, adjutant (Beamish no. 417).
132 Lieutenant August Muller (Beamish no. 402).
133 Lieutenant Henry Wilding (Beamish no. 404).
134 Ensign Charles August von der Hellen (Beamish no. 414).
135 Beamish records 6 sergeants and 63 men wounded; he also counts another lieutenant wounded, which would be Lieutenant Diederich von Einem (Beamish no. 394).
136 Beamish records 16 men missing.
137 Major (at Waterloo) George Muller (Beamish no. 423) was made a lieutenant colonel for Waterloo.
138 Colonel E.von Vincke; 5th Hanoverian Militia Brigade.
139 These were probably Hanoverians or Nassauers; as at the time, no Brunswick troops were yet involved in the action at Hougoumont.
140 Captain George Tilee (Beamish no. 984).
141 Captain William von der Decken (Beamish no. 425).
142 Captain Frederick Purgold (Beamish no. 427). One of his letters has been published in the author's *Letters from the Battle of Waterloo* (no. 132).
143 Captain Frederick von Wenckstern (Beamish no. 430).
144 'N. N.' in German is a customary abbreviation for *nomen nescio* which translates as 'I am ignorant of the name'. The description would seem to indicate Genappe, but it is very unlikely that they proceeded this far that night.
145 All told the battalion lost 106 killed, wounded and prisoners.
146 Note by Pflugk-Harttung. The same report with many minor changes exists in the *Journal der acht Linien-und Veteranen-Bataillone K.G.L.* which was collected and assembled by several officers at the initiative of Major Christopher Heise of the 1st Light Battalion of the Legion for Beamish's *History of the German Legion*.
147 This confirms the receipt of late orders by this brigade.
148 Cambron-casteau.
149 Actually the Bois de Bussières.
150 Lieutenant Colonel George Charles Augustus du Plat, 4th Line Battalion KGL, died of his wounds on 21 June 1815.
151 Lieutenant Colonel Frederick von Wissell 3rd Line Battalion KGL (Beamish no. 470).
152 Major Gottlieb Frederick von Lutterman (Beamish no. 471).
153 Captain Frederick Didel (Beamish no. 990).
154 Major Everhard Charles Boden (Beamish no. 472).

155 Lieutenant Frederick von Jeinsen (Beamish no. 1037) died at Brussels of his wounds on 28 June 1815.
156 Beamish shows Charles Leschen (Beamish no. 477) as captain.
157 Lieutenant Augustus Kuckuck (Beamish no. 490).
158 Lieutenant Harry Edward Kuckuck (Beamish no. 494).
159 Beamish only lists two lieutenants wounded (the Kuckucks) and 31 men missing.
160 6 km north-west of Binche.
161 10 km south-west of Ath.
162 A roundabout route.
163 I have been unable to identify this location.
164 5 km north-east of Ath.
165 His timings now appear to be about two to three hours too early.
166 Scheuch's figures only appear to list the killed, Siborne lists a further 4 officers and 17 men wounded and 2 officers and 7 men missing. Given their losses came from distant cannon fire, one must conclude that the missing probably fled.
167 The short title of the Osnabrück Battalion has been used to avoid the confusion of the three Duke of York Battalions.
168 Major Lewis von Dreves (Beamish no. 474).
169 Both a few miles north of Ath.
170 Bull's and Ramsay's batteries were virtually alongside each other here and it is possible he mistook them for a single strong battery of 12 guns.
171 The Third Brigade of Major General Frederick Adam.
172 The evidence is clear and strong that Cambronne was captured and did not utter the immortal phrase (even this appears to be a later invention). 'The Guard dies but never surrenders'.
173 Siborne lists 3 officers and 17 men killed.
174 Siborne lists 6 officers and 62 men wounded.
175 Siborne lists only 6 men missing.
176 Pflugk-Harttung note. Colonel Halkett is meant.
177 The larger calibre of the British Brown Bess muskets than that of the French muskets permitted the use of their cartridges.
178 Major George Lewis Rudorff (Beamish no. 297).
179 Captain Otto von Hamerstein (Beamish no. 105).
180 Siborne lists 1 sergeant and 19 men killed.
181 Siborne lists 2 officers, 3 NCOs and 57 men wounded with 1 man missing.
182 Karl Count von Alten had fought throughout the Peninsula, serving at Albuera, Salamanca, Vitoria, Nivelle, Nive, Orthes and Toulouse. He was severely wounded at Waterloo.
183 Pflugk-Harttung's footnote: The map is missing from this document.
184 Commanding the Grubenhagen and Verden Field Battalions respectively.
185 William of Orange Nassau, 'The Silent', liberator of the Netherlands from the Spanish yoke (1533–84).
186 He signally fails to mention that it left the battlefield during the fighting, for which the colonel was cashiered.
187 Pflugk-Harttung's footnote: Pencil notation on the margin: The other two cavalry regiments as well as the 6th Infantry Brigade of Major General Lyon

were part of the corps of General Hill [at Halle].

188 This praise is in marked contrast to Alten's earlier report to Wellington, which appeared to blame Kielmansegge for the retiring of the Hanoverian Brigade under his command just after La Haye Sainte was captured and thereby threatening Wellington's centre. Kielmansegge was placed under arrest following the battle, but following the intervention of Captain James Shaw (later to be Shaw-Kennedy) 43rd Foot AQMG to the 3rd Division was released without any blemish on his character. See Gareth Glover, 'A Very Unfortunate Business: The Arrest of Count Kielmansegge', *Journal of The Association of Friends of The Waterloo Committee*, vol. 27, no. 2, Summer 2005.

189 He would appear to have been wrongly recorded in the Waterloo Medal Roll as Frederick Lindemann: he served in No. 4 Company of 2nd Light Battalion KGL and was discharged on 24 August 1815. James Bogle in *A Waterloo Hero: The Adventures of Friedrich Lindau* (Frontline, London, 2009) states that he was in the 1st Company on joining but it is quite possible he moved later and there is no one of a similar name in the Waterloo Roll in that company.

190 1 Mariengros = 8 Pfennig.

191 There is no one of this name listed in the Waterloo Medal Roll for this battalion, which includes those killed, but it might be Private Gabrial Tiefer (as in the Roll) of No. 1 Company who was killed.

192 Here he seems to indicate that his brother was in the same battalion, he could be misrecorded as George Lindner, who appears in the Waterloo Medal Roll in No. 4 Company as well. It is known that his elder brother's name was George.

193 His younger brother was named Christian but there is nobody listed in the KGL Artillery with a similar name. As it was not unusual for middle names to be used in preference it could possibly be Gunner Henry Linneman (as in the Waterloo Medal Roll) of Captain Kuhlmann's troop.

194 Mentioned previously in his memoirs, not printed here, his youngest brother had followed Lindau against his parents' will.

195 A pun on the mountain range of the same name in central Germany.

196 This seems unlikely: where were these to come from?

197 Captain Frederick Melchior William Schaumann (Beamish no. 988).

198 Captain Adolphus Bosewiel (Beamish no. 975).

199 Lieutenant George Drummond Graeme (Beamish no. 354) was wounded at Waterloo. Two letters from this officer were published in Siborne's *Waterloo Letters* (nos 179 and 180). He became a captain in later life, hence Lindau's reference to this rank.

200 Sergeant Christian Poppe of No. 6 Company was killed at Waterloo.

201 Ensign George Frank was severely wounded at Waterloo.

202 Captain Ernest Augustus Holtzermann (Beamish no. 340) was slightly wounded at Waterloo.

203 This appears to be Sergeant Frederick Forstermann (in the Waterloo Medal Roll) of No. 2 Company.

204 The coach was eventually sold to Madame Tussauds in London and was an exhibit there until destroyed in a fire in 1925.

205 There is some confusion here. Lieutenant William Timmann (Beamish no. 370) was adjutant at Waterloo and was severely wounded. Lieutenant Bernhard Riefkugel (Beamish no. 348) may have taken over as adjutant but is recorded as having been wounded himself, according to Baring and 'severely wounded' at Waterloo by Beamish. It is possible, however, that the wound was not serious and that he remained with the battalion.

206 A Captain Arnaud Baron Twent (Beamish no. 1216) did serve with the 2nd Light Battalion in Spain. He resigned on 1 March 1814 and clearly joined the Dutch/Belgian army. He died in Holland in 1818.

207 Captain Lord John Somerset, brother of Lord Fitzroy Somerset.

208 Lieutenant Colonel William von Linsingen (Beamish no. 559). A letter of his has been published in the author's *Letters from the Battle of Waterloo* (no. 166).

209 Beamish only lists 3 officers 6 sergeants 1 drummer and 40 men wounded which agrees with the first casualty return published in the London Gazette on 8 July 1815. It is clear that this return is based on later knowledge of what had happened to the missing.

210 Beamish shows fully 74 men missing. It would appear that Beamish's records are based on the Gazette return, before many more had been returned wounded rather than 'missing' as originally listed.

211 Captain Ernest Christian Charles von Wurmb (Beamish no. 981).

212 Lieutenant and adjutant John L Schuck (Beamish no. 1012).

213 Captain Frederick Sander (Beamish no. 562).

214 Charles Berger (Beamish no. 571). Beamish who shows him as a captain.

215 Charles Bothmer (Beamish no. 568) became a captain on 27 June.

216 Lieutenant George Klingsohr (Beamish no. 577).

217 Lieutenant Charles von Witte (Beamish no. 574).

218 William Meyer (Beamish no. 563) was not recorded as wounded in the first return; Beamish also correctly shows him as a captain.

219 Ensign and adjutant William Walther (Beamish no. 597).

220 Ensign Charles Christian Winckler (Beamish no. 588).

221 Lieutenant Edmund Wheatley (Beamish no. 581). His memoirs were published as *The Wheatley Diary* by Christopher Hibbert in 1964.

222 7 km south-east of Soignies.

223 4 km south-west of Nivelles.

224 Ensign William de Moreau (Beamish no. 724).

225 Sergeant Ferdinand Stuart survived to receive a Waterloo medal.

226 Lieutenant colonel John Christian von Schroder (Beamish no. 1018) died on 22 June of his wounds. Beamish shows him as belonging to the 2nd Line. He replaced Colonel Charles Best in command as he commanded the 4th Hanoverian Brigade at Waterloo.

227 Major Charles von Petersdorff (Beamish no. 696) was slightly wounded.

228 Captain Thilo von Werterhagen (Beamish no. 992).

229 Captain Augustus William von Voigt (Beamish no. 982).

230 Lieutenant William von Marenholz (Beamish no. 998).

231 Sergeant Trangott Adam.

232 Sergeant Christian Waldmann.

233 Drummer Christian Hentze.

234 Beamish lists 24 killed.
235 Adjutant Frederick Brinckmann (Beamish no. 733) was severely wounded.
236 Captain Charles Emanuel W. Rougemont (Beamish no. 702) was slightly wounded.
237 Lieutenant Johann Christian Sattler (Beamish no. 711) was slightly wounded.
238 Beamish says 76 rank and file wounded which again proves that he quotes Waters's return from the Gazette of 8 July for his casualty figures. The figures quoted in these letters are more accurate later returns.
239 Beamish says one sergeant missing.
240 This order was received in the Prince of Orange's name but not actually from him, as at this time he was dining with Wellington and was ignorant of affairs.
241 Actually placed on the road to Mons to guard against any movement by the French on this wing.
242 This was nothing more than skirmishing.
243 A number of batteries removed their guns from the line instead of bringing up reserve ammunition wagons to the guns, this is probably the main cause of Wellington's later complaints regarding the artillery in the battle. See letter no. 16 in this volume for evidence of Cleeves's and Sinclair's batteries doing this.
244 As ordered by the Prince of Orange, that regiment's 2nd Battalion and the remnants of the much weakened 1st Battalion made a bayonet attack against a strong enemy column. While riding by their side and encouraging the men, the Prince was wounded and fell off his horse. This and the impact of the violent enemy fire threw the Nassauers into confusion and led to their retreat. See 2nd Lieutenant H. von Gagern's 'Waterloo Letter', no. 54 in this volume.
245 More than three-quarters of the battalions consisted of recent conscripts, the troops of the 1st Nassau Regiment had received only minimal training and were not led through formation drill and were thus unable to form square. According to a witness 'throughout the battle they stood in closed column. They never formed square', and, in the words of the same observer, 'their losses were obviously quite considerable [from enemy artillery fire] . . . since they were formed in a close column.' See Captain C. von Scriba's letter, no. 29 in this volume.
246 Siborne records losses totalling 40 officers and 921 other ranks killed, wounded or missing from a total of 3,189 men thus losing a third of its complement.
247 5 km west of Soignies.
248 Siborne states that the battalion numbered 512 men.
249 Actually commanded by Major Bülow.
250 Capital city of Jerome's former Kingdom of Westphalia.
251 Von Muffling was the Prussian liaison officer to Wellington's staff.
252 In fact, 960 men of the 1st Battalion, 1st Duchy of Nassau Regiment; eyewitness proof that a Nassau force was part of the first line from the beginning of the battle.
253 Firing high was a common problem, but it was normal practice to fire at the horses rather than the rider; a cavalryman without his horse is useless and blocks the path of following horses.
254 He is mistaken: the general advance did not occur for another three hours.

255 For this reason, Wellington in Spain had banned men from leaving the ranks to aid their wounded comrades until the fighting was over. The musicians were employed to carry the wounded back to the dressing stations, but in an intense battle such as Waterloo, they soon became overwhelmed.

256 Lieutenant Colonel William Langrehr (Beamish no. 1222).

257 Ensign Gustavus Hartmann (Beamish no. 457).

258 It is generally assumed by British writers that this brigade remained virtually inactive alongside Best's Brigade on the left wing throughout the battle, they are clearly in error. These troops were moved to the centre well before Vivian and Vandeleur's cavalry moved

259 On the Ferraris & Capitaine map of 1797, Gros Fromage is shown to be just north of Glabais on the Genappe road.

260 No general of that name fought in Napoleon's part of the French army; at this time, General Comte de Vandamme, commander of the 3rd Corps, was fighting the Prussians at Wavre under Marshal Grouchy.

261 It has to be said that the German reports are more candid regarding the fact that some troops deserted from the hard fighting; it is impossible to believe that such things did not happen in British units to some extent, but is never mentioned.

262 Von Strube was a major at the time of Waterloo and was wounded in the battle.

263 Should be 4th Hanoverian Brigade.

264 The times stated in this report are consistently at least an hour and a half in advance of the accepted timings of major events.

265 Montroeul-sur-Haine west of Mons.

266 Pflugk-Harttung footnote: 'See Colonel Vincke's report on the 5th Infantry Brigade [no. 26 in his book and vol. IV of *The Waterloo Archive*] 1 July 1815.'

267 This statement is confirmed completely by Scovell himself, see his memorandum in vol. III of *The Waterloo Archive*. It is strange however, that Westphalen was able to understand this order written in English, given his earlier statement.

268 Pflugk-Harttung note: 'The piece is written by Count von Westphalen in his own hand and signed by Lieutenant Collmann. Added at the end was "and to join Count von Kielmansegge", which was crossed out with the same ink that was used for the signature.'

269 Cleeves's battery certainly retired to get more ammunition. See his own account, letter no. 16 in this volume.

270 Colonel Charles Best (Beamish no. 695). Another letter of his has been published in the author's *Letters from the Battle of Waterloo* (no. 194).

271 Siborne lists him as Lieutenant T. Fenisch.

272 Lieutenant C. E. Wegener.

273 Siborne spells his name Plati.

274 Major Kuhlmann's Troop.

275 Major General Sir Edward Barnes, Adjutant General.

276 Captain Siegmund Brauns, 8th Line Battalion KGL (Beamish no. 699).

277 Ensign C. A. Schanz.

278 Such a candid report on the failings of certain individuals is a feature of these German reports and is one that is noticeably lacking from British reports,

when it is certain that individuals from these units also failed in their duty.

279 Translator's note: the author's expressions of his patriotic sentiments on the first three pages have been omitted since they do not include any historically relevant information.

280 Jacobi's footnote: Hanover received English subsidies for its troops that were based on English rates; but the troops themselves were paid only the meagre Hanoverian rate. In the Field Battalions the amount per month for a captain was 50, for a lieutenant 15 and for an ensign (most junior company officer) 12 thaler; added to that were allowances for field service. In the beginning, the Landwehr battalions were paid even less, and only with a great effort did General Alten succeed during the campaign in obtaining for them the same rates as those of the Field Battalions.

281 Jacobi's lengthy footnote here deals with his efforts to be paid the higher rate for field service, as against that for depot service that he received at the time.

282 Jacobi's footnote: 'At that time, brigades were identified by the name of their brigadiers; in the field this is much to be preferred over numbers.'

283 7 km north-east of Mons on the road to Soignies.

284 I have discussed the identity of these 'hussars' in depth with Andre Dellevoet, an expert on the Belgian cavalry in the Waterloo campaign. The timing appears to be around 15.30 to 15.45 when the 5th Belgian Dragoons would be returning victoriously (hence shouting 'Long live the King!' and also possibly to avoid being shot at by mistake) from their long-standing fight with the 6th Chasseurs north of Gemioncourt. The Dutch hussars, who were the only hussars from the Netherlands force to reach Quatre Bras, had retired earlier, but it is possible that some had remained to become embroiled in this fight and hence the misidentification. The Belgian Dragoons withdrew to re-assemble north of Gemioncourt.

285 Sart-Dames-Avelines is actually set off to the north of the main road, references to the French occupying this village actually refer to the small group of houses actually on the main road and sometimes called Paradis.

286 Jacobi's footnote: 'According to the regulations at the time, the place of the peloton commander was on the side of this unit; Lieutenant Volger was next to me on the enemy side; he thus received the shot which would have struck me without fail.'

287 Jacobi's footnote: 'When later I wandered in Paris through the Palais Royal I unexpectedly met this Brunswick comrade. He affirmed that I had saved him from total exhaustion, and now asked me to be his guest to commemorate the event. I gladly accepted, and we then partook in a happy mood of a trifle more than what we had shared in the wood near Quatre Bras.'

288 Captain C. T. Korfes was returned as killed.

289 This refers to the Duke of York 1st Battalion (Osnabrück) in the 1st Hanoverian Brigade and should not be confused with the Osnabrück Landwehr Battalion in the 3rd Hanoverian Brigade. See footnote 9 for further clarification of the three Duke of York Battalions.

290 Jacobi's footnote: 'We learned later that the division could have used a shorter road to the highway, which, however, was not found by the not very circumspect officer who had been sent ahead to reconnoitre for the best way. We were often reminded later of the presence of the Duke of Wellington

when the marching arrangements of the different arms were discussed. A cavalry regiment moved towards us on the highway and would have forced the entire division to move off the roadway to continue its march. Wellington had observed this and had ordered in sharp terms, the cavalry to advance over the open fields, because the hard surfaced roadway was to be reserved for infantry and artillery.'

291 Jacobi's footnote: 'The men had to give up their overcoats several weeks ago, and every man had received a woollen blanket that was strapped to the top of the knapsack. The blankets were provided with eyelets so that five men, each, could set up a tent supported by rifles and held down by bayonets stuck into the ground. The blankets turned out to be very useful although they were quite heavy when wet; their use for building tents soon proved to be impractical.'

292 Jacobi's footnote: 'When we marched up to the position, my orderly and many other officer orderlies and their horses were still at the rear of the brigade, as it turned out later. As some balls were striking the area behind the troops during the cannonade, these faint hearted fellows hurried off on the Brussels highway to the wood. Undecided on what to do, they spent the night there, and were caught up in the morning of the 18th in the disorder and flight, in which the entire baggage train of Wellington's army became entangled, as is well known. Everybody had fled in a wild rush towards Brussels, and partly even to Antwerp. It was from the latter place that my orderly returned to the battalion when we had a day of rest on 23 June; he had only one horse but it carried all my belongings; the second horse which had gone lame, was left in Antwerp, and later returned to me.'

293 Jacobi's footnote: 'One of the officers offered a glass of brandy to the highly respected and esteemed Lieutenant Colonel von Wurmb, commander of the Grubenhagen Battalion, and asked him to drink it up. The lieutenant colonel responded with grave foreboding: "I drink this glass to your health; it will be my last one." In the afternoon he was mercilessly struck by a mortal bullet.'

294 Jacobi's footnote: 'Here is the end of my notes that I wrote down soon after the battle; all of the following is based on my always vividly retained memories and later written communications. I do not intend to provide an overview of the battle which is impossible to describe on a few sheets; instead, I will give an idea of my personal experiences, tying them to Hulsemann's History of the 4th Infantry Regiment.'

295 The louis (or Napoleon) d'or was a 20-franc piece.

296 This must refer to Captain Gerlach von Schlutter, 1st Line Battalion, who was severely wounded at Waterloo, but did not die until June 1818. He is not officially listed as an aide de camp but it was not unusual for senior officers to employ 'extra' aides de camp.

297 Jacobi's footnote: 'The unfortunate outcome of our bold advance has since provoked considerable criticism. Lieutenant Colonel von Klencke was deeply envied by many in the legion. At the end of the year 1811 he had left that corps as one of the more junior captains, and was now met by his former comrades as one of the more senior lieutenant colonels. They later expressed the opinion that von Klencke had tried to outshine others in front of the army by his bold sortie, without properly considering the adverse situation. The

lieutenant colonel, on his part, affirmed later to have received the order to attack from an adjutant of the Prince of Orange, the commander of our corps. General von Alten later told me that he had admired the calm courage with which the battalion had advanced, but had also noticed the riskiness of the undertaking; he had been unaware of any order from the Prince of Orange. A further clarification of the circumstances has never occurred.'

298 Jacobi's footnote: 'Captain von Bobarth and Ensign von Platho were cut down; 18 rank and file had been killed, 137 were wounded and 47 were missing. Major von Dachenhausen, always ahead of the line and encouraging the men, was taken prisoner by French infantrymen who had grabbed the reins of his horse.' Siborne records losses of 29 rank and file killed, 137 wounded and 48 missing over the full three days. Jacobi's figures are very similar indicating this was not the loss specifically at the time of being overrun by the cuirassiers. Dachenhausen was recorded as missing and did not return until late July.

299 Jacobi's footnote: 'I later received several letters from disabled non-coms and soldiers who recounted these events in their naïve manner. They extolled their own performance to obtain a recommendation for the award of the Guelphic Medal. In one of these letters it is said more or less truthfully: "I will never forget your honour's words to Captain Rall at that time: 'Captain, we will have to attach ourselves again to some unit', who then said: 'Where could I go with this small group?', and you then said: 'Men, even though most of you have bloody heads, I nevertheless believe that we have not yet done enough for the Fatherland, and that we will have to join the others again.' Not a single one of us stayed behind on hearing these grand words." '

300 Jacobi's footnote: 'If the general had had more war experience, he probably would not have given this kind of order. The matter came to the attention of the Duke of Wellington, it is not known in what way, and the general experienced some unpleasant consequences. Had we been more familiar with the general situation, we might have asked for different orders; our Adjutant von Pentz asserted that he had already done this but without effect.'

301 A senior magistrate.

302 Siborne incorrectly states that he was a lieutenant at Waterloo; Hanbury was actually recorded as killed, therefore he must have succumbed soon to the wound.

303 Jacobi's footnote: 'The city had been ordered to build huts of wood or straw for the Prussians' camp.'

304 Jacobi's footnote: 'In the case of the English troops, a commission of officers was formed whenever foodstuffs were received; if it rejected these, the commissary had to supply better ones.'

305 Jacobi's footnote: 'When Count Munster visited Paris some time later, he was informed by his relatives and friends, who served with us, of the troops' condition. He immediately issued an order in the name of the Prince Regent for the payment of money from the *Feld-Kriegs-Casse* [War Chest] for the purchase of vegetables by the battalions. Those commanders who knew how to take care of their men now sent off officers with train wagons to more distant areas for the purchase of vegetables.'

306 Jacobi's sarcasm: 'For the greater glory of the Duke'!

307 Jacobi's footnote: 'The following parody of the song "Ein freies Leben führen wir" [We live an unencumbered life] was often sung by the soldiers at that time for their amusement:

> We live the life of slaves;
> A life without delight;
> The accommodations at night are hard,
> We dwell in the bois d'Boulogne,
> Tormented by dust and the sun.
>
> Today we drop by at Longchamp,
> And tomorrow at the Provost General's;
> Here we're treated with whips, and there with sour wine,
> For the rest we will well allow
> the stern Milord to provide.
>
> And when with juice from the Seine
> We have cleaned out our throats,
> Then we will drink full of courage and vigour
> To our brotherhood with hunger,
> Who cooks and fries for us.
>
> To our burden and pain, Victory
> Was given us by the good God,
> Oh Lord! take the Victory unto Thyself,
> Oh Lord! take the pain off myself,
> Lead us to our homes in peace!'

308 Jacobi's footnote: 'My older sister Dorothea was married to a Herr Bastide who at first was Payeur [Paymaster] with the French troops and was later an employee of the Imperial Field Administration at Hanover. My sister passed away in September of 1812, shortly after she had given birth to a daughter. Bastide returned to Paris in March 1813; the daughter remained in the care of my mother in Celle; my brother in law travelled there in September 1815.'

309 Major General Sir James Lyon had been with the reserve at Halle on 18 June.

310 Canaille.

311 Jacobi's footnote: 'When several of our men were arrested by the English Provost because they had taken vegetables from nearby gardens, the lieutenant colonel immediately visited with General Colville and assured him that he would have the men most severely punished. The general was much satisfied with this sign of prompt action and responded: "Have compassion with the poor fellows." '

312 The Luneburg Battalion wore dark-green jackets and had black leather equipment.

313 Jacobi's footnote: 'It was of interest to us to find in the harness room a lady's saddle with the label of the Saddlemaker Narten of Hanover. Another oddity that I found in the castle I have preserved until today; it was an old newspaper sheet which showed the 37th Bulletin issued during the war of 1805, dated

von Schonbrun, le 5 Nivose an 14. Among other matters it said: "General Saint-Cyr will march at a rapid pace to Naples, in order to punish the treason of the queen, and to depose that criminal woman from the throne who without shame has violated all that is sacred to mankind. The queen of Naples has ceased to rule." I read this at a time when the haughty Emperor was already a prisoner on board of an English ship.'

314 Jacobi's footnote: 'The first Royal Officer, who was sent to order the fortress to surrender, was shot dead in front of the gate.'

315 Prince Bernhard of Saxe-Weimar (1792–1860), a son of the reigning Duke of Saxe-Weimar-Eisenach; he entered military service with the Prussian Army in 1806, only to be caught up in its defeat at Jena by Napoleon. He transferred to the Army of Saxony in 1809, and distinguished himself in the Battle of Wagram against the Austrians, as ADC to Marshal Bernadotte, and in 1810 was decorated with the Cross of the Legion d'honneur. The Saxon Army went over to the allied side after the Battle of Leipzig in October 1813. Prince Bernhard then became Colonel of the Saxon Regiment of Grenadier Guards, who participated in General Bülow's Corps in driving the French out of the Netherlands. On 16 January 1815, he joined the Netherlands Army with the rank of colonel and was put in command of the Orange Nassau Regiment. At 23 years of age, he led the 2nd Brigade, 2nd Netherlands Division, in the Waterloo Campaign, after its brigadier had suffered a disabling accident a few days before the battle. After the war, he remained in the Netherlands service and eventually became commander-in-chief of the Dutch Army in the Netherlands East Indies. He was retired in 1853.

316 Quoted in R. Starkloff, *Das Leben des Herzogs Bernhard von Sachsen-Weimar-Eisenach* (Gotha, 1865), pp. 185–6.

317 At the time of Waterloo, the Duchy of Nassau, today a part of the German State of Hesse, had a population of some 275,000; it covered an area of 1,900 square miles (about one-fifth the size of Wales). With Wiesbaden as its capital city, it extended northeast from the merger of the Rhine and Main rivers, and bordered on its north side on the hereditary German possessions of the House of Orange Nassau.

In all, the Duchy and the Orange Nassau territories contributed 7,200 soldiers to Wellington's army. Of these 3,000 served in the Duchy's 1st Light Regiment; 2,500 in its 2nd Light Regiment, being under Netherlands command; and 1,700 in the Orange Nassau Regiment, it being an integral part of the Netherlands Army.

After Waterloo, the Duchy of Nassau, as enlarged by the Congress of Vienna, saw its population doubled. It found an infamous end in 1866, when after fighting, and losing, in the war against Prussia on the side of Austria and other members of the Austrian dominated German Federation, it was turned into part of a Prussian province. Duke Adolph found refuge at the Habsburg court and, in 1890, was made a hereditary Grand Duke of Luxembourg.

318 According to Wacker p. 679 and 683, regimental strengths were actually 1st Light – 2,900, 2nd Light – 2,710, and Orange Nassau 1,742 (including the Volunteer Jäger Company) for a total of 7,352 men.

319 See below for the full loss in killed after the 'missing' have either returned or were presumed dead.

320 Major Johann Friedrich Sattler was put in charge of the 2nd Nassau Regiment. Sattler had originally joined the service of the Archbishopric of Mainz in 1799 but transferred to the Nassau service in 1802 as a lieutenant.

321 Colonel Friedrich Wilhelm von Goedecke (1770–1857) had been commander both of the 2nd Regiment Nassau and the 2nd Brigade, 2nd Netherlands Division. Major Johann Friedrich Sattler (1782–1842), until then commander of 1st Battalion, 2nd Nassau's, was given the command of the 2nd Regiment after von Goedecke's disabling accident.

322 Major Philipp von Normann had actually begun his military career as a cadet in the Austrian army in 1801, but transferred to Nassau service in 1803, becoming a captain in 1809 and major in 1813. He became a lieutenant colonel in 1820 and retired as a colonel in 1832.

323 Major Gottfried Hegmann, commanded the 3rd Battalion during the Battle of Waterloo, one of his legs was shattered by a cannonball, he underwent two amputations but died a few days later. He originally joined the Dutch army in 1793 and transferred to the Nassau force in 1806 and fought with the French in Prussia and in Spain.

324 Captain Carl August Frensdorf eventually took command of the 3rd battalion 2nd Nassau Regiment, when Major Hegmann was severely wounded. He had commenced his military career in the Dutch Brigade on the Isle of Wight and then fought against the British at the Cape of Good Hope in 1805. He was promoted major in 1817 and retired in 1821.

325 Captain Carl F. E. von Mulmann had joined the Nassau service in 1808 as a cadet. He died in 1823.

326 Strangely, he omits to mention the Guards, who took the woods towards the end of the day.

327 Statements were made that they were forced out of these farms, but were emphatically refuted by the officers of the regiment. See also letter 46 in this volume.

328 Vivian's Brigade of the 10th and 18th Hussars and 1st Hussars KGL.

329 For further in depth research on the role of the Nassau troops at Hougoumont, the reader is referred to Martin Mittelacher, 'The Nassauers at Hougoumont', *Journal of the Society for Army Historical Research*, vol. 18, no. 327, Autumn 2003, pp. 228–42.

330 Büsgen's 'vegetable garden' was actually the park-like large garden of Chateau Hougoumont. The complex was unoccupied except for the families of the tenant farmer and gardener. Its owner, a Chevalier de Louville, resided in Nivelles. It is thus entirely possible that much of the garden had been planted with vegetables by June 1815.

331 According to Nassau Sergeant Andreas Buchsieb, the battalion colours were displayed on the roof of the house, but then were quickly taken down upon the commencement of the action. Later, accompanied by an escort, he brought the colours to the safety of the regiment stationed in the Papelotte area. His arrival there coincided with the British cavalry driving the French prisoners from d'Erlon's Corps over the crest to the rear. A. Buchsieb, *Denkwürdigkeiten 1808 bis 1815*, pp. 75–6, published 1867. For parts of this work that relates to Waterloo see vol. IV of the *Waterloo Archive*.

332 It might seem strange that there were no defenders within Hougoumont at

this time, but the two light companies of the Guards initially looked to defend the wood and gardens and would retire into the buildings when pressed, hence the obvious preparations for defence, only later were the buildings occupied by the Guards.

333 The 'Brunswick' Jäger were actually Hanoverian Feldjäger of Kielmannsegge's 1st Hanoverian Infantry Brigade. Although the Electorate of Hanover (later a Kingdom) had split off from the Duchy of Brunswick in 1692, Hanoverians were often referred to as Brunswickers until well into the 1900s.

334 Büsgen had no specific knowledge regarding the deployment at Hougoumont of the British Foot Guards. The four light companies posted there since the eve of the battle consisted of those of the Coldstream Regiment (100 men) and the 3rd Guards Regiment (100 men), and of two companies of the First Guards Regiment (165 men) The two First Guards companies rejoined their regiment on the main position, hence at the beginning of the action, there were thus only 200 Guardsmen posted at Hougoumont. The First Guards companies were ordered back to the chateau after the first French attack and were defending the orchard until relieved in mid-afternoon by line companies of the 2nd Battalion, Third Guards Regiment. Of the Coldstream Regiment, all of its further seven available companies (the colours could not be hazarded in the complex and one company stayed on the ridge to protect them) were eventually sent into the Hougoumont complex. They joined their light company who earlier, with the Third Guards light company, had defeated the French in their first incursion through the North Gate.

335 The buildings in question were the gardener's house, and offices and stables adjoining it on either side. They formed part of the southern boundary of the chateau complex, which faced the French positions.

336 The troops defending the wood included also 100 men, each, of the rifle armed Luneburg and Grubenhagen Battalions of the 1st Hanoverian Infantry Brigade, apart from its Feldjäger company and the two Nassau companies.

337 After the first French attack by one brigade of Jerome's 6th Division, the orchard was cleared of the enemy by the two First Guards light companies who had been ordered back to Hougoumont. They were assisted by Hanoverians and Nassauers who had earlier taken refuge in the hollow way behind Hougoumont [A. Schmidtborn, *Antheil der Herzoglich-Nassauischen Truppen in den Kampfen des 16., 17. und 18. Juni 1815*, Wiesbaden, 1865]. Together with the Coldstream and Third Guards light companies and some Hanoverians, operating from the western side of the chateau, they forced the French back into, and then almost completely out of, the wood. The allied troops were driven back again in the second French attack carried out by both brigades of Jerome's 6th Division.

338 This would appear most likely to be the 2nd company 2nd French Horse Artillery battery.

339 This second incursion by the enemy, through the side door next to the Great Barn at a much later period than the earlier (and famous) one at about 1 p.m. through the North Gate has been omitted by previous historians of the battle. The claim is fully confirmed by Private Matthew Clay of the Third Guards, although he thought that the French had penetrated through the South Gate at the gardener's house rather than through the side door as described by

Büsgen (see Clay's account, Gareth Glover, *A Narrative of the Battles of Quatre-Bras and Hougoumont*, 2006). Clay confirms the timing as being at the moment they are forced to abandon the burning chateau at around 3.30 p.m. The barricaded South Gate however remained securely closed throughout the battle.

340 Johann Peter Leonhard, was a conscript in the Duchy of Nassau's 2nd Light Infantry Regiment, which was in the Netherlands service since July 1814. He participated in the Waterloo campaign as a private in No. 3 Company of the regiment's 1st Battalion. That battalion had been despatched to Chateau Hougoumont in the morning of 18 June 1815 to reinforce its garrison of British Foot Guards and Hanoverian riflemen. Three companies of the six company Nassau battalion, some 400 men, became the entire force inside to repel the initial French attacks on the buildings and garden. Soon, however, most of the troops of the 2nd Guards Brigade, some 1,600 men, joined the defence of the chateau against the persistent attacks of the French infantry of General Reille's 2nd Corps.

    The 2nd Nassau Regiment, returned to its garrison in the Netherlands in December 1815, where it was to remain until 1820 in accordance with the 1814 agreement between the Duke of Nassau and the Sovereign Prince of Orange Nassau of the Netherlands.

341 There were no thunderstorms in the area on the day of battle; exploding shells may have overly impressed Leonhard's imagination

342 Original in Hessisches Hauptstaatsarchiv Wiesbaden, File No. 130 II 7,238.

343 Friedrich Ernst von Reichenau (1789–1865); a cadet in the Duchy of Nassau's Chasseurs à Cheval as of 1809, he fought in Napoleon's army in Spain until 1813 and, after the Duchy joined the allied side, became a captain in the Nassau infantry and served at Waterloo as brigade adjutant of 2nd Brigade, 2nd Netherlands Division.

344 This excerpt from von Reichenau's private letter was passed on from Lieutenant Koch to one Lieutenant Colonel von Oberkamp, who in his turn brought it to the attention of the Duke of Nassau on 10 July 1815.

345 Major General August von Kruse (1779–1848), highest ranking officer of the Duchy of Nassau. After the battle on the march to Paris, the 2nd Nassaus were removed from Netherlands command to form, with the 1st Nassau Regiment, the Nassau Division under General von Kruse in Lord Hill's 2nd British Corps. The two regiments were renamed brigades as they each were of brigade size strength. Kruse had originally served with the Hanoverian Garde Regiment in 1793, joining the Nassau forces in 1803 as a captain. His rise was pretty meteoric, becoming major in 1806, lieutenant colonel 1807 and colonel 1808. He eventually retired in 1837 as lieutenant general.

346 A harsh comment on one of those credited with the decision not to abandon Quatre Bras against orders on 15/16 June. It is clear in a number of letters that he was not loved by his officers, who openly disagreed with some of his statements.

347 He is mistaken, the correct name was Ter la Haye, not to be confused with the heavily embattled farm of La Haye Sainte before the centre of the Anglo-Allied line.

348 Captain George Ludwig Ahlefeld (1798–1856) commanded at Waterloo the

grenadier company, 2nd Battalion, 1st Nassau Regiment.

349 Major Wilhelm von Weyhers (1775–?) (although his actual name appears to have been von Ebersberg), had joined the Nassau staff in 1806 as a captain, he was promoted to captain while fighting in Spain in the French army with the 2nd Nassaus, and to major after the Duchy joined the Allied side in December 1813. At Waterloo, as commander of the 1st Battalion, 1st Nassaus, on 18 June he caused his grenadier and No. 1 Companies to be overwhelmed by French cuirassiers by ordering an ill advised abortive attack against a nearby French battery. He was severely wounded in the action and pensioned off in 1816.

350 Lieutenant Friedrich von Trott (1798–1815), a cadet in the Duchy of Nassau 2nd Regiment December 1813, he was promoted to lieutenant in 1814 and served in that regiment at Waterloo, where he was killed.

351 Lieutenant Carl Magnus von Holleben (1794–?) joined the Duchy of Nassau's Chasseurs à Cheval as a cadet in 1813 and fought with the French in Spain, he was promoted to lieutenant in March 1813. After the Duchy's change to the Allied side in December 1813, he transferred to the infantry to become a 1st lieutenant in the 2nd Regiment. Having fought in the Waterloo campaign he retired in 1818 and was granted a pension and the nominal rank of captain.

352 Original in Hessisches Hauptstaatsarchiv Wiesbaden, file no. 202/1015.

353 The author of this report, Carl Friedrich von Rettberg (1788–1844), a captain at the Battle of Waterloo, had begun his military career as a cadet in the Duchy of Nassau's Chasseurs a Cheval, who fought in Spain as part of Napoleon's troops of the Confederation of the Rhine where he was made an officer of the Legion d'honneur for his bravery, but was also wounded twice. He joined the 2nd Duchy of Nassau Infantry Regiment in 1814 with the rank of captain. At Waterloo he was nominally in command of his battalion's flanqueur (light) company, he kept defending with a five company detachment the Papelotte farm, on the army's extreme left wing, against superior French forces. In later life, he attained the rank of colonel and served as an ADC to His Highness Duke Wilhelm of Nassau. Some of the information in this report was used by Captain William Siborne in his *History of the War in France and Belgium in 1815*. It had been part of a summary report on the role of the Duchy of Nassau troops in the Waterloo campaign which had been sent to London in 1836.

354 It could not have been the 18th regiment: this formed part of Major General von Losthin's 15th Infantry Brigade and was in the Smohain area

355 See note 343.

356 Doring was a sergeant in the Grenadier Company of the 1st Battalion of the Orange Nassau Regiment. A tanner by trade, his memoir of military service between 1813 and 1817 shows him as an acute observer of events at Quatre Bras and Waterloo. In later life he was mayor of Herborn, his native city, in the heartland of the German hereditary possessions of the House of Orange Nassau. Incorporated by Napoleon into the Grand Duchy of Berg, these lands had been returned to their Netherlands sovereign by the end of 1813.

In mid-January 1814, the Orange Nassau Regiment was formed with several hundred soldiers of the former Grand Duchy of Berg and by conscription of new recruits. In July 1814, it became part of the Netherlands Army as the 28th Regiment of the Line. Its uniform was that of the Dutch

infantry; blue coats, grey overalls, white bandoliers, and black shakos. It was
armed with French muskets and bayonets. In the Waterloo campaign,
together with the 2nd Light Regiment of the Duchy of Nassau and a
volunteer Jäger company, it made up Colonel Prince Bernhard of Saxe
Weimar's 2nd Brigade in General Perponcher's 2nd Netherlands Division.

357 The periods before and after the Waterloo campaign contained in the memoirs
of Sergeant Doring have not been included. In editing the document, some
lengthy personal comments referring to his uncle, Major Gottfried Hegmann,
commander of the 3rd Battalion, 2nd Nassau, and his brother, Albert Jacob
Doring, a surgeon in his Orange Nassau Regiment, have been omitted.

358 The regiment's full name was Duchy of Nassau 2nd Light Infantry Regiment.
The Duchy's area extended south from the southern boundary of the German
possessions of the House of Orange Nassau towards the confluence of the
Rhine and Main rivers. Today it is part of the German State of Hesse. Most of
the regiment's officers and many men of the rank and file were veterans of
Napoleon's Spanish war, where they fought as part of the troops of the
Confederation of the Rhine.

359 The author erred on the high side. In the morning of 16 June, about 7,500
men of Netherlands and Nassau infantry and 16 guns faced around 11,000
French infantrymen, 1,900 sabres and 22 guns.

360 Field Surgeon Johann Gottfried Neuendorff served with the Volunteer Jäger
company at Waterloo. He became a divisional surgeon and retired in 1843.

361 This would appear to be in error as it was nearly ten o'clock in the morning
before Wellington knew of the Prussian retreat. However rumours of this
defeat do seem to have been round the camp fires that night.

362 Major General August von Kruse, commander of the brigade size 1st Duchy
of Nassau Light Regiment, apparently took it upon himself to press British
cavalrymen into Nassau service in order to expedite the retreat of his troops
to Waterloo.

363 Clearly refers to the Scots Greys.

364 Although the author mentions Waterloo at this and other places, he obviously
refers, in fact, to the Mont St Jean complex of farms.

365 The rapid movements of this campaign precluded regular supplies to the
troops of all nations. Only national prejudice can blind to the fact that troops
of every nation were guilty of plundering in the desperation of hunger and
that their officers overlooked their demeanours.

366 This indicates that Frischermont was captured by the French.

367 Major Wilhelm von Dressel was commander of the 1st Battalion, Orange
Nassau Regiment.

368 Sergeant Doring's brother, Albert Jacob Doring, was the battalion surgeon of
the 2nd Battalion, Orange Nassau Regiment.

369 A jurist by profession, Friedrich Ernst Eberhard (1782–1835) appears in the
Officer List of the Orange Nassau Regiment with the rank of first lieutenant
as of 16 February 1814. No prior military service is shown in the biographical
data of a list of Nassau officers. After the battle he transferred to the Duchy
of Nassau military establishment, was promoted to captain but pensioned in
1816 due to the impairment from the wound suffered at Waterloo. From 1818
to 1832 he was a representative in the second chamber of the Duchy's Estates.

370 These were troops of Best's brigade and specifically the Osterode and Munden Battalions which stood at the crossroads throughout.

371 The lack of an ample supply of infantry ammunition for the Orange Nassau Regiment was a problem both at Quatre Bras and at Waterloo. The regiment was under the direct command of Prince Bernhard of Saxe-Weimar until 15 June. (He then replaced Colonel von Goedecke as commander of 2nd Brigade, 2nd Netherlands Division.) It is unclear why the regiment was low on ammunition on that day at Quatre Bras, even though it had been kept on alert for several days in expectation of the French attack. That the same problem occurred again at Waterloo can only be explained by poor leadership. The Orange Nassau were part of Prince Bernhard's brigade. One should have expected that one of his first orders before the battle would have been to assure an ample supply of ammunition for his former regiment.

372 General Durutte's 4th Division, the 2nd Brigade of General Brue attacking the Papelotte-Frischermont area operated almost at right angles to the Division's 1st Brigade of General Pegot, which attacked the British 5th Division in a northerly direction.

373 Lieutenant Friedrich Muller was wounded in the arm while defending the Smohain area. He had originally served with the Garde Regiment of Hesse, became a cadet-sergeant in Dutch service and then served in the Prince of Orange's Garde du corps from 1787 to 1792. He then seems to have disappeared until 1814, when he appears as a lieutenant in the Orange Nassau Regiment. He finally retired in 1820.

374 Note that Eberhard had described their wounds as not dangerous in his letter to his wife, written shortly after the battle.

375 Captain Ignaz Morenhoffen accompanied the lightly wounded Prince Wilhelm of Nassau-Weilburg to the rear at Waterloo. He was promoted major and ennobled in 1830 and retired in 1849 as a lieutenant colonel.

376 Captain Carl Willibald Bruno von Bose, served at Waterloo as adjutant to Major General von Kruse. He had originally been in Wurttemberg service, but joined the Nassau cavalry in 1810, serving with the French in Spain. In 1816 he retired as a major and in 1835 he became Equerry and Chamberlain at the Ducal court; he then retired in 1843.

377 The records actually show him as First Lieutenant Hermann Count Walderdorff, who served at Waterloo as a volunteer adjutant on the staff of Major General Kruse. He was promoted to captain in September 1815 but died later that year.

378 Major à la suite Anton Philipp Breidbach-Burresheim served as adjutant to Prince Wilhelm of Nassau who was on the Duke of Wellington's staff. He had started in the Nassau cavalry in 1809 serving with the French in Spain. He became a lieutenant colonel in 1830 and colonel in 1848 when he also became Equerry to the Duke of Nassau. He was active in the German National Parliament of 1848 and then became the representative of Archduke Stephan of Austria at the Diet of the Germanic Confederation.

379 Colonel Eranst L. H. von Steuben. He had joined the Hanoverian service in 1801, joining the Jäger corps of the Archbishopric of Mainz which was acceded to Nassau in 1802. He became a captain in 1803, major in 1806 and lieutenant colonel in 1809. He served in Prussia and Spain, receiving the

Legion d'Honneur. Von Steuben retired in 1816 but died that year from a wound sustained in a duel.

380 Lieutenant Colonel Adolph Ferdinand von Hagen served on the Nassau General Staff at Waterloo. He took command of the 1st Battalion 1st Nassau Regiment after Major Weyhers was severely wounded. He had originally served in the Prussian army but in 1807 he transferred to the Nassau Chevau Legers in 1807, serving with the French in Spain. He retired in 1830 and became Chamberlain at the Ducal court.

381 Major Friedrich C. D. Preen commanded the 3rd or Landwehr Battalion at Waterloo. He had joined the Dutch service in 1801 and joined the Nassau service, serving in Prussia in 1806 and Spain from 1808–11. He became a captain on the Nassau staff in 1810 and became a major in 1813. He became a lieutenant colonel in 1817, colonel 1820, major general 1840 and retired as a lieutenant general in 1848.

382 Captain Carl Joseph von Weitershausen a cadet in the Guards Regiment of Hesse in 1804, transferred in 1807 to the Nassau service, and by 1814 had risen to the rank of captain in the 1st Regiment Nassau.

383 This war diary account omits that the inept battalion commander had ordered his men to charge at two enemy guns, and that after an advance of about 50 paces from the position, the two leading companies were overwhelmed by the cuirassiers waiting nearby. The remnants of the two companies and the rest of the battalion returned to the position. See 'Report of Major General Weiz', no. 51 in this volume.

384 According to an eyewitness, General von Kruse led this detachment and the Prince of Orange rode at its side and then fell from his horse wounded. See H. von Gagern's 'Waterloo Letter', no. 53 in this volume

385 It is clear that the much weakened 5th Brigade of Halkett was pushed back by the Guard.

386 Captain Peter Gottlieb Schuler commanded the Grenadier company, he was severely wounded at Waterloo and not fully recovering, retired in 1816. He had begun his military career in the Nassau service in 1806 as a lieutenant, becoming a captain in 1810. He fought against Austria in 1809 and in Spain from 1810–13.

387 This report was submitted by Major General Friedrich August Weiz to his sovereign, Duke Adolph of Nassau, in 1863, many years after the great battle. At Waterloo, he was a captain and company commander in the 1st Battalion of the Ducal 1st Light Regiment.

388 The author here laments the fact that the young men no longer serve in blind obedience under an autocratic ruler. Duke Adolph had reneged in 1851 on the basic freedoms of speech, of association, and of the press, which he had been forced to grant in the revolutionary year 1848. The author's identification with the old order is reflected in the submissive and effusive style of his covering letter to Duke Adolph.

389 In 1848–9, some Nassau troops participated in the army of the German Federation in its armed conflict with the Kingdom of Denmark over the possession of the Holstein border province.

390 Some Waterloo historians claim that the 1st Nassau Regiment had initially been posted in rear of the Anglo Allied first line. However, from the

beginning of the battle, its 1st Battalion had been positioned in the first line between Halkett's 5th British Brigade and Kielmannsegge's Hanoverian Brigade in General von Alten's 3rd British Division.

391 At the time of Waterloo, the battle formation of a Nassau battalion of six companies had a right wing consisting of the Grenadier and the next numbered two companies, and a left wing of the following numbered two companies and the Voltigeur, or light, company. In its 'division' order of two companies side by side, the Grenadier and No. 1 Companies were at the front of the battalion and thus directly exposed to enemy fire.

392 This would be Cleeves's battery.

393 The 2nd Battalion 73rd Foot were to their immediate right.

394 Captain Peter Joseph Rohm commanded No. 1 Company at Waterloo and was wounded in the critical phase of the battle. In 1816 he transferred to Prussian service as his homelands were transferred to Prussia by the Congress of Vienna.

395 This is almost certainly First Lieutenant Wilhelm J. J. Niess of No. 1 Company, who was severely wounded at Waterloo. He was promoted captain in 1816 but ended his own life in 1831 following an altercation with Major Büsgen.

396 Lieutenant Ernst Menzler of No. 1 Company was wounded during the critical phase. He was discharged at his own request in 1818 and later became Mayor of the City of Diez.

397 The odd-numbered Nassau battalions had their companies numbered in odd numbers, and the even numbered battalions had theirs designated in even numbers. Thus, the six companies of the 1st Battalion had the designations 'Grenadier', 1, 3, 5, 7 and 'Voltigeur' Company. In their battle order of two company divisions, the 'Grenadier' and No. 1 Companies were in front, Nos 3 and 5 Companies in the middle, and No. 7 and the 'Voltigeur' Companies in the rear.

398 First Lieutenant Theodor Koehler was promoted to captain two days after the Battle of Waterloo but died August 1815 at the Bois de Boulogne.

399 Lieutenant Carl Macco commanded No. 5 Company late in the day as all senior officers had been wounded or seconded to other leaderless companies. As his native region became part of Prussia as a result of the Congress of Vienna, he transferred to the Prussian army in 1816.

400 Lieutenant Ludwig Wollmerscheid served with the Grenadier company of the 1st Battalion at Waterloo and was wounded. It is possible that he had risen from the ranks as his record shows service in Prussia in 1806, Austria 1809 and in Spain from 1810–13. He became a first lieutenant in 1828 and captain in 1838, retiring in 1844.

401 This decoration is mentioned in Sir Bernard Burke's *The Book of Orders of Knighthood and Decorations of Honour,* London, 1858, p. 163, as the 'Military Decoration of Honour'. It was awarded in gold and silver versions and only to sergeants and lower ranks; the reverse bearing the inscription *Der Tapferkeit* (For bravery). Clearly they were awarded the Gold Military Decoration of Honour.

402 General von Kruse's report, dated Malplaquet, 21 June 1815, was for the information of the Duke of Nassau. He sent a second report, dated

Wiesbaden, 7 January 1836, to the Hanoverian Captain Lewis Benne, to be forwarded by Benne to the British General Staff, apparently in response to a request from Captain William Siborne for information on the Duchy of Nassau troops' participation at Waterloo for his battle history and large model of the battle.

403 Siborne states 24 officers.

404 The son of a high-ranking official in the German Duchy of Nassau, Heinrich von Gagern began his military career as a cadet in a Bavarian military academy. Upon Napoleon's return from Elba in March 1815, with its renewed threat to peace in Germany, the 16-year-old Gagern volunteered for service in the 1st Duchy of Nassau Light Infantry Regiment and was given the rank of second lieutenant on 2 April. A day earlier, on 1 April, the regiment had been put on a war footing and was built up to brigade size strength of 3,000 men in the following weeks. It became part of the Duke of Wellington's Army Reserve after its arrival in the Brussels area on 7 June.

As the allied army retreated to Mont St Jean the next day, two of the regiment's flanqueur [light] companies were left behind for skirmishing duties. Gagern belonged to one of these companies. As told by him, they were among the last allied units to leave the Quatre Bras area, and only narrowly escaped being taken prisoner by the French. At Waterloo his regiment was posted between Hanoverian and British brigades, with its 1st Battalion in line and Gagern's 2nd Battalion in the second line. Wounded himself, he misses being sent with his flanqueur company to the support of the garrison of La Haye Sainte, where an uncertain fate awaited his fellow Nassauers, his company commander among the first being killed.

In later life, Heinrich von Gagern became a well respected jurist who, eventually, was elected president of the German National Assembly of 1848. Lacking executive power and the continued support of its member states, this body's attempt at creating a unified Germany was doomed to fail. Von Gagern's name is still remembered in history books as Germany's first Reich President.

405 The Duchy of Nassau 2nd Light Infantry Regiment fought at Quatre Bras as part of Prince Bernhard of Saxe-Weimar's 2nd Brigade of the 2nd Netherlands Division. The regiment had become part of the Netherlands Army in July 1814 by agreement between the Duke of Nassau and the Sovereign Prince of Orange Nassau (as of 9 June 1815 King William I of the United Netherlands; they were cousins).

406 Duke Friedrich Wilhelm of Brunswick (1771–1815). Known as the 'Black Duke', he wore a black uniform like most of his men, as a sign of mourning over Napoleon's seizing his Duchy in 1807. When holding off a strong French attack towards Quatre Bras on 16 June, the Duke tried to steady his Leib-Battalion by riding twenty-five paces in front of his men. It was then that an enemy ball ended his life. At the beginning of the Waterloo campaign, his army consisted of 5,700 infantrymen, five cavalry squadrons, and two 8-gun batteries. Most of them were poorly trained recruits and they suffered severely at Quatre Bras and Waterloo.

407 Beginning in late afternoon of 15 June, the 2nd Battalion of the Duchy of Nassau 2nd Light Infantry Regiment was the first unit of Wellington's army,

together with a battery of Belgian horse artillery, to engage and stop the vanguard of Marshal Ney's wing of Napoleon's army on its advance on the Brussels road. This regiment and the Orange Nassau Regiment, with a volunteer Jäger company, formed the 2nd Brigade of the 2nd Netherlands Division under the command of Colonel Prince Bernhard of Saxe-Weimar. The vigorous musketry of their 4,000 infantry and the artillery fire of the attached eight gun battery impressed their adversary enough to suspend further action that day. Early on 16 June, Prince Bernhard's Brigade was reinforced by most of the remainder of 2nd Division and by a foot battery. These troops held on to their position throughout the morning and, as best they could, after Marshal Ney's superior forces started a powerful attack at two o'clock in the afternoon. Beginning at about three o'clock, a build up of allied reinforcements, by then commanded by the Duke of Wellington, prevented further advances of Marshal Ney's troops.

408 Colonel The Hereditary Prince Wilhelm of Nassau-Weilburg (1792–1839) served on Wellington's staff during the Waterloo campaign. He became Duke of Nassau upon the death in March 1816 of his uncle, Duke Friedrich August.

409 Bois de Bossu.

410 Captain Carl Friedrich von Waldschmidt (1789–1818), commander of the Flanqueur (Light) Company, 1st Battalion; Captain Karl Joseph von Weitershausen (1789–1815; killed at Waterloo), commander of the Flanqueur Company, 2nd Battalion; both 1st Duchy of Nassau Regiment.

411 It does seem that these troops were forgotten when the troops retired as the cavalry did not cover their retreat.

412 Major Adolph L. H. von Nauendorf (1781–1842), commander of 2nd Battalion, 1st Duchy of Nassau Regiment.

413 A gross misrepresentation of the opposing forces.

414 Karl Friedrich von Ibell (1780–1834), Director of the Ministerial Cabinet, Duchy of Nassau. The name sounds in the local dialect like the word *Ubel*, or 'injury' in English.

415 Gagern's company was the Flanqueur Company, 2nd Battalion, of 160 men, which was sent to La Haye Sainte in support of the KGL troops. The KGL men were Hanoverians, in common usage still referred to as Brunswickers, even though Hanover had split from Brunswick more than hundred years earlier.

416 At this time, the attacking French troops were most likely infantry of Donzelot's division of d'Erlon's 1st Corps, and not of the Imperial Guard.

417 While Gagern uses the word 'Square' (*Karree* in German), other sources indicate that these Nassauers advanced in attack column. The three battalions of the 1st Regiment were never put through formation drill, which would involve changing from column to line to square. As a result they suffered higher losses in their compact column formation from artillery fire than neighbouring troops who formed into line or square, depending upon circumstances.

418 The injury suffered by the Hereditary Prince Wilhelm of Nassau-Weilburg was apparently of a minor nature. According to the memoirs of Frances Lady Shelley, when in Paris less than a month later, 'I remembered [his] chivalrous devotion – for he was in those days my most active attendant. I remembered

how he used to mount me on my horse at the reviews.' *The Diary of Frances Lady Shelley 1818–1873*, ed. R. Edgcumbe, London, 1913, p. 322.

419 Major Friedrich von Preen (1787–1856), commander, Landwehr Battalion of the 1st Duchy of Nassau Regiment. Captain Caspar Dern (1775–1815), commander of the grenadier company, Landwehr Battalion. He was 40 years old when killed at Waterloo. First Lieutenant Johann Friedrich Ruckert (1792–1819), company officer, No 4. Company, 2nd Battalion; promoted to captain after the battle.

420 At Waterloo, officers of the Duchy of Nassau and the Netherlands infantry wore sashes, unlike officers of other nationalities. Gagern could easily be mistaken for a French officer with his French-style shako with, in addition, its white protective cover, and being without his characteristic orange sash. On his shako he had the Duchy of Nassau plate and not the Napoleonic eagle, as suspected by the so called 'Katzbach' officer who insisted on closer inspection. 'Katzbach' refers to the battle of that name, in which Marshal Jacques MacDonald's French Army of the Bober was caught by Blücher on 26 August 1813 with its back to the Katzbach River and nearly destroyed. Gagern apparently meant to hint at the brash, impetuous manners of Blücher's officers.

421 Gagern refers to the victory of the allied forces of Prussia, Austria and Russia over Napoleon at Leipzig in October 1813, which put an end to French domination over Germany.

422 Colonel Olfermann commanded the Brunswick contingent in the campaign.

423 Major von Wachholtz was chief of staff of the Brunswick contingent.

424 Major von Cramm had commanded the Brunswick Hussars and was killed at Quatre Bras.

425 Major von Rauschenplatt had commanded the Avantgarde or Jäger battalion.

426 Heinemann was their quartermaster general, killed at Waterloo.

427 Commanding the Brunswick Light Brigade.

428 Commanding the 2nd and 3rd Light Battalions respectively.

429 Commanding the 3rd Line Battalion.

430 Pflugk-Harttung footnote: 'This proves that the Report was still written in June.'

431 Pflugk-Harttung footnote: 'This entire passage proves that the Report was authored by a Brunswicker.'

432 Pflugk-Harttung footnote: 'This indicates that it is probably written by a participant.'

433 The report was prepared in Brunswick based on information received shortly after the battle. It includes much misinformation, the most egregious being the claim that Wellington fought with one part of the army at Genappe and the Prince of Orange with his Corps at Nivelles, the Prince being attacked by Generals d'Erlon and Reille.

434 Footnote by Pflugk-Harttung: 'This indicates that the report is based on information available until about the 19th. It apparently represents the official Brunswick account, prepared in Brunswick and based on reports as received. This also explains the factual errors.'

435 This document is Pflugk-Harttung's untitled excerpt from a Brunswick history book of 1890.

436 Only officers names are listed; no information is shown on how and where these officers distinguished themselves.

437 Pflugk-Harttung footnote: 'Schutte's father was a merchant in Gandersheim. See the information in the album of the Wolfenbüttel Gymnasium, 2nd issue, p. 3f and Braunschweigisches Magazin, edited by Dr P. Zimmermann, 1912, No. 7 p. 73f.'

438 'Jette' = short for Henriette.

439 Pflugk-Harttung footnote: 'Heinrich Wilhelm from Dankelsheim, soldier in the Leib Battalion.'

440 Pflugk-Harttung footnote: 'Major August Mahn, Commander of the [Brunswick] Artillery, died 30 April 1853.'

441 Pflugk-Harttung footnote: 'Johann Friedrich Vorlop from Schoppenstedt, company surgeon with the Uhlans.'

442 Pflugk-Harttung footnote: 'Heinrich Kruger from Brunswick, also a company surgeon with the Uhlans.'

443 Pflugk-Harttung footnote: 'Julius Schmidt from Vechelde, battalion physician with the 2nd Light Battalion.'

444 Pflugk-Harttung footnote: 'August Meinecke from Brunswick, battalion physician with the Avantgarde.'

445 Pflugk-Harttung footnote: 'Theodore Franz Dietrichs from Holzminden, lieutenant with the horse artillery, born 1795.'

446 Pflugk-Harttung footnote: 'Uhlan John Heinrich Bringmann from Stroit.'

447 Pflugk-Harttung footnote: 'Gunner Wilhelm Keitel from Gandersheim.'

448 Pflugk-Harttung footnote: 'Friedrich Schumann from Gandersheim, corporal in the 3rd Light Battalion.'

449 Pflugk-Harttung footnote: 'Friedrich Huhne from Gandersheim, sergeant in the 1st Line Battalion.'

450 Pflugk-Harttung footnote: 'There was no military physician of that name with the Brunswick corps, only with the hussars, a cavalry Captain Christian Schnelle from Wolfenbüttel.'

451 Pflugk-Harttung footnote: 'August Pockels became Staff Physician of the Field Corps and Chief of the Military Medical Service in 14 November 1813; he passed away on 9 December 1840 a Senior Staff Physician.' Peter Hofschröer incorrectly reads this name as Lockels.

452 Printed as Soirlen in the original article, but clearly refers to this town near Namur.

453 Interesting he heard cannon fire this far east while the Belgian troops at Quatre Bras remained oblivious. Not the only example of this during the campaign.

454 Lieutenant John Tatter (Beamish no. 753).

455 Veurne in West Flanders.

BIBLIOGRAPHY

In any work of this kind, a great number of books have been used for reference, but a few have been particularly helpful and I list these here. The date of publication shown shows the version seen by me. The source and references for original, unpublished material has been inserted at the relevant points for greater ease.

Anon. *The Army List*, War Office, various edns
Anon. *The Royal Military Calendar*, T. Egerton, London, 1820
Anon. *The Battle of Waterloo by a Near Observer*, 10th edn (2 vols), London, 1817
Anon. *The Waterloo Medal Roll*, ed. C. J. Buckland, Naval and Military Press, Dallington, 1992
Adkin, Mark *The Waterloo Companion*, Aurum Press Ltd, London, 2001
Beamish Ludlow, N. *History of The King's German Legion*, London, 1832–7
Chandler, David *Dictionary of the Napoleonic Wars*, Arms and Armour Press, London, 1979
Dalton, Charles *The Waterloo Roll Call*, Eyre & Spottiswoode, London, 1904
Glover, Gareth *Letters From the Battle of Waterloo*, Greenhill Books, London, 2004
Glover, Gareth *A Narrative of The Battles of Quatre-Bras and Waterloo; with the Defence of Hougoumont by Matthew Clay*, Ken Trotman, Godmanchester, 2006
Hall, John *History of the Peninsular War*, vol. VIII, Greenhill Books, London, 1998
Hofschröer Peter *1815, The Waterloo Campaign* London, Greenhill Books, 1998–9
Lachouque, Henry *Waterloo*, Arms and Armour Press, London, 1975

Bibliography

Mullen, A. L. T. *The Military General Service Roll 1793–1814,* London Stamp Exchange, London, 1990

Pawly, Ronald *Wellington's Belgian Allies, 1815,* Osprey, Oxford, 2001

Pivka, Otto von *Dutch Belgian Troops in the Napoleonic Wars* Osprey, Oxford 1980

Pivka, Otto von *Brunswick Troops 1809–15,* Osprey, Oxford, 1985

Siborne, H. T. *The Waterloo Letters,* Arms and Armour Press, London, 1983

Siborne, W. *History of the Waterloo Campaign,* Greenhill, London, 1990

Wacker Peter and Guntram Muller-Schellenberg, *Das herzoglich-nassauische Militar 1813–1866,* Schellenberg'sche Verlags-buchhandlung, Taunusstein, 1998

INDEX

of correspondents

It should be noted that some of the reports in this volume are not signed and therefore cannot be included in this index of correspondents.

INDEX

of officers and places mentioned in the letters